OAKLAND COMMUNITY COLLEGE
3 2355 00133671 8

D0991930

LINDSAY

A Man for Tomorrow

LINDSAY

A Man for Tomorrow

BY

DANIEL E. BUTTON

Preface by BENNETT CERF

RANDOM HOUSE · NEW YORK

FIRST PRINTING

 Published in New York by Random House, Inc., and simultaneously in Toronto, Canada, by Random House of Canada Limited.

Library of Congress Catalog Card Number: 65-26991

Manufactured in the United States of America by
H. WOLFF, NEW YORK

DESIGN BY TERE LO PRETE

To All Those Who Helped

PREFACE

Publishers seldom write introductions to books they publish. Sometimes they have a lurking feeling that they shouldn't be caught loitering near the scene of the crime. Sometimes they fear damaging comparisons of their style with that of the author. Most often it's because they're smart enough to know that a good publisher should be keen and not heard.

In any event, with Dan Button's permission, I'm stepping out of line and writing a preface for this book for what I think are two very good reasons:

First and foremost, I think it is imperative to have men like John Lindsay in public life today—though I hasten to add that this "study in legislative independence" is not a campaign biography. This book was planned when Congressman Lindsay had no notion at all of running for Mayor of New York City. Its publication during the New York mayoralty campaign is coincidental—an accident of time and events which may or may not help him.

My interest in John Lindsay, in fact, is oriented primarily to his service in Washington and to a point which this book's telling of his story makes very clear—that individual action is the key to civic betterment at all levels, and that he, the individual, is needed; that the way to check the natural arbitrariness of government is to keep government close to the people, and the only way to achieve this is for the people to stay close to government.

No one I know has fought harder against the arbitrariness of government than John Lindsay. And few have brought more people close to government, as evidenced by the extraordinary numbers and quality of volunteer helpers he attracts, whether in campaigns or in special community undertakings such as the unique volunteer task force on housing that he formed in his Congressional District.

John Lindsay has represented me in Congress for almost seven years—along with about half a million other citizens of Manhattan. The book publishing industry is almost totally located in his Congressional District, and it is refreshing to be represented by one who believes in the written word, who is sympathetic to the world of authors and publishers, who does a good deal of original writing himself.

John Lindsay is one of the strongest voices in Congress against invasion of free speech and of the rights guaranteed by the First Amendment, which is the basic protection of authors and creative people in general. He is a strong and effective advocate of the right to communicate. He has battled for years and sometimes alone against the myopic forces in Congress which try periodically to restrict use of the mails—always, of course, in the name of such unassailable causes as anti-communism and literary decency—but with a curious obtuseness as to the importance of avoiding infringement on the right to communicate. Just recently, the U.S. Supreme Court confirmed Lindsay's position by unanimously striking down one of the mail-restriction laws that Lindsay and a handful of others had fought.

The second reason for my writing this preface, and one which is entirely relevant, is the fact that we are friends. My wife, Phyllis, and I have found John and Mary Lindsay to be delightful companions, and we have had great fun on the occasions that John has appeared with me as a panelist on the "What's My Line?" television program.

I know that John has enjoyed serving in the House of Representatives. He has given the Congressional District in which I live, and have my place of business, an intimate and personal representation which his constituents must approve, since each of his re-election pluralities has been substantially larger than the previous one.

Now John Lindsay has announced his willingness to take on what many people consider to be the second most difficult job in the land, that of governing New York City. The important fact of his candidacy is that he genuinely believes it *can* be governed. I heartily agree with him.

A municipal campaign is difficult under any circumstances. In New York City, with its eight million people and enormous variety of complications, it is about as tough an undertaking as one could imagine. However he fares, John Lindsay is at least providing the service (as I write this preface) of shaking up the City of New York and making its citizenry think a bit as to whether this city or any city has a worthwhile future and if so, what it wants to do about it.

The events which have brought John Lindsay to this point make this an interesting and instructive book which hopefully may also be inspiring to all citizens—and an antidote to that political apathy which, in the final analysis, is freedom's worst enemy.

Bennett Cerf
FALL, 1965

Contents

LINDSAY

A Man for Tomorrow

❦ ❦ I ❦ ❦

The Country Will Remember . . .

A DERISIVE din rocked the cavernous Cow Palace on the second night of the 1964 Republican National Convention, a session that continued for eight contentious hours. The delegates would, on the next night, "get on with the business of the convention," Barry Goldwater's spokesmen announced. They awaited confidently the anticlimax of his nomination.

But this night, the night of the party platform's adoption, set the tone and style of the entire convention. Standing in the middle of raucous howlers, I heard a woman's voice say, "They're animals!" It would have been hard to disagree.

John Lindsay, who was going to face this mob within minutes, had milder though no less troubled words: "It's a crowd that has its own brand of conservatism. It's hostile to any opposing force, even ferociously so. In fact, it is in danger of embarrassing the Goldwater faction, with these outbursts which reveal the anxieties and resentments of the faction beyond anything its spokesmen have done."

The Goldwater management was at that moment droning through

a two-hour reading of the eighty-five-hundred-word platform. The maneuver served to delay until late evening in San Francisco, and after midnight for Eastern TV-viewers, the efforts of pro-Scranton moderates to offer amendments on three key sections: extremism, nuclear controls, and civil rights.

The amendment on extremism was shouted down and Governor Rockefeller withstood a torrent of abuse as he told the delegates, as he put it, "the truth." Senator Hugh Scott of Pennsylvania, leader of the Scranton forces, offered the amendment on civil rights. "The overwhelming Republican support of the Civil Rights Act of 1964 in Congress," he said, "reflects our party's deep belief that the federal government has constitutional responsibility. . . . The Republican Party assumes special responsibilities by virtue of the fact that it is the party of Lincoln. . . ." Five supporting and five opposition speakers were to be heard. On the negative side was Congressman McCulloch of Ohio, with whom Lindsay had worked so long to get a strong civil rights bill.

It was late at night when John Lindsay strode to the rostrum to appeal to the party to honor its century-old "covenant with the American people." He reminded the delegates of the task of safeguarding the rights affirmed in the Constitution; he told them that if the national government has any purpose at all, it has this purpose. And in a tense delivery, he told them their party had been faithful for a century to this ideal in its platforms. He invoked the once-magic name of Taft, the Thirteenth Amendment, and the Fourteenth and Fifteenth; he asked if they were prepared to abandon the platforms of the past. Much of his rapid-fire talk was a restatement of his appeal to the platform committee, but he added some pungent reflections on the platform's language. Though specific in a hundred areas, he commented, it seemed unable to stress the need in the most basic of human rights,* and he reiterated

* The platform statement on civil rights was limited to the pledge of "full implementation and faithful execution of the Civil Rights Act of 1964, and all other civil rights statutes, to assure equal rights and opportunities guaranteed by the Constitution to every citizen; improvement of civil rights statutes adequate to changing needs of our times; such additional administrative or legislative actions as may be required to end the denial, for whatever unlawful reason, of the right to vote: continued opposition to discrimination based on

his plea not to "deny our tradition" in favor of "a political dead end." And then, just before the end, he offered stern words of warning to this bored and scornful and inattentive convention: "The country will note well what we do here today—and might even remember."

On a roll call the civil rights amendment was defeated better than two to one; the negative vote disclosed that Goldwater had the nomination sewed up.

"Neither the conservative nor the moderate speeches," said Lindsay, "including my own, could have hoped to influence delegates whose votes had been decided for them before the opening of the session. The Goldwater forces had decided that they would not allow the convention to adopt any amendment to their platform and saw to it that it happened that way. Lack of respect for the traditions of free deliberation was apparent."

If the effort on the convention floor was futile and frustrating, the Scranton-Rockefeller-Lindsay forces suffered many another defeat and humiliation and rebuff.

"Governor Scranton's moderate forces, myself among them, were met by an overwhelming conservative majority not only on the floor of the Cow Palace, but in the important convention committees," Lindsay recalled a little later.

It was only a week after Lindsay had stood in the President's office as he signed the Civil Rights Act that he came before the party's platform committee.

Most of his appeal involved recommendations on civil rights and urban problems, but he touched also on a range of other items including, as he put it, "matters put in issue by Senator Goldwater himself." Then, in an appeal to the committee, he addressed them in words that had a beseeching quality in the smoke of the hotel room: "I ask you to chart your course wisely. . . . Do not be

---

race, creed, national origin, or sex. . . . Elimination of any such discrimination is a matter of heart, conscience, and education, as well as of equal rights under law."

afraid of the new, lest you abandon to others the task of charting the untraveled mountain peaks and valleys and infinite spaces that lie ahead, nor be scornful of the old, lest you turn your back on history, a history and tradition that for more than a century have made our party the great center core of America.

"Lastly, I ask that you do not treat this platform as a cynical exercise—to be viewed as a pacifier with one eye, and winked at with the other."

And he spoke of problems of the elderly, of housing, of schooling, of the arts, of immigration and of foreign policy, of Congressional reform.

He told the committee that he strongly believed only the President, with the advice and consent of the other civilian heads of state of NATO countries, should make a decision on using tactical nuclear weapons. He spoke of the United Nations, and the need to have confidence in it while seeking ways to improve and strengthen it. And he decried the emergence, in some corners of their party, of the extreme rightists—"the kind that have attacked the loyalty and patriotism of men like former President Eisenhower and Chief Justice Warren."

And a hundred committeemen from all over the nation heard John Lindsay describe with feeling the work of earlier platform committees that pledged their party to use federal strength to guarantee civil rights. They also heard his plea for an affirmative and unequivocal declaration holding constitutional the 1964 Civil Rights Act (Senator Goldwater and some of his backers had raised the question).

Lindsay had earlier come up against the Goldwater adamancy in another committee encounter. As one of New York's two members in the convention's rules committee, he presented an amendment to a rule concerning election of delegates. The amendment sought to overrule the Goldwater clique which had refused to seat a Negro in the lily-white Tennessee delegation. The convention itself had shouted down an appeal for an end to discrimination in selection of delegates. Lindsay and other Scranton supporters worked out a straightforward anti-discrimination clause and took it before the rules committee in the Mural Room of the St. Francis

Hotel. "I knew, judging from Goldwater's strength in the platform and other committees, that we would probably not be able to muster enough votes to pass the amendment," he said. "But it was still a sharp disappointment when the sixty-nine dissenting votes were compared to the eighteen generous 'ayes' our proposal attracted.

"We have set our teeth grimly," John Lindsay said, "to meet these rebuffs, to fight the negative forces threatening these fundamental principles."

Lindsay declared that the Goldwater forces had known for at least two weeks that they had the necessary delegate strength to have their man nominated. Meanwhile, the Scranton forces, including Lindsay, combed delegations for the few undecided votes and racked their brains to uncover a floor strategy that might breach the massive Goldwater vote.

"Few of us deluded ourselves," Lindsay said later, "into thinking that our efforts could make any difference to the outcome of the convention." The inevitability of the outcome might have led Goldwater's strategists into some sort of compromise with the moderates that would have led more easily to party unity. But the Scranton forces never saw evidence of any spirit of conciliation. "We were allowed to beat our heads against a wall."

When the inevitable did come about, and Goldwater's nomination was clinched, most delegates rushed to join. Amid the pandemonium in New York's ninety-two-member delegation after the Goldwater nomination was assured, one of history's most informal caucuses was held. State Chairman Fred Young, acting as head of the delegation in Governor Rockefeller's absence, was pressured both to throw all the New York votes to Goldwater in the usual effort to signify unity, and, on the other hand, to hold out, retaining the votes in the Scranton column. One thing was certain: some members of the New York delegation would never voluntarily permit their votes to go for the Arizonan. Chairman Young jumped on a folding chair, scanned the faces that reflected shock, disappointment, disgust (and, in a few cases, pleasure). Delegates—John Lindsay among them—were shouting at him, their voices almost unintelligible; but a decision had to be made almost immediately. This was Fred Young's "caucus"; he grabbed the microphone and announced that eighty-seven delegates were switching to Goldwater, but that five were abstaining. Who were they? The number was wholly arbitrary, and Young with sardonic caprice left it up to the delegates to fight it out for the now almost meaningless and unofficial distinction of being "one of the five." Lindsay was among those who had tried to be heard in the din of the "caucus," and he quickly claimed rank among the five—but so did "a hundred others," Chairman Young reported the next morning.

Having anticipated the outcome of the convention, not to say the attendant problems of running on the ticket with Barry Goldwater, John Lindsay and Bob Price, his campaign manager, had opened their own headquarters in familiar rooms at the Hotel Roosevelt in midtown New York, five weeks before the convention. The date coincided with Governor Rockefeller's withdrawal following his California primary defeat. Now, with the party in the hands of those who stood for "uncompromising resistance to other opinions," who had rejected out of hand the traditional course in civil rights that he had proffered, Lindsay left San Francisco, saying of the campaign ahead, "I will be staying aboard and I will be fighting." He added, "I am disappointed, of course, that there was not the strong endorsement of the civil rights bill that I'd hoped for. A firm civil rights plank would have lent stability in the national picture. It would have aided in the effort toward curbing the street violence that Senator Goldwater spoke of. And even Senator Russell of Georgia now is urging compliance with the new law. It doesn't help him at all in the South, where his voice commands great respect, to have the Republicans turn out to be wishy-washy on the subject. But despite the disappointment I am not going to retreat from my principles. This is a matter of conscience with me and I shall treat it that way throughout the campaign. . . ."

John Lindsay's staying aboard and fighting was a stance difficult to reconcile with the "matter of conscience" about the nature of the Goldwater campaign that had so troubled him. Some three weeks after the convention he resolved the problem by running on his own record "without reference to the national ticket." It was a controversial position and it put him in peril of being branded as a maverick, subject to discipline and ostracism within his party. But he pointed out that one source of opposition to him was from New York's Conservative Party, which was, in the words of GOP State Chairman Fred Young, "publicly committed to campaign for the defeat and destruction of the Republican Party in New York.

"Thus," he added, "the Conservative Party and its early organizers for Senator Goldwater in New York State are bent on a course of destruction . . . and I have no choice but to fight back with all the strength at my command."

The Congressman, in his declaration of personal independence, recalled that at the San Francisco convention he had "fought for certain principles that I believe are embedded in the Republican Party's history and tradition—and from which I have no intention of retreating." He recounted again the items that the Goldwater forces had spurned in the floor fight, and commented: "These and others are long-established tenets of the party, and yet the convention would not acknowledge them even when their merit had been put directly in issue. To those who are deeply disturbed as I am over the existence of these uncompromising circumstances and attitudes . . . it should be clear that I have no choice but to run in this election on my own record without reference to the national ticket. To do otherwise, as long as these circumstances exist, would be to retreat from principle and to assist the Conservative Party and its organizers who in New York seek to defeat me and the historic Republican Party principles that I represent."

But the Lindsay declaration that August afternoon looked beyond his own campaign. He stated his intention to work for and with candidates "who have kept faith" and with like-minded Republicans throughout the nation. His statement of position became a call to action by "Republicans across the country who believe in the party of Lincoln."

He summoned them to "join hands and work together for the rededication of the Republican Party to those principles which have made the party in the past the great center core of America. . . . I have found many thousands of Republicans all over the United

States who feel as I do and who will also work within the party for their beliefs. I intend to work tirelessly with them, as I have in the past."

An editorial writer noted approvingly: "Clearly, here is a man who expects much of his party—more than he finds it offering at the moment. He apparently feels that the voters themselves expect more than the current national ticket and platform seem to promise. Despite these disappointments, he will work within the party for beliefs and principles to which he subscribes, and this is encouraging, for certainly his party stands in need of such articulate voices for reason as his is."

John Lindsay, then, stood at the crossroads even as his party did. How did he reach the crossroads?

❦❦ 2 ❦❦

What Makes Him Run?

WHEN John Lindsay became a national political figure in the spring of 1965, the dashing and aggressive antagonist in the nation's prime political contest of the year, the attention focused—as it has frequently—on appearance rather than substance.

Few references to Lindsay fail to mention his height (impressive), his features (inclined toward the heroic), or his personal charm (depending on the point of view, quite considerable or monstrously so).

One rave notice introducing the candidate to a breathless public even remarked that he has good teeth. The nation's barbers have named him one of the ten best-groomed men in spite of the fact that the *New Yorker* has called him tousled and virtually every profilist has made much of his casual appearance. Depending on which paper you read, you can find him curly, wavy, or just attractively windblown on top, blond or dark, sandy blond or light brown or somewhere in between. The first time John Lindsay turned up in a national magazine was in January, 1959, the month he entered Congress; the occasion was a photograph in *Glamour*.

Even the bitterest of his political enemies, William Buckley, who continued his personal vendetta against Lindsay and his liberal views by entering the mayoralty contest as Conservative candidate, has used such terms as "classically Grecian" and a "Cecil B. DeMille President" to describe him. A wide-ranging critic, Richard Watts, Jr., wrote, after meeting Lindsay for the first time, "I can understand why he is almost impossible to defeat. He is a man of vast personal attractiveness." Murray Kempton, one of the least susceptible of commentators, who can reject the ordinary and resist the humble without even a lingering thought, wrote of Lindsay as he entered the 1965 race: "You're never safe in running against simple charm. . . . He has the face that could make New Yorkers hope again."

But all these observations miss the mark. Some suggest that there is no substance to John Lindsay—that it is all shadow puppetry involving a lean, elongated doll contrived by some master magician. Others imply that even if there is substance, John Lindsay must wish to capitalize on the external and to be the candidate or congressman or mayor who causes hearts to flutter. Others propose that, in any event, the public wants public figures who look the part, who are, in effect, the living version of the DeMille statesman.

In justice to John Lindsay it must be said that he rejects all these variations on the stuffed-man theme. His record in public life demonstrates surely enough that he is his own man, free of strings twitched by other hands, free also of doctrinaire compulsions.

Lindsay the person is equally free of pretense and sham—direct and simple in his approach to other people. He does not seem to be a man who would contrive to employ superficial appearances at the expense of significant matters. "Conspiring, even within his own mind, to be the matinée politician is just about as foreign to John as anything you could mention," a friend remarked upon reading several of the "personality" stories—including some featured on covers of the largest national magazines.

If John Lindsay is not a paper politician, what is the inner substance? "Directness" seems to be the key that unlocks much of the answer.

Surely no man is wholly what he aspires to be, but we can safely presume that any man strives to make his own existence more meaningful to others and more acceptable to himself. Contemplating this, John Lindsay quoted Martin Buber one day. "Buber, you know, told us, You shall not withhold yourself.* He said something like this: that there is an imperative on each of us to break out of the forms that surround us, break through the bonds of pride, and establish a directness of communication with others, so that every other person has a significance to each of us without reservation or limitation. . . ."

This very directness of communication between men is actually where John Lindsay excels. Probably this characteristic is instinctive and inherited; according to family, it is a trait that has been his since his earliest years. In part, of course, it may have been cultivated unconsciously and necessarily as part of his roles as barrister and politician. "I love the give-and-take of the courtroom," he has exclaimed. And in the House of Representatives his mastery of the skills of communication under the most difficult circumstances was underscored sharply by an onlooker one day during the civil rights debate. "Time and again I noticed that the noisy House grew still when Lindsay rose to explain a complicated point at issue," said Herman Edelsberg, director of the Anti-Defamation League.

John Lindsay's ability to communicate with men is vastly deeper, however, than mere volubility or articulateness. In conversation with another he is direct; he "has contact with man," in keeping with Buber's dictum. Direct in communication, with barriers down, the exchange is open, free, and personal. The talk is not small, the formalities are minimal, the pleasantries pleasantly observed but far from dominant. If you have a thing to say to John Lindsay, he has a response for you.

He is a communicator but it is far from a one-way passage. In trite terms, he is a good listener as well as a ready talker, but he does not make you pour yourself down his well before offering a single reaction or constructive thought in return. Lindsay's listening is the reflexive participation of a devoted conversationalist. His

* Lindsay's reference apparently was to Buber's essay "What Is to Be Done?" in which he said, "You, imprisoned in the shells in which society, state, church, school, economy, public opinion, and your own pride have stuck you, indirect one among indirect ones, break through your shells, become direct; man, have contact with men!"

reaction is responsive and his responsiveness is open and outgoing. He is blunt, his directness is combined with a pungency. The Lindsay opinions are forceful, vigorously and flatly expressed. His voice is deep and it reflects the tones of his native city with more than an occasional suggestion of the sidewalks of New York. His words almost fall over one another. He tends to repeat a phrase, habitually, as if emphasizing for himself the point he is hoping to make with it: "A first-rate man, first-rate man," he may exclaim of some Washington colleague whose name is tossed to him conversationally. But occasionally his expressions seem molded into a format of campaign clichés.

His concentration is so industriously worked at that it impresses the onlooker as neither withdrawal nor taciturnity but a form of participation. There is in John Lindsay an impatience with the peripheral and inconsequential, a distaste for the sloppy and inaccurate and slovenly in mind as well as in being. The impatience sometimes shows itself abruptly. He is direct, so he tends to be frustrated by indirection in others; the frankness of his response is tempered only by an obvious considerateness of nature. He does not willingly or cheerfully suffer fools; yet his passion for the game of politics is such that he can endure many of the agonies of that game's rules with a smiling stoicism. A friend has been quoted as being impressed by his distaste for bullies: "He is passionate about minority groups, and if they're being bullied, he explodes." *

Despite the outgoing nature and the politician's professional need to relate with the handshake and the smile, there is a strong element of reserve in John Lindsay. It is essentially akin to his instinctive sense of the fitting and decent approach to a man's inner self. He must reserve some of his being for himself and for his family, for he cannot be wholly a public man. Different men draw this line at different places. John Lindsay is "John" to family, to friends, to any who know him; he is not the "Johnny" that some clubhouse politicians would have him be out among the people, nor is he a

* "On occasion," says Mary Lindsay, who has had sixteen years of opportunity to observe at a wife's point-blank range, "he can become extremely annoyed, but I suppose it's common to politicians. Whatever temper he has, he doesn't really lose it very often—at least, not at home."

"Jack" ("no one who knows him would think of calling him 'Jack,' " one staff member said, "though there are those who don't know him and try it"). Over-familiarities are unthinkable with a man of this degree of reserve.

Many of John Lindsay's other contradictions are, of course, political. He is the one of all the predictable breed of Republicans who turned out to be most unpredictable: he was a young and promising trial lawyer, on his way in a career which he relished immensely and which he gave up for a fantastically more chancy affair; he is the advantaged Yalie who explodes when the less advantaged are bullied; the Congressman with only a small number of Negroes in his District who is strongest on civil rights; who, as a Republican, might be the loser through a change in New York State law to allow Spanish-speaking residents to vote, but advocates that change. He is the man who has publicly changed course in the middle of a political season. He is a man whose detractors will say lacks any humor at all. (His wife says that the most compelling thing about him is "his ability to always be able to laugh at himself." And, she adds, "I can make him laugh when other people cannot.")

"Some people's community is themselves; others', their family," John Lindsay observed one day when someone asked him about his own purpose in life. "Others' community will be General Electric, figuratively speaking; others', their law firm. Others go beyond that into the state. That's for me. I think I always wanted public life," he recalls now.

But it may well be that the war gave direction, as it did for so many other men, to his vague stirrings of involvement.

He mentions frequently that a fourth of the boys who were graduated with him from St. Paul's School in New Hampshire were killed in the war. One of his college roommates was killed, as were several of his closest friends. Every word that John Lindsay speaks of them implies a commitment to a life that would help to make their own short lives seem less in vain.

On the other hand Lindsay seldom refers to his own war experiences, which may have been as significant. He hurried through Yale, graduating as a class of one in an accelerated program (his elapsed time as an undergraduate was only about two and a half years). Immediately after, he entered the Navy, at twenty-one, with an ensign's commission, and for nearly three years he lived on the destroyer *Swanson*. He saw action in the Mediterranean at the invasion of Sicily that same summer as a gunnery officer. The *Swanson* nearly sank in a collision with another destroyer. Then, after nine months in the Atlantic and Mediterranean, the *Swanson* sailed for the Pacific, and for more than two years was with the 7th Amphibious Fleet in the Southwest Pacific (landings on Biak, Hollandia, and Admiralty Islands) and in the Western Pacific with the 5th Carrier Strike Fleet (the Philippine invasion). By the time he left service, he wore five battle stars, was a full lieutenant, and was the *Swanson*'s executive officer.

He became a civilian again in the spring of 1946 and he took a six-month breather. The lieutenant shucked the uniform and the battle stars, picked up his final pay, and went skiing as long as the money held out. Then he tried a bank clerkship and learned, with a certainty beyond any possible future regret, that this career was not for him though his father had thrived on it. And as it happened, the Republican Congressman in the family's area of Manhattan was confronted at this time by a primary contest. For a pair of relatively idle hands, waiting to enter the Yale Law School in the fall, the opportunity to work for Congressman Joe Baldwin during the midsummer primary campaign was first a novelty and very shortly an absorption. But it was to be disappointing, for Baldwin was outpointed in the primary voting by a newcomer more palatable to the orthodox thinkers of the GOP organization in Manhattan. The newcomer's name was Frederic Coudert, who re-enters the Lindsay story later.

There had been an earlier exposure to politics. Some fast footwork at St. Paul's had wangled for John and his twin brother David the two page-boy assignments allotted to the school for the 1940 Republican National Convention. And a visit to City Hall with schoolmates one day in his early teens, during the LaGuardia tenure, had made a lasting impression. It was his first exposure to the men and forces that make government work.

Discussing LaGuardia's Republicanism, maverick though it was, Lindsay observes: "It was quite natural for me to become a Republican. He was with the good guys, fighting the bad guys—Tammany Hall."

As might be expected in a banker's family living on Park Avenue in the Eighties, the young Lindsays had sprung from a Republican background. But a great deal more than the weight of custom and economics and patriarchal influence helped shape John Lindsay's early Republicanism.

"I decided to be and stay a Republican," he says now, "but it was after study and after thought. It seemed to me that it was important that this was the party of the individual—as I saw it, and as I still see it. It's the party of Lincoln, of civil rights, the protection of the person and his liberties against the majority, even against big business or the federal bureaucracy."

By this time, in any event, John Lindsay was deeply committed to the law and, in keeping with his temperament, trial work already attracted him. Involvement in the conflict between Baldwin and Coudert seemed a good place to prepare for some courtroom exchanges.

Late in the war Catherine Drinker Bowen had published her penetrating study of the great dissenter, Justice Oliver Wendell Holmes, and John Lindsay on shipboard had picked up and read *Yankee from Olympus* with absorption; he read it again. "No question," he says, "but that that book influenced my decisions at that time."

But was there already a plan? Lindsay discounts this completely. "You can't plot out such a thing in advance," he says. "You don't know the things you are going to do." Nearly twenty years after the event a Navy shipmate told Lindsay in a chance encounter that during their service in the Pacific he had mentioned a desire to enter politics after the war. "But I have no recollection of that," says Lindsay.

The record shows, in any case, that the political commitment developed slowly. In that year of 1946, when he was getting his feet damp in a primary campaign and casting his first vote, John F. Kennedy, only four years older, and Richard Nixon, nine years older, were running for Congress, as were many young war veterans.

But Lindsay still had law school ahead of him; and then the beginnings of the practice with a good firm (Webster, Sheffield, Fleischmann, Hitchcock and Chrystie); some effort with the New York Young Republicans and then with Youth for Eisenhower about the time he turned thirty; and finally, the decision to run for Congress when he was thirty-six—hardly a juvenile escapade.

But even though the signs had been pointing in this direction, his entry into the Republican primary turned out to be something of a surprise to the family; his father questioned the wisdom of the move, John Lindsay recalls. But if he was surprised to realize that his son preferred the rough-and-tumble of politics to high-level appointive jobs in Washington executive offices, he ultimately lent his support to the son's political emergence with a will.

His influence on the early development of John and his three brothers was considerable from the earliest days. A vigorous and strong-minded man, he started at fifteen as a runner for a Wall Street firm. The way to the top for George Lindsay—whose father had emigrated to America from the Isle of Wight—was through initiative and determination.

George Lindsay, born in New Jersey, was studying law at New York University while working with the Wall Street investment house. But if his son John, and two other sons, were to find a vocation in the law, this was not for George Lindsay; he never practiced, though he won the LL.B. in a typical odd-hours study regimen. He chose banking and rose to a partnership with Blair & Co., a large investment firm; later he joined in the organization of the Swiss-American Corporation, a banking firm, and became its president and board chairman.

Meanwhile he had met a Wellesley alumna from Newark, Eleanor Vliet, a contractor's daughter who aspired to a career on the stage (Jo in a production of *Little Women* was one role she did get) but who was willing to give up the entire idea to marry George Lindsay, the young Wall Streeter. They were married shortly before World War I and lived in an apartment on quiet and unspectacular West End Avenue in the Eighties. Their first child, a daughter named for her mother, was born there; and a son, named for his father. It was on Thanksgiving Day of 1921 when twins—John and

David, who are fraternal rather than identical—were also born there. Four years later a fourth son, Robert, was born—the only one who didn't become a lawyer, though like all the other boys he attended Yale. (Sister Eleanor, Mrs. Cooper Schieffelin, was a Vassar girl. She died in 1965.) All the younger Lindsays except John now live on Long Island.

Some fatuous efforts have been made to liken the Lindsay brothers to the Kennedy brothers. The comparison does not have a basis for existence. Only one brother is involved in political life; their father did not have his own life as a public man nor did he aspire to project himself vicariously in the public careers of his sons. Nor was his own modest success in business comparable to Joseph Kennedy's fortune. The son who did enter public life did so on his own without patrimony. His brothers, with individual careers and lives of their own, have been interested in and generally helpful to John Lindsay in the various stages of his political career, but are completely without political ambitions of their own. In 1965, when John Lindsay faced the fight of his life, they pitched in as volunteers, somewhat as any brothers probably would if one of them were about to tangle with the kid down the street who had a three-to-one advantage in height, weight, and reach.

Similarly, some comparisons are drawn between John V. Lindsay and John F. Kennedy. Apart from the fact that each, in widely disparate ways, has intellectual appeal for voters, there appears to be little validity for such comparison. John Lindsay, whose hallmark is independence, is neither "the new Kennedy" nor "a Republican Kennedy," nor any other variety of Kennedy; he is an authentic original, and whatever his value may be, it is to be assayed in such terms.

The Lindsay family tended to both books (they are all omnivorous readers) and athletics. "I spent most of my time on the Mall in Central Park," John Lindsay has recalled, "under the benches, playing hide-and-seek—and most of the time getting trapped." He remembers, too, playing football in the park under Queensborough Bridge. John likes to sail and indulged the hobby whenever there was free summer time out at the family's former rambling summer home near Cold Spring Harbor on Long Island Sound. He was good enough to stroke the Yale freshman crew in the spring of 1941 (they were defeated by Harvard). Then he lent his 6′3″, 180-pound frame to freshman football. Winter sports are perhaps even more fascinating for him, and he and his family go off for skiing weekends with or without excuse. And George Lindsay passed along a fondness and skill for skating; in his seventies he still sped around the Rockefeller Center rink. John Lindsay is a much above average figure skater who keeps a pair of skates at that same rink; he has been known to enliven a political rally by adding a skating exhibition to the speechmaking.

While all these athletic inclinations were being honed in competition, first around the corner from home at the Buckley School (until 1935), then at St. Paul's (until 1940), academic and intellectual skills were being sharpened and nurtured. At St. Paul's he became president of his class; there was a taste of public speaking and of dramatics, to which he turned a willing hand.

But it was in the hurry-up schedule at Yale, from the fall of 1940 to the spring of 1943, that John Lindsay found himself. He majored in English history (his major thesis was on Cromwell and his religiosity) and he was marked as more of a student by the time he received the B.A. than when he entered, when his mind was as much on freshman football and the crew as on the academic routine. One of his professors recalls his "tremendous strength of mind and character—you could see he was a fellow who could take charge." *

And law school, also at Yale, was similarly on an accelerated schedule for him—two years instead of the customary three. He finished there in the spring of 1948, the year in which Thomas E. Dewey was being measured for the White House desk under the tutelage of a manager named Herbert Brownell. There is a legend that says that Brownell, on a visit to Yale while John Lindsay was

* Lindsay's association with Yale has continued. He served on the executive committee of the Yale Law School Association for five years, was a Ralph Hill Thomas Visiting Fellow (for lectures) in 1961, a Chubb Fellow in 1963, and is a Fellow of Jonathan Edwards College (his undergraduate college). In 1964 he was elected by vote of Yale alumni from among four candidates to the Yale University Corporation, the sixteen-member governing body of the university.

a law student, spotted him as a comer. The trouble with the legend is that there is nothing to it; Brownell and Lindsay didn't meet until three or four years later, when the younger man was active in the Young Republicans and helping to shape up an early Eisenhower-for-President group, an activity that did, then, get Brownell's favorable attention. In another few years Lindsay became his assistant in the United States Attorney General's office.

But at law school John Lindsay did make one most important acquaintance, not a politician, nor even a political type, but a very feminine, dark-haired, dark-eyed Vassar girl from Greenwich, Connecticut, born in Richmond, Virginia—Mary Anne Harrison. If John Lindsay could go through Yale in three years, Mary Harrison could finish Vassar in three. While she taught in Providence and at the same Buckley School in Manhattan that he had attended for years, she was courted by John Lindsay. They were married in June, 1949, and their first home was a small apartment in Stuyvesant Town, the huge development on the East Side that later became a part of the 17th Congressional District. Mary taught again, briefly, in the community nursery school, then retired to have children of her own (as of 1965, these were Katharine, fourteen; Margaret, twelve; Anne, nine; John, five).

"He has such tremendous power of concentration that sometimes even I have trouble getting through," Mary Lindsay has said. She has had trouble "getting through" in other ways, too; the life of a public man can become so public that at times he is all but invisible to his family. To break the barrier of inaccessibility, Mary Lindsay, "Mare" to her husband, once made an appointment through his secretary to have an interview on a household matter. She was seen promptly (Mrs. Franklin D. Roosevelt has recounted similar experiences).

Mary Lindsay plunges with exuberant enthusiasm into her husband's campaigning (she opened four district headquarters in a single day for him early in his mayoral drive) and participates readily in other parts of his career. She is unaffectedly herself: soft-voiced, natural in manner, friendly and outgoing, yet far from noticeably assertive. She conceded having been "scared to death" by the idea of campaign speeches, yet the first reviews of her 1965 efforts were highly complimentary. Her self-described title as "sounding-board" for her husband clearly is incomplete; "backstop" might be added to it with some justice, if the reference were to be extended. In a time when a public man's wife is so thoroughly screened as part-of-the-act, Mary Harrison Lindsay must be rated as a plus-factor in the Lindsay act. She is an attractive woman without even remotely attempting the overpowering chic of a Jacqueline Kennedy; she is competent without thinking of competing with a Lady Bird Johnson in the business world. Yet she is far from the shy Bess Truman or Mamie Eisenhower, to name other women who have been in the public eye. And to make further comparisons, there is not the slightest hint of the undue power of Florence Kling Harding or Edith Galt Wilson. There is no question as to who takes charge in the Lindsay family; the male lead is exactly that, and this in no way derogates any supporting player. To his family John Lindsay delegates those things that properly fall outside his province or which must somehow take second place when his schedule demands that he be hundreds of miles away. But the most meaningful decisions must be his, even with the benefit of an understanding "sounding-board."

After he had been in Congress for some four years, commuting to the East Seventy-second Street apartment as many weekends as possible from his Washington office—and being interrupted and detoured by constituents and associates with pressing problems—a small incident changed the family's life drastically. Nine-year-old Margie asked, "Why is it, when Daddy comes home, everyone gets to see him except us?"

John Lindsay, who has told the story many times, admits that he was greatly affected ("I wept when I heard that . . .") by the pathos of the child's question. Shortly afterwards the Lindsay family moved its headquarters to Washington (a white-brick Colonial house built into the side of a hill), while at the same time taking a smaller apartment on West Fifty-eighth Street as a New York City residence.

From the house-in-the-hill the Congressman drove his 1949 Plymouth (it collapsed in 1965) to the House Office Building; too often, the day has ended for him in a banquet hall or a conference room in Cleveland or Waterbury or Utica. He is tireless when on the go, but occasionally he stops for more than a few hours' sleep.

Total in all his responses, this is a man whose restlessness for action is mirrored in his quickness of movement as well as alertness of intellect and fluidity of emotion. In his reading he plunges into an *avant-garde* novel with almost the same relish with which he attacks his long-established favorite, history. Frequently, he writes reviews of new books for the newspapers and magazines; these, like his magazine articles and almost all his speeches, have habitually been pounded out by Lindsay himself in the recesses of a den at home; until the multi-speech demands of the mayoralty, there was no "Lindsay writer."

His mayoralty campaign leaves little enough time for reading of any sort, much less for creative writing; for his reading, he tends to dip while on the run. One book that he carries with him on his dashes about the city is Saint-Exupéry's posthumous *A Sense of Life;* one afternoon, while relaxing for a few moments in a station wagon between rallies, he quoted from it.* "Give ourselves; give ourselves," he was saying—and it is this deep response to the demands of life upon man that characterizes John Lindsay's attitude toward life.

John Lindsay can master the intricacies of a civil rights bill and make the House of Representatives pause to listen to his voice; can plunge overnight into a campaign against the greatest of odds and follow through with the energy of a man who believes in what he is doing, despite the restraining clutch of fatigue and discouragement; who, on a little girl's quiet question, uproots the family

* The Saint-Exupéry observations, published originally at the time of the Munich crisis of 1938, were these: "What all of us want is to be set free. . . . We ourselves cannot draw a free breath unless we are bound to others by a common and disinterested ideal. We are the children of the age of comfort, yet we are filled with an inexpressible happiness when we share our last crust with others in the desert. . . . We will win our way through to freedom if we can help each other recognize a common aim that unites all men, rather than look for abstract solutions. . . . What have we to do in order to be born into life? Give ourselves. We have sensed dimly that man can commune with man only in terms of a shared image."

residence and turns his life upside down; who picks up his sturdy little boy and carries him over Manhattan's long crosstown streets at the end of a tiresome afternoon in the park. All these are John Lindsay.

❦ ❦ 3 ❦ ❦

The 17th: Myth and Reality

ONE of the oddest elements of the country's political mystique and mythology is John Lindsay's 17th Congressional District. It is variously described as the richest in America, which it is not, the best educated, which it is not, the "Silk Stocking" District, which is an exaggeration, and the most renowned and glamorous, which by all odds, it is. Lindsay calls it the "most exciting."

The 17th takes in the few square miles of Manhattan real estate best known throughout the nation and the world: the United Nations, Times Square, Central Park, Rockefeller Center, Greenwich Village; the Empire State Building and other skyscrapers; the principal theaters, hotels, shops, clubs, restaurants; the "Madison Avenue" of the advertising world, the greatest concentration of publishing, television, and radio headquarters; universities, museums, and a variety of other spots ranging from Welfare Island to Madison Square Garden to the garment center. Most of the 17th is confined to the area between the East River and the Fifth Avenue boundary which designates Manhattan's East Side. And it extends in a rather narrow finger from Third Street, below Washington

Square, to the northern end of Central Park and the southern boundary of Harlem at 110th Street. John Lindsay's New York residence is almost precisely in the center of the District—in an apartment building on West Fifty-eighth Street, just back of the Hotel Plaza and a block away from Central Park.

Amid the towers and the bright lights are packed an amazing number of people, nearly 400,000, of whom about 190,000 were voters in 1964. Individual family incomes range from the very high to low: their median is about $8,600, fourth highest in the country. And their educational achievements also rank fourth in the country among Congressional Districts: they have completed, on the average, a half year beyond the high school level. Nearly half the households consist of people who live alone, and four out of five homes have no more than two persons, so the average family is small (1.88 persons). Five out of six residents are over twenty-one, nine out of ten are white, and they include some of the nation's most familiar names in literature and the arts, in entertainment, finance, philanthropy, and politics. "I represent brains," Lindsay has observed. Among the 17th District's residents, for example, are former Governors Thomas Dewey and Averell Harriman, as well as Richard Nixon and present Governor Nelson Rockefeller. Robert Kennedy, by taking an apartment near the UN, became a 17th District resident, thereby joining New York's other Senator, Jacob K. Javits. Herbert Hoover, Douglas MacArthur, and Eleanor Roosevelt all were 17th District residents.

Democrats heavily outnumber Republicans.* In recent Presidential elections they have been Democratic (President Johnson carried the 17th by about 70,000 votes), but Republicans have

* The 17th was established in a 1917 reapportionment, and has retained its distinctive area since then, despite expansion in size and population. In 1917 the District had not more than 200,000 residents, a figure which has nearly doubled in the half century since. A major adjustment occurred in 1961, after the 1960 census, when about 120,000 people (some 50,000 voters) were added. Some 13,000 of these were in the huge Stuyvesant Town development alone, and these were nearly two-to-one Democratic in enrollment. The strength of the Democrats, as measured by their enrollment of voters in comparison with Republicans and the non-enrolled, increased sharply, despite the fact that the reapportionment was in the hands of a Republican-controlled Legislature (some Democrats had accused Lindsay of influencing the legislators to keep some Democratic areas out of the 17th or to eliminate others).

carried it for Congress each time since 1936, though the margin has ranged from a scant few hundred in 1954 to John Lindsay's 80,000-plus over two opponents a decade later. An indication of the independence and sophistication of the 17th's voters is dramatically drawn by the 1964 returns which show that some 75,000 of them, far more than half of those who voted for Democrat Johnson, switched to the Republican line for Congressman Lindsay.

As for the "silk stocking" label, it is a survivor of some bygone age when silk stockings were enough of a rarity to warrant comment and to cause this strange tag to be hung on a portion of a cosmopolitan city. Manhattan's East Side itself, it must be noted, is not known as a "silk stocking" area; this is a name applied, oddly, only to the Congressional District.

Historically, apart from the illogic involved, "silk stocking" as applied to the 17th Congressional District derives from an assembly district, no longer in existence, which covered part of the upper middle East Side in Manhattan. But the crowning aspect of the misnomer is that the District, in Lindsay's words, "contains the most varied mixture of people and incomes and living conditions of any Congressional District in the United States."

The Census Bureau marks it as the District that has the largest number of nationalities living within its borders. Lindsay points out: "From block to block the contrasts are sudden and striking. Around the edges of Central Park and down the avenues on the East Side are big luxury residential buildings. In this part of the city many of the buildings have large rooms, penthouses, every modern-day comfort, and doorman protection. The apartment houses on Fifth Avenue have breathtaking views of the park and the entire skyline of Manhattan. Along the side streets there is good living, too."

But he adds, "There are also the refuse-strewn blocks where the sun never enters. It is always gray, and one can sense fear and tension. At night you want the day. And in the day you want the night to hide you from it and it from you."

In any event, the "silk stocking" name, which John Lindsay has tried in vain to avoid and to discourage, is exceedingly misleading when applied to today's 17th District, with the implication that all those 400,000 people—those who live alone, the pensioners and the clerks and the starstruck girls from Menomonie, the drifters in the cheap hotels of the near West Side, these and all the others who may live almost cheek-by-jowl with, or who are, the famous and notorious—are cut from the same privileged cloth. Actually, the District is one of the most varied in the nation.

As Congressman John Lindsay's home base it is worth special note not only for its theaters and skyscrapers, the UN, and the glamor and grime, but because its very heterogeneity generates the will to support a Congressman of independent mind and voice.

As John Lindsay told groups of them who came to hear him explain his views, and especially to explain away Barry Goldwater on the same ticket, "This is an extraordinary District . . . in enrollment nearly two-to-one Democratic—but liberal enough to send a Republican to Congress . . . and liberal enough to give him the opportunity of exercising great freedom.

"Which he should do in any event."

4

. . . As Lindsay

IF John Lindsay is almost devout in his respect for Abraham Lincoln, the sire of the Republican Party, he is often accused of holding his party itself at arm's length. His campaigns play down "Republican" identification almost to the point of disappearance, and he follows a highly irregular party line in Washington. Amazement and amusement followed his 1965 declaration he would run "as Lindsay" for Mayor of New York City.

But if this freedom from label is characteristic of John Lindsay, he is still both ardent and articulate in delineating a future course for the Republican Party. He tries not to disassociate himself from Republicanism in this role, but to shore it up and bring in supporting timbers to buttress sagging walls. Some elements in his party decry him as a poor Republican, or no Republican at all. With at least equal vigor, a growing number of Republicans and independent voters see in John Lindsay a man, perhaps *the* man, who will one day emerge as the party's greatest hope to win national office.

What is the quality of John Lindsay's Republicanism? How good a Republican is he? The word "Lincolnian" drops frequently and easily into any conversation or speech in which he has occasion to talk about his party, his politics, his philosophy. "I am Lincolnian," he says, "in that I believe when an individual or a locality can't help itself, it is the function of the federal government to help it . . . to live in dignity and to live decently as human beings. This is the ancient tradition . . . of Republican thought."

And this, basically, is where John Lindsay's Republicanism begins and where it is visible—the worth of the individual. This concept has marked his response on issues, programs, and legislation. At the 1964 convention he cited repeatedly the Lincolnian origins of the party. And in March, 1960, in one of the most important speeches he has delivered in the House, Lindsay ended an impassioned plea for a strong civil rights bill by quoting Lincoln at Springfield in 1857 as, "reminding us that the authors of the Declaration of Independence 'intended to include all men.' "

In lighter moments John Lindsay has tended to dismiss his Republicanism casually. His family voted Republican as he grew up, though, as he frequently adds, his father was a supporter of Al Smith, "perhaps because he was a New Yorker, with a derby and a cigar." But when he talks about his "Republican heritage," he means intellectually rather than by family tradition. He says, "I can't imagine being anything other than a Republican." Clearly his belief in Lincoln's Republican Party is substantial, not really shaken even by the trauma of 1964, and one of his great tasks as a promising leader and spokesman for that party is to convey the basis of his faith to a growing number of not necessarily convinced voters.

Since he is a man of action as well as ideas, the answer to the widely expressed and perplexing question, "Why is John Lindsay a Republican?" has to be found in his reactions to immediate political dilemmas.

In the Democrats, he says, he sees "the very opposite of Lincolnian philosophy, for the most part. Lincoln forswore both power for its own sake and motion for its own sake. When he used Presidential power aggressively and bluntly, he publicly acknowledged regret at having to do so."

• • •

In Congress, Lindsay's votes turned out to have been the same as the majority of other Republicans' three times out of five in his first two terms; he supported most Eisenhower bills that were opposed by the dominant conservative Democrats and Republicans. In his third term (1963–64), he found himself in agreement with the majority of GOP members on only one vote in three. This trend apparently reflected his readiness to vote for an incumbent President, Republican or Democrat, on key issues involving foreign and domestic policy. In his first term, when President Eisenhower was in the White House, Lindsay supported him four times out of five, well above the overall Republican record, but he was frequently at odds with Eisenhower on issues like public housing, aid to education, and a national minimum wage.

In the first two years of the Kennedy Administration he supported the President two times out of three on such key issues as liberalized immigration policies, trade expansion, social welfare measures, and foreign aid; in the next two years he increased his support on liberal measures (aid to education and to Appalachia) to about three out of four, which was almost as often as he had supported Eisenhower. His backing of the White House, whichever party holds it, remains far higher than the overall Republican figure.

From 1961 to 1964, as William Buckley's *National Review* pointed out, Administration-sponsored bills were saved by Republican votes in forty-five instances. In thirty-one of these Lindsay's vote was cast with the defecting Republicans'. His support was also invaluable in a major showdown of 1965: the crucial Administration housing bill of late June might have gone down to an unanticipated defeat at the hands of a conservative Republican-Democratic coalition but for four New York Republicans, including Lindsay. On a key vote the four made the difference between victory and defeat.

"I have a careful money-voting record," Lindsay has said of himself. Early in his first term he told his constituents, "I intend at all times to keep a watchful eye on federal spending." He feels that "All federal programs should meet the test of necessity and need. Necessity for maintaining our defensive strength and our leadership position in the free world; the need of our people to live decently and without fear of economic calamity that is not of their own making and which they themselves cannot overcome." Again, defending the Eisenhower "pay-as-you-go" formula, he declared: "The policy is sound, even though it is painful and possibly unpopular to insist upon paying for what we get." And: "The President is correct in insisting upon the Congress' paying for the programs it enacts; spending should be according to priorities of national needs, and pork-barrel approaches to legislation must be avoided." His "careful money" record was not unrelated, in some of its aspects, to other votes over the years (as fruitlessly cited by his 1964 Democratic opponent): against area redevelopment and public works, extensive agriculture subsidy, a veterans' housing loan program, food stamps, and extension of the Food for Peace program. Partially on the basis of such votes, Lindsay was branded as a "phony liberal" by New York City Council President Paul Screvane after he entered the mayoralty race of 1965; this was before the Liberal Party rejected Screvane as a candidate in favor of Lindsay. *New York Post* editor James Wechsler wondered whether such critics "can offer any comparable examples of fidelity to principle under fire."

Though he was an organizer and is uncrowned leader of the "Wednesday Club"—a score of younger liberal Republicans—he was named in the spring of 1965 to the Republican Policy Committee in the House. A unanimous vote of the seven-state Northeastern delegation selected him as that twenty-two-member group's representative on the committee. It was a significant designation (that he was unopposed underscored its meaning not only for the Northeasterners but for the House as a whole). The committee is one of the more prestigious in the Congressional machinery; in the past, in fact, John Lindsay had found himself in conflict with some of its decisions, as on the 1961 enlargement of the Rules Committee. As indicated by its name, the Policy Committee is intended to determine the party's positions on outstanding legislative items. To be selected for its membership gave Lindsay a new forum on Capitol Hill for his voice and views. That this was conferred by vote of other Congressmen, rather than simply coming about through the inevitability of seniority, was also significant.

The "Wednesday Club" was organized by only seven junior Republican members, all but one from the East, in the opening days of the Eighty-eighth Congress in 1963, to "discuss issues, exchange information, and have a few drinks together." It was enlarged to fifteen a year later, and it was only when they sent a letter to Secretary of State Dean Rusk proposing a Johnson-DeGaulle conference that their existence as a group even came to light.

Three days after the 1964 election debacle (with one of their members, Sibal of Connecticut, defeated in the Nov. 3 action) the Wednesday Clubbers met on a Friday to discuss the party's future. John Lindsay said afterwards: "We are among the Republicans who will have to rebuild the Republican Party out of the ashes. We hope we can work with other moderate groups throughout the country to return the party to the tradition of Lincoln."

Originally it was a progressive group; all of the charter members had voted for permanent enlargement of the Rules Committee. The membership now is more representative of the liberal-to-moderate House Republican membership, and its behavior in the minority leadership contest showed this. After a period of indecisiveness as to whom they would support, three quarters of the group voted for Congressman Gerald Ford, the winner, while Lindsay and four others voted for the defeated leader, Charles Halleck. One of the Club's recruits, Peter Frelinghuysen of New Jersey, was the Club's choice as Party Whip and he was defeated. Lacking empathy with much of their own party (they number about one seventh of the current Republican membership), the Wednesday Clubbers are likely, under Lindsay's informal leadership, to continue to cross party lines frequently.

The 1964 national ticket and campaign—and the election defeat in which they culminated—were major tragedies for any man who so firmly believes, as John Lindsay does, in his party as "the party of responsibility."

He has foreseen a "vast struggle" for dominance within the party, of which the 1964 trauma among Republicans was but a small piece, "to see whether the Republican Party will move back to a moderate position."

If it does not, "a splintering reconstruction of the political system" may occur, he has said. Foreseeing "a multiplicity of parties if one of the major parties is too rigid," he has spoken of an "efficient flexibility" as a suitable posture for a party. The 1964 campaign, Lindsay points out, was "the first time in history that a major party has failed to find a middle ground. . . . It is essential that the party assume proper direction, think of itself as the party of Lincoln."

If John Lindsay considers his Republicanism Lincolnian, how does this translate meaningfully to others, in a day when only a fourth of all Americans consider themselves Republicans? It must be noted, first, that the quality of his Republicanism might be said to have been written by the voters of his 17th District. In 1964 they overwhelmingly elected him, on the Republican line, while rejecting overwhelmingly the national brand of Republicanism offered simultaneously. Of every ten voters who approved of him in 1964, about six turned away from the Republican Presidential candidate.

It should next be noted that in Washington he is anything but a party regular. The Republican leadership cannot count on his vote but, as an astute observer noted, neither can the Democrats. He himself has admitted, "I'm sufficiently independent to have come close to the edge of being ineffective." He has exercised this independence of conscience and expressed an independence of judgment on issues as they came separately before Congress and confronted him. He has bucked the party's leadership frequently on major issues but has just as often provided his party with stalwart leadership and voice as well as vote. Time and again he has spoken out on principle more vigorously, more tellingly, against the Democratic Administrations and Congressional policies than has any other Republican in Washington.

Lindsay speaks articulately not only in Washington but all over the nation as a Republican legislator. As such, he is one of the party's speakers most in demand—his dais engagements average about four a week and these represent only a fraction of his invitations. One of his principal themes is "The Republican Challenge" or a variation on it, and to audiences all over the country from Boston to Milwaukee, Philadelphia to Kansas City, Washington to Minneapolis, after conceding his party is more of a minority than at virtually any time in its history, he says:

First, the Republicans have the task of recapturing the political center they once owned. This would be a purpose not for its own end but to discharge a social obligation; use of government to provide enough order in society that every human being may live in dignity, respect law, and receive justice—and exploit to the limit the best in himself.

But being in the center means the door must be open to everyone, with an active welcome. He is frank to note where the most important falling-away has occurred: "We must see to it that our Negro citizens come back to the Republican Party and that scholars, writers, teachers, and intellectuals in every occupation find a political home here. Neither businessman nor laborer, professional man nor farmer, should ever feel a sense of discomfort in turning to Republican candidates. It must be an open society, this Republican Party. . . ." He includes city-dwellers among those who must be embraced within the party, if it is to survive. "We cannot turn our backs on the cities. . . . I hope my candidacy [in New York, 1965] will demonstrate that the Republican Party cares deeply about the people of our cities."

Different shades of opinion must be able to thrive in both parties, Lindsay warns, if the two-party system is to survive. "Without sufficient intra-party flexibility, a big country-wide party will break. There must be sufficient bend in the arc that embraces the party in order to allow for differences, and respect them."

He points out, too, that the opposition must see a much greater role for itself than merely to oppose; it must want to govern: "This means programs, as programs are always required to meet different conditions."

Most important, pragmatically, in his desires for his party is "the significance of running candidates." And here there begins to emerge what must be the key to his own concept of himself as Republican, politician, office-holder, candidate, and a man who would be hard put to let his ambition outrun the ambition of others for him.

"Policy has little meaning in the abstraction," says Lindsay in his talks about the Republicans. "It needs flesh and blood. It is right and proper that the political systems of each community develop and organize themselves around local candidates; this is meaningful. Abstract policy will not sell in the absence of the personality of candidates to put it around. The shape of the party will be controlled by the extent to which local candidates for office are developed, educated, supported, and tested."

And perhaps Lindsay's most important single statement involves theory, practicality, and the essence of a determined realism. It had immediate application to the problem of New York City politics as he found it in 1965: "You discover the meaning of the loss of power only when a candidate is lost in a local, or other, election."

In other words, if you can't win, you can't govern; your ideas are sterile, for they are destined not to be placed in practice, and you are a theoretician romancing the idea of government but unwilling to come to grips with the essence of government, which is holding office to exercise power. Not merely the candidate's basic quality and character, but also his ability to find and express, even through a projection of "personality," the heart of the matter, enable voters to be willing to entrust power to him.

"Power lost is power gained by others, and here the control of parties and the formulation of issues and policies take place. Those who wish to shape the government will do so by their involvement in local campaigns, and with the daily headache that people in office —or standing for office—have. Involvement is the answer, and involvement is the obligation."

Implicit in his approach is the free and independent choice, freely and independently exercised, by the voter-at-large. He believes and expects that the discriminating voter will seek out and support the supportable candidate. Party lines will be crossed if not ignored; the pressure will be on the parties and on the leadership—on the "bosses," where they may still exist—to search for and choose candidates, bearing in mind that if they appeal to small interests rather than to the great cross section, they will lead that party into a permanent minority status. What is involved is ticket-splitting—a kind of selective process which in fact enhances the dignity of the citizen-voter and improves his chance of finding choices of a higher quality next time.

"I detect a growing sensibility on the part of the American public," Lindsay said midway between his overwhelming re-election to Congress by a record-breaking exercise in ticket-splitting and his high dive into the New York City mayoralty contest, "and it is a very healthy one. Parties must shape themselves to the expectations of the people pretty quickly if they are to survive. Voters increasingly are exercising discriminating independence in their choice of political leaders. Party lines are not as readily accepted as they were a few years ago. People like unbossed candidates, and more and more assign priority to caliber and competence rather than party espousal."

John Lindsay, who has hugely benefited from the trend he describes, finds this encouraging: "A happy development in the face of massiveness in almost every other area of American life. It is," he suggests, "as if Americans were exercising some instinctive countervailing force."

On the other hand, of course, there is the relation of the office-seeker and office-holder to a party which has lent him its name and support and whatever material aid and reservoir of reputation it can summon. What is Lindsay's responsibility to his party?

Part of John Lindsay's answer must be found in his behavior. In 1964, for example, he performed high feats in Washington on the Civil Rights Act. Throughout the year-long struggle for its enactment he functioned—in committee deliberation, in floor management and debate, in exposition and exhortation all over the country—very specifically as a Republican legislator. He was willing to co-operate with the Democrats to produce an enactable and desirably strong law, yet he stood distinctly apart from them in approach and strategy. "The bill is largely Republican," he proudly told audiences after the effort had brought conspicuous success and wide acclaim. Lindsay sought to persuade the Republican National Convention through the platform committee and on the convention floor, to "honor its heritage" and stand strongly behind the law. He was turned down, and the party nominated a man who was in turn scornful, dubious, and tolerant of the law—an attitude which had finally provoked his principal convention foe, Governor William Scranton, into his belatedly determined stance.

Unable to reconcile this behavior on this and other issues by party and candidate with traditional party doctrine, Lindsay chose to run a campaign "without reference" to the national ticket. It was an elementary question of survival which drove right to the heart of Lindsay's commentary on "the loss of power when a candidate is lost . . . power lost is gained by others."

Facing a Republican in his position was the need to preserve principle and integrity while at the same time preserving his own ability to hold office, to exercise the "power" of the man who wins. Some, notably Arthur Krock, have argued that such a candidate who participated in the convention's deliberation and choice should be bound by that choice, deprived of his own discretionary judgment. But such arguments in fact are linked to the inflexibility against which John Lindsay raises his voice not only for himself but for all within the party: "Without sufficient intra-party flexibility, a big country-wide party will break . . . the party must allow for differences, and respect them."

In one important interpretation, it is more important for the party to have the flexibility to accommodate divergence and diversity than to be the exclusive province of a single-minded, small-minded club. The latter is the end product of the splintering of which John Lindsay has cogently warned—the progenitor of the multiplicity of parties he would avoid. It is very much one with the spirit of "In your heart you know he's right" (and everyone else is wrong); and the assurance given the 1964 GOP convention by one of its anointed, "You are the salt of the earth." And it is akin to the exclusiveness of the proposed rightist organization, shucking off, if not exactly splintering from, the Republicans, with Barry Goldwater taking a leading part in mid-1965.

A major part of the remainder of John Lindsay's response on this question of the politician's responsibility to his party was written in 1965.

As the mayoralty campaign shaped up he was raising eyebrows and questions, and creating controversy as well as gaining commendation with his "I am running as Lindsay" statement.

In keeping with his basic philosophy that it is a duty of the office-seeker to find winning ways, Lindsay has emphasized "the candidate"—the individual, the personality, and his exposition of issues—rather than party label. In his Congressional campaigns it has been a subject of comment, amused or tart depending on the point of view, that Lindsay campaign posters and pamphlets failed to display the word "Republican" prominently if at all. A typical piece of literature might not include the party's name, but the reader would have no doubt about who was "the District's Pride, the Nation's Hope."

The proof was in the result. For John Lindsay, the device of playing up "the candidate" rather than "the party" has been startlingly successful.

In his campaign for mayor he sought and accepted the Republican designation. Again there is a downplay of the constricting label "Republican," though one would search fruitlessly in 1965, as in previous Lindsay campaign years, for any disavowal of the party as such. Entirely to the contrary, Lindsay was publishing articles with variations on the theme of "The Challenge to the GOP," and making speech after speech on the problem of the party at low ebb in reviving its fortunes within its traditional lines.

Though he talked of "fusion" (as in 1961) and contemplated a city-wide ticket with Democrats or Liberals as running mates, he chose the state's Republican senior Senator as his campaign chairman. Though he established an impressive, ambitious network of district campaign headquarter outposts to be manned by volunteers, he identified himself with Senator Javits, former Mayor LaGuardia, and others—"they are Republicans and I am a Republican." * Though he drew some startled attention by brushing off possible campaign support from such out-of-town party bigwigs as General Eisenhower, this was clearly a device to neutralize the Democrats'

* In a variation on this, he once remarked to a clergymen's group: "I am a Republican, but don't hold it against me."

ability to use the President, Vice-President, and an entire battery of Democratic campaigners from Washington and elsewhere.

Though he did exclaim that he would campaign "as Lindsay" (actually, what more could a voter ask than that a candidate be himself?), he stopped far short of disassociating himself from any of its important local elements. This strategy was promptly endorsed by virtually every national leader of party—Nixon, Romney, Scranton, and others except, understandably, Barry Goldwater. Though he fell back, at one uninspired point, on the cliché that there is neither a Republican nor Democratic way to clean the streets, he also declared "I am a Republican." Though confronted on the one hand with an enrollment bulge in favor of the Democrats of about three to one, he was confronted on the other with a dormant if not comatose Republican organization which has been accused of liking to lose elections. Though in Washington he had departed from the party line on many issues when he disagreed with the leadership or majority on matters of principle, he never qualified to rank with the fence-jumping "sons of the wild jackass"—Norris, LaFollette, Hiram Johnson in another day and Morse, on the one hand, or Thurmond, on the other, in our own.

The answer to the question of "How good a Republican is John Lindsay?" must be: Intellectually he is a strong Republican; emotionally, he is fiercely independent; spiritually, he is a progressive and in that sense frequently finds common cause with the Democratic liberal group. But much more importantly, he is morally and ethically committed to principles he holds to be paramount in value to all other considerations. Thus he is entitled to run, in a campaign of his own making, not merely as a Republican but "as Lindsay," in keeping with his tenet that the office seeker has a responsibility to survive in the struggle for power—*responsible* power, as delegated by the people.

The Lindsay brand of Republicanism has proven overwhelmingly acceptable to the voters. There are skeptics just as there are rivals among the party's pros. Yet even before Lindsay began to "win big," a voice from within the House of Representatives campaign committee was heard to say: "A few more like Lindsay, and all we'd have to do is wave some flags to carry the House and Senate." This, of course, reflects a projection of the Lindsay "image" and the Lindsay "profile" or the Lindsay "charm" much more than it represents an understanding of the Lincolnian Lindsay.

In Washington there is a saying that if John Lindsay were a Democrat, he would rank among the dozen men running the House of Representatives. As an urban liberal Republican, however, he finds himself in a minority within the minority on Capitol Hill. To Lindsay himself the supposition that he could be much more a decision-maker, a doer and a shaper, a mover and a shaker as a Democrat—is idle and it is preposterous.

5

It Proved I Am a Free Man

As winter turned into a slushy early spring in 1958, very few people anywhere cared whether a thirty-six-year-old lawyer named John Lindsay became the Republican nominee for Congress in Manhattan's 17th District. And in the District itself many people clearly preferred almost anyone else.

The seat had been held since 1946, rather shakily in recent years, by Frederic (Fritz) Coudert, and before that by a string of rather familiar names.* It was in the style of some of them that the District had gained the never valid but incredibly indelible stamp

* These included Democrat Claiborne Pell immediately after World War I, soon after the District's establishment; Ogden Livingston Mills in the twenties; Ruth Baker Pratt in the Hoover period; Bruce Barton in the late thirties (he was the middle man in FDR's 1940 slogan of disdain for "Martin, Barton and Fish"); and liberal Kenneth Simpson and Joseph Clark Baldwin during and after the war. Coudert beat Baldwin in a 1946 primary fight in which Lindsay was a volunteer worker for the losing candidate. Among the unsuccessful aspirants for the 17th seat over the years was Heywood Broun, Socialist candidate in 1930.

"silk stocking" that was to pain John Lindsay and others in more recent years.

Coudert (the name is given a Gallicized pronunciation—Coo-*dare*) was a stodgy politician, not of the derby-and-cigar stodginess, but of a curly-coifed, rimless-spectacled stodginess whose remoteness of manner put many a voter edgily in mind of high-collar Hoover Republicanism. Coudert had gone to Washington with the same freshman group of Representatives that included John F. Kennedy, Richard Nixon, Jacob Javits, Kenneth Keating, and others who went on to win their spurs as masters of politics. But the 17th District's representative apparently viewed his principal mandate as going to Washington to vote against Harry Truman, and he voted against Truman measures with a will while that era lasted. After that he voted with a will against much of the Eisenhower program. And Coudert voted, seemingly with conviction, for what McCarthyism stood for in the 1950s. His was not a popular posture in the cosmopolitan 17th. In 1954 he survived the challenge of a youngish Democratic PT-boat hero, Tony Akers, by a mere 314 votes. Two years later, with Eisenhower leading the ticket to smashing majorities almost everywhere, Coudert was able to hold onto the 17th seat, once more against Akers, by a slim 2,500-vote majority.

No wonder, then, that restlessness was stirring within at least a small cell of the 17th's Republicans, in the New York Young Republican Club, and in a few other spots. This included Joseph Macchia, a lawyer; Charles Metzner, another lawyer who now is a federal judge; John Ellis, a broker; and a law student named Robert Price, a name to remember.

Their man they hoped—the hope was just a bare glimmer—was John V. Lindsay. Not long back from Washington service in the Justice Department, he was re-establishing himself in an interrupted law practice with one of the city's larger firms, and reaccustoming himself to apartment life on the East Side with his wife and their three little girls. He had served an active term as president of New York's Young Republicans (a rather tenuous distinction, as events later showed) and had been an enthusiastic Eisenhower Republican when most young lawyers everywhere were Eisenhower enthusiasts. He had helped found the Youth-for-Eisenhower movement in 1951, and cashed much of the credit for this activity when he took the Justice Department job, but he felt some credit remained; he drew on it (and on the "credit" analogy) that spring of 1958.

During the winter he had huddled with Price and Ellis and Macchia and other anti-Coudert dissidents who were willing and even anxious to be pro-Lindsay. There were rumors that the seat was going to be vacated, that the solution for Fritz Coudert and his rigidity and his unpopularity would be an ambassadorial appointment. Names of potential successors began to appear occasionally in political columns: Eric Javits, nephew of the Senator; Elliott Goodwin, another former Young Republican Club president; a State Senator named MacNeil Mitchell who, it was said, might well get the organization's support; and John V. Lindsay. Last of all, John Lindsay.

By late winter it was evident that if Coudert chose to try to remain in Congress, he would probably face a fight within his own party. And there loomed again the specter of tough Tony Akers in November. Manhattan's GOP County Chairman, Tom Curran, also of the complacent and nostalgic backward glance to Good Old Republicanism, was a Coudert man, and his bravura words in these days declared that the Congressman could win a primary fight if anyone was disposed to give him a contest. But, he added warningly, that would be damaging in a district that had become as close as the 17th under Curran-Coudert leadership. And while Tom Curran was saying that, Fritz Coudert was saying a halfhearted "Count me in"; simultaneously John Lindsay was making what was virtually his first public utterance in politics: "I am under a considerable amount of pressure to run."

The pressure was from Price, Ellis, Metzner, and the others in the private little anti-Coudert, pro-Lindsay rebellion. But to the likes of Tom Curran and Fritz Coudert, and to the Javitses and the Goodwins and the Mitchells and many more, the existence of actual support for John Lindsay seemed invisible and slightly incredible. And the Congressional nomination still seemed one to be handed out by the Organization as it chose—Tom Curran's Organization, which by no definition now included John Lindsay and his friends.

"I'm called, politely, an insurgent," John Lindsay said of himself, and then he explained with earnest precision: "That word is built around the word 'surge.' According to Webster" (and here the pros must have groaned as one, "Oh, no, not a Webster-quoting candidate") "to surge is to swell. That noun is used, Webster says, as in the surge of the sea" (from the pros, sighs and more groans) "and that's what this is—a rolling groundswell."

The Curran-Coudert Organization pros might concede the insurgency, but they surely could find no urgency in it, nothing resembling a groundswell; and they surely could resist whatever "pressures" John Lindsay found building up. That was as of early March in that comfortable Eisenhower spring of 1958.

And this was still the situation as of mid-April, when John Lindsay called his first press conference as a politician. It was a far cry from that spring day seven years later when he held five widely covered press conferences in five boroughs to say, "Yes, I am going to run for mayor." John Lindsay called reporters, and many showed up, to his pleasant, smallish apartment on East Seventy-second Street near Third Avenue. With an assurance belying the large uncertainties, he announced his candidacy for the 17th District seat, whether or not Congressman Coudert chose to try to stay. "I'm in all the way to the August primary," said John Lindsay, while former national chairman Herbert Brownell nodded approvingly.

Why was he going for Congress against the obvious wishes of those Republicans who were Anybody in the District? "I am especially concerned with the loss of Republican strength in this traditionally Republican stronghold," said the new candidate, as he cited the woeful figures of 1954 and 1956. Alluding to Congressman Coudert without mentioning his name, he added, "We have not seen the type of aggressive leadership that is needed in Congress to carry forward the Eisenhower program—active support for sound legislation." With at least a surface confidence, he expressed optimism—a "certainty" in his own mind—that "many Republicans" would "swing over" to him.

But Fritz Coudert, with the prestige of an incumbent Congressman finishing a dozen years on Capitol Hill, was in a position of strength. He was the leader of the 9th Assembly District, the very heart of the 17th Congressional District. Through this and other connections he could control the loyalty of most of the Election District captains who formed the core of workers needed to win a primary.

This, then, was Fritz Coudert's hill to fight on, if he chose to fight for himself. If he preferred to pass the crown on (they were all saying publicly the day John Lindsay announced himself), the Organization's support would go to Lindsay's friend Elliott Goodwin, who wasn't yet even a professed aspirant. Or Eric Javits might conceivably come off with it. And one political columnist wrote that the party's brass in Washington—including not only New York's United States Senators Jacob Javits and Irving Ives, but also National Chairman Meade Alcorn and Vice-President Richard Nixon—would ultimately select MacNeil Mitchell as a compromise.

Anyone, anyone but Lindsay, seemed to be the message from his party's leadership. And on the big day of his own announcement, yet another political force nosed in for some prime attention. Carmine DeSapio chose that day to announce that the Democratic candidate would be Tony Akers. While Republicans wrangled among themselves for the next four months Akers, with a state patronage job behind him, could get into high gear and then coast.

But if the weight of the opposition and its seeming determination to turn elsewhere impressed John Lindsay, he surely was not overly impressed, for his own determination never wavered visibly. A week after announcing, he made his first speech, at an alumni reunion of the Horace Mann School, on behalf not of himself but of progressive legislation under the auspices of a progressive Republicanism.

He attacked the working coziness between Northern liberals and Southern Democrats in Congress and the resultant "smothering of progressive legislation." Speaking for his own party, he proclaimed it "the party of progress" that had "stolen the show and blanketed the sails of the opposition party." (The awkwardness of metaphor was not true to John Lindsay's accustomed ease of phrasing.) And when he sent off a letter to the *Times,* it dealt not at all with local issues but with a proposal in the Senate to curb the powers of the Supreme Court.

Then, less than a fortnight after announcing his candidacy, Lindsay stood up before the Young Republicans and declared that he opposed Coudert because of the Congressman's repeated support of legislation constituting "a severe hamstringing of executive powers" in the federal government. And John Lindsay unveiled again for Republicans the specter of losing the 17th, as Fritz Coudert had come so perilously close to doing, and observed tartly that if the party did indeed lose the District this year, everyone then would be asking, "Why wasn't something done about it when there was yet time to do it?" He proposed to be the doer.

Having paid his respects to Coudert, Lindsay then tried within a week the tactic of projecting himself ahead by leapfrogging over his immediate foe and addressing himself directly to the man whom he hoped would be his *ultimate* opponent. He demanded a debate with Tony Akers, asking, "What do you stand for, besides being against Coudert?"

The Lindsay tactic and the Lindsay manner and the Lindsay organization finally were attracting some more than tolerant attention. One political commentator found him a "young man in a hurry," and gathered the impression that if County Chairman Tom Curran were to block him from the 1958 nomination, Tom Curran would live to regret it, for John Lindsay would lead a fight against the Curran leadership come another year. And one newspaper noted with not unapproving surprise Lindsay's "determined bid and fast breakaway," and reported that enough young doorbell-ringers were out for John Lindsay to make genuine his threat of a contest all the way to the August primary.

Tom Curran must have thought so, too, for he said a contest would be unavoidable. His man, Coudert, began his own effort to justify and retain his seat in Washington with an announcement mentioning, rather belatedly, a need for support of the Eisenhower program. And then, just a week later, Fritz Coudert withdrew from the contest because of "private interests" that would make it impossible for him to give enough attention to Washington.

But if the avenue to the 17th GOP designation thereby seemed opened up, Tom Curran moved swiftly enough to close it off by declaring a choice would be made "right away" from among a group that included Elliott Goodwin and MacNeil Mitchell, but now also took in Pepsi-Cola's Walter Mack and Harold Riegelman, who had submitted to an earlier pasting from Mayor Wagner for the party.

"I'm glad my candidacy forced an early decision by Coudert," said John Lindsay, with some justifiable satisfaction. "It doesn't alter my decision to see it through to the primary," he added promptly.

A month after declaring his intentions at that Seventy-second Street apartment press conference, the still managerless John Lindsay made what for him was an historic move: he opened a headquarters at the Hotel Roosevelt, where a couple of rooms on an upstairs residential floor became the hive for that swarm of volunteers who were to become his campaign trademark.

The headquarters underscored his permanence in the fight and gave credibility to his aspiration. (The hotel, once the site of Thomas E. Dewey's headquarters, was to become a fixed location for every Lindsay campaign thereafter.) He sat there that day with an interviewer, a foot propped against the desk edge, a wry smile on his lean face that had somehow grown a bit leaner and just a shade less boyish ("boyish" was the political writers' term for John Lindsay that surprising season) and confided: "This is killing me—this campaigning. I've got to earn a living at the same time." (In fact, he barely found time to look in at the law firm, and he never really returned, though he has retained an association with it.)

He employed his "credit" analogy now. The 17th District, he asserted, should have been "a cradle for the new Republicanism," but in the hands of Coudert and Coudert-minded followers, it hadn't turned out that way. Anything but, in fact.

"It was embarrassing to us who were working very hard," John Lindsay said, meaning people who had gone down the line in the 17th for Eisenhower and the reforms that the new Republicanism had seemed to promise. "I've got a credit card here," he added, referring to his own bustling activity for the Eisenhower cause in the earlier days. "I think this is the time to redeem the pledge a lot of us made to our party at that time."

And the next day a District leader came in with enough green stamps to help the redemption along, at least several steps along the way. On the day Tom Curran said that he would defer the "immediate" choice he had promised (from among that group which specifically did not include John V. Lindsay), the leader of the "6th Assembly District North" Vincent Albano, Tom Curran's ultimate successor, declared for Lindsay. Here was the first real break of this campaign.

Albano's 24 Election District captains could be of much help in insuring that the 750 voters' signatures needed on Lindsay nominating petitions, the legal minimum, would be obtained before the July deadline. And Albano brought along two other Assembly District leaders, who controlled between them seventeen more Election Districts. Together the three represented one fifth of the 17th's Republicans. Even if these leaders couldn't demand the nomination for Lindsay, they would be of great aid and comfort as the realities of a primary contest became more urgent, as petitions took priority over press releases, and as voters became more than statistics in a canvass book.

The pro-Lindsay leaders were only three out of nine, and a week after they had thrown their hand in for the insurgent, it became finally and fully evident that no more defections were forthcoming. At Tom Curran's bidding the other six leaders chose Elliott Goodwin, who thus became the GOP's designee for the nomination. To become the Congressional candidate John Lindsay would have to buck Goodwin and overcome all the work that Tom Curran's six leaders and their scores of Election District captains and their scores upon scores of precinct workers could do to turn out the vote for Goodwin.

Lindsay declared as vehemently and as publicly as he could that Goodwin's selection was that of Curran and Coudert. They had done their "hand-picking without soundings" among the party's rank-and-file who would, he implied, have preferred him.

A continuation of the Curran-Coudert rule, as reflected in the

Goodwin designation, offered no visible hope for a change in the status quo, and they had "misjudged the time and the temper of our party," said John Lindsay, with considerable heat. He envisioned the party in the District as "weakened almost to the point of no return."

Lindsay petition-carriers were soon out on the streets, circulating through the apartment houses and the park areas of housing projects. Within a week they had a thousand signatures, more than enough to guarantee their man a place on the primary ballot, if all were valid and could withstand the kind of scrutiny that organizations are wont to inflict on troublemakers.

And troublemaker John Lindsay refused to be silent. He criticized the party's leadership under Tom Curran for having co-operated with Democrat Adam Clayton Powell in the Congressional District just north of the 17th. He asked for debates with Elliott Goodwin in the clubhouses where the pros and the hangers-on gathered and where they would be able to hear from John Lindsay what he had to say for himself. He demanded voting machines for the August primary and came out for Nelson Rockefeller as the nominee for Governor the day after Rockefeller announced his candidacy, saying that sentiment in the District was behind him. His people passed out 40,000 copies (more than one for every Republican) of a leaflet called, "Why this Man Should Represent You in Congress." It was the first use of what was to become a favored Lindsay campaign technique—snowing the voter under reams of printed material.

He attracted some telling support: Herbert Brownell, his old boss in the Justice Department, brought the prestige of a former Attorney General and Republican National Chairman to the Lindsay camp; the Young Republican Club endorsed him over Goodwin in a close but favorable ballot; John Roosevelt's Metropolitan Political Club overwhelmingly supported him.

Meanwhile, his petitions were circulating. At the end of six weeks of work they were in and filed with the election board. The Curran-Goodwin captains had amassed three signatures for every two the Lindsay-Albano forces could muster. The count, mildly challenged by both sides, was recorded as 5,972 for Goodwin and 4,147 for Lindsay.

The contestants were actually friends of long standing and were superficially similar. Both were Ivy Leaguers (Goodwin had gone to Harvard, Lindsay to Yale) and had been Navy lieutenants with combat records; both were lawyers; both had been Eisenhower Republicans for years; they were members of the same church—St. James's Episcopal, on upper Madison Avenue.

It was these peas from very similar pods who met as antagonists one hot night, forty-eight hours after their signed petitions had made them official opponents. In shirtsleeves, on a low dais at one end of a room crowded by six-score curious Republicans, they debated over the whir of a single electric fan at the Coliseum Republican Club on the western fringe of the District, on starkly drab Broadway near Sixty-seventh Street.

Lindsay swung out at the "decline and decay" under Curran and Coudert in the District, at least, in Republican fortunes in the District, and deplored a "loss of confidence" by the voters in response to "do-nothing policies."

Goodwin complained that Lindsay seemed to have a predilection to attack only Republicans. And though the occasion had been heralded as the first of a series, the "debates" collapsed, for the issue—discontented progressive insurgency against the conservative complacency of the Organization and its designees—was not clearly enough drawn.

To an interviewer who visited his headquarters John Linsday seemed "intense" with an "on-target drive" as the days dwindled down to a few before the primary vote—but despite the intensity he found him easygoing; his mind, quick, precise, spring-driven; his look, competent, though boyish, a look the reporter thought must be "disarming" to others.

Whether disarming or convincing, John Lindsay's appearance, his manner, his message, his words proved effective. When the primary votes were tallied, they reversed almost exactly the totals claimed by each man when the nominating petitions were filed. Lindsay was able to claim his victory before midnight. The count was 6,129 to 4,052. One quarter of the District's Republicans had voted and they had turned in a decision now considered an upset by the "experts" who had never conceded John Lindsay a winner over the Organization.

By the next morning one newspaper tagged him a "Man to Watch" and described him as boyish, charming, an intensely serious man under an apparently relaxed exterior, lacking the "surface characteristics of a giant-killer," and, more to the point, a candidate who fought with the relish of a man who loves to fight against odds. Another newspaper recalled that John Lindsay was told early in the game that the Organization would "take care of him," that he had been warned of pressures to withdraw on the promise that perhaps he could run for a seat in the State Assembly, if he behaved. But, they concluded, John Lindsay had refused "to be taken care of."

By the morning after, the new Republican candidate was forecasting that he would win in November and would beat Tony Akers "badly." He described his campaign strategy as citing what he called the Republicans' emphasis on the individual and his freedom and security.

In lighter vein, to someone who persisted with questions on the long-range ideas of this new demi-champion, he responded:

"Do I want to be Senator? Sure.

"Do I want to be Governor? Sure.

"Do I want to be President? Let's wait" (a Lindsay guffaw interrupted) "until I've at least won this election."

As for the primary campaign itself, in which he had taken on the Organization's Man and the Organization itself, and had won, in which he had won not only a political victory but a name for himself, the candidate had this to say:

"It proved I am a free man."

Ten thousand had voted in the primary; the November election would poll ten times as many ballots. As Lindsay said tersely after his midsummer: "I met the Republicans during the primary; now I want to meet the Democrats."

And meeting them, just as many of them as he could find the

hours and the energies to seek out, occupied his furious pace for the next dozen weeks. He plugged away at his task with monumental hard work; in one graphic expression, it was "shirtsleeves and sandwiches and doorbells all the way." *

Lindsay and Akers locked in one debate. The Democrat preferred to discuss foreign policy while Lindsay pressed hard on local and domestic issues. His high pitch was characterized when one observer saw him "rising from his chair like a fighter leaving his corner" answering a question.

In one significant respect, however, John Lindsay's role that fall was that not of the battler but of the peacemaker. Much of his time was spent patching wounds and sores opened during the primary warfare. "You can't run in politics with open wounds," the candidate observed. He moved on another front, too. Recognizing the danger that the core of Republican voters would desert him if they felt they had a young whippersnapper progressive on their hands (the words were John Lindsay's own), he took a hard Republican line. Aside from the obvious tacks of belaboring Tammany Hall and calling for a Republican Congress to work with President Eisenhower, he reiterated again and again that, "The national interest is best served by the Republican Party. Neither shackled by illiberal Southern committee chairmen nor committed to policies which overemphasize the role of government over the individual, it is the party of individual rights."

The weeks and weeks of tireless campaigning, of "shirtsleeves

* A development midway in his campaign proved to be one of the most significant single events of the Lindsay political career. Joseph Macchia, his campaign manager, became ill and withdrew. Robert Price, a twenty-five-year-old law student who had been assisting in the campaign work and who was one of the original inner circle, stepped in. Though the loss of Joe Macchia was unhappy, Bob Price was never displaced; he has managed all subsequent Lindsay campaigning. (Macchia has been chairman of the Congressional re-election drives.) An indefatigable worker, Price has never been paid; in the spring of 1964, he took off six weeks to manage Nelson Rockefeller's only successful primary effort, in Oregon. When he made Price the manager of his 1965 campaign for the New York City mayoralty, John Lindsay called him an "organizational wizard" and "one of the most discerning leaders in politics today." No one familiar with the Price operation of a campaign doubted Lindsay's observation that "selecting Bob Price was the first and easiest decision of the campaign."

and sandwiches and doorbells," paid off; a dividend was declared on November 4, not only for the brand of Republicanism that John Lindsay espoused and for the personal magnetism he conveyed but also for the tramping along the miles of Manhattan streets and trudging up and down the endless apartment building stairs, the handshakes by the tens of thousands, and the long, long days of driving effort.

Though the total vote dropped by nearly one fourth from the peak reached in the Eisenhower outpouring of 1956, John Lindsay trebled the 2,500-vote victory margin that Fritz Coudert had counted that year. The official vote was: Lindsay 53,674; Akers, 45,956, and this was the last of Akers' candidacies.

If the pundits had tended to brush off John Lindsay as a candidate, they turned effusive for the Congressman-elect: "He knows how to win votes," asserted one, with what was now scarcely clairvoyance. "He knows the political scene. His ability to take care of himself is proved. . . . He emerges as one of the bright hopes of the Republican Party." (The term "bright" has become so associated with John Lindsay's political future as to be almost patentable.) Another commentator found his victory the more lustrous because the 17th had been rapidly losing its Republican status. (Actually, despite its GOP tinge, the District had chosen Democratic Congressmen in five elections since its creation in 1917.)

As for John Lindsay, he spoke now not of the 17th but of Congressional Districts everywhere that his party might aspire to: "Republicans must build locally," he advised, only a day after his election. "Of course it can be done. The leaders must put up strong candidates, and do it early.

"Elected Republicans must listen to local needs, and they must perform. They must continually point out and define the issues. They must be affirmative, forceful, and unafraid when they believe they are right. And they must have the courage when it comes to saying 'No.'

"In short, they must lead. There is no room for sham in politics. It will be sensed immediately by every intelligent citizen.

"In other words, if Republicans will stick to basics and remember the origins of their party, and work hard, they will win."

He spoke as a winner, but the words were big ones for a young man who had yet to prove himself in office. Washington was all in the future, and Washington has a way with self-assured young winners, a place for them, and a way of putting them in their place.

6

As Long as I Have Voice in My Body

THERE is probably no more cherished rule on Capitol Hill than that a freshman member shall be respectfully silent during his first session. Part of Sam Rayburn's dictum was "to get along, go along," and going along means acquiescence to the proposition that the new member obviously knows little and is ill prepared to participate.

In his first month as Congressman, John Lindsay rose to take sharp issue with a senior Republican. It may have cost him acceptance by and advancement in his party in the House; still he was unable to sit silent in the presence of a blistering attack on the Supreme Court. (In a second instance during his first year in Washington, he challenged one of the most influential men in the House; he even cast aspersions on the way Congress conducted its business—and what it knew about some of that business.)

Late in January of Lindsay's first session as a back-bencher Noah Mason, a downstate Illinois Congressman with a quarter-century seniority, had launched into a rambling diatribe against the court and many of its decisions. The Warren Court was brazenly substituting "Socialist doctrines" for cherished precedents, Mason said. "How can our citizens respect present-day decisions of that court?" he asked, with what was intended as rhetorical conclusiveness. Several other members joined in the attack after Mason finished; but no voice was raised to object or to defend the court.

Lindsay paid Congressman Mason his due by acknowledging his respect for "the remarks of my distinguished senior"; but he added firmly, "I am constrained to disagree with him." Though he had come unprepared for debate Lindsay launched into a discussion of a case he had helped to argue as a Justice Department lawyer. He emphasized his own disagreement with the Supreme Court's ruling in the case, which dealt with a defendant's access to FBI materials (he found it "painted too broadly") but he declared nonetheless: "I will defend as long as I have voice in my body the jurisdiction of the Supreme Court in every area involving the personal rights and liberties of our people, including the area of internal security. I would oppose," he continued, "any effort to cut down the jurisdiction of the Supreme Court when there is a disagreement because of the result in one particular case."

Historians will deem the Warren Court "one of the great courts of our country," he prophesied; and he vigorously defended Eisenhower appointments, including that of the Chief Justice, as meeting "the highest standards of the legal profession."

In remarks foreshadowing many of his later addresses on constitutional questions, he closed with this declaration: "I subscribe to the theory that the Constitution is a living and growing document."

Within the House, no member rose to join his outspoken defense of the court. A few members did drop by to voice sympathy with his ideas (and condolences also, perhaps, for his future within the party's hierarchy) or to congratulate him on his courage and forthrightness. But the House chose, for the most part, to overlook Lindsay's indiscretion.*

* Lindsay's deep involvement with the integrity of the Supreme Court and its inviolability was foreshadowed in a letter published in the *New York Times* early in his effort to get the Republican nomination for Congress in 1958. He attacked a proposal by Republican Senator Butler of Maryland to deprive the court of its jurisdiction in important areas concerning the citizen's constitutional rights. The proposal provided that Congressional committees should be the final judge of whether questions put to witnesses are pertinent to a valid

Elsewhere the Lindsay break with Congressional tradition and his spirited defense of the court attracted attention, some of it enthusiastically encouraging. One of the country's great newspapers, the *St. Louis Post-Dispatch,* termed his speech "in the best of constitutional traditions," and added:

"This is the first time that the country as a whole has heard his name. If his defense of the Supreme Court is a sample of his thinking and his courage, the country will hear from him again."

While still in his first months in Congress, John Lindsay took on one of the Congressional powerhouses, Chairman Howard Smith of the Rules Committee, in vigorous combat over the so-called "anti-preëmption" bill.* This proposal sought to limit the scope of Congressional acts so as to avoid their invalidating states' laws not in direct conflict. The primacy of federal law is said to "preëmpt" the particular area from state action; thus, the "anti-preëmption" bill was intended to limit federal powers. Though the subject was technical and involved, it became the vehicle for one of Lindsay's most impassioned speeches in Congress—one in which, among other things, he intimated that Congress doesn't always know what it is doing.

"It would," Lindsay argued before the committee, "make a shambles of the federal supremacy clause of the Constitution by emasculating the doctrine of federal preëmption by judicial interpretation. . . . It would cut the power of the courts to invoke the doctrine of preëmption in cases of conflict between federal and state laws. Yet nothing has been adduced . . . which would warrant so drastic a measure. . . . This bill, without any demonstrated need, would substitute the sledgehammer for the scalpel."

Lindsay argued in the House against even considering the bill

---

legislative purpose, and also prohibited the court from reviewing any case involving state requirements for membership in the bar. Noting that attacks on the court dated back to the time of Chief Justice Marshall (*Marbury v. Madison*), Lindsay reviewed two previous ideas for putting limits on the court's powers, and deplored the Butler proposal as retaliatory, imperiling the independence of the judiciary, and holding out a threat of further punitive action.

* In the next Congress he provided crucial vote and voice to break Smith's stranglehold on legislation, and has consistently voted for proposals to curb Rules Committee powers.

and asserted, "We ought not to torture ourselves with debate on a proposal so unnecessary in basis, so irresponsible in concept, so uncertain in meaning, and so chaotic in operation."

He scolded his colleagues for devoting three days to the proposal when, with the session approaching its close, "appropriations bills remain untouched by us; the labor bill languishes, civil rights legislation awaits us; omnibus immigration legislation is overdue; the President has asked us for new fiscal powers.

"Isn't it ironic," he asked, "that legislation of such huge importance as the Mutual Security Act was given only four hours of debate—whereas this bill is given five?"

Lindsay told the House that "the doctrine of preëmption is the necessary lubrication in our federal system. We have enjoyed it since the beginning of time in this country. It has not been altered by the Supreme Court."

He urged members "not to be fooled" by arguments advanced by Chairman Smith and the Rules Committee, and advised them: "Before you vote 'aye' on this bill, realize exactly what you are doing."

He held one of the volumes of the United States Code as he exclaimed: "And I would recommend that you take all six volumes of the Code and go through them from cover to cover so that when the time comes, you can explain to the folks back home exactly what you have done. Otherwise you will not know.

"Is it heresy to suggest in this chamber that we do not sometimes know the full impact of what we do here when we legislate?" he demanded of the House.

The Lindsay language was bitter medicine for the ancient body to hear from one of its most junior members—Lindsay's speech referred to "my limited time here"—and the House itself was adamant. Having once before passed Howard Smith's measure (which the Senate killed in 1958), the House doggedly jumped through the same hoop. It rejected a Lindsay motion to recommit the bill to committee and another he proposed to kill the heart of it, then approved it.

So on this first day of summer in 1959, Howard Smith could sit back benignly as the House of Representatives endorsed this favored pet to "preserve States' rights." John Lindsay turned away in dismay as the "unwise, unnecessary" bill went whistling through and the House turned back with unhurried insouciance to the appropriations, civil rights, and labor bills, and the fiscal legislation that the freshman from New York had tried to prod them on.

Another outspoken defense of the Supreme Court by Lindsay occurred in 1964 after a Virginia Congressman, William Tuck, proposed to strip federal courts of jurisdiction over apportionment of state legislatures. This was a recoil reaction to decisions by the Supreme Court and lower federal courts bearing on states' prerogatives. At issue was the one-man, one-vote proposition, held by the Supreme Court to be applicable for both houses of each legislature and enforceable by district courts.

The Tuck proposal attracted sympathetic support from men with a wide range of motivations: the stern States' righters, those of thoughtful bent who wondered aloud about propriety in the federal judiciary's mandating of arbitrary rules for states, complete with deadlines, blueprints, inflexible standards, and from traducers of the Supreme Court, its members, and its theories and decisions.

"We're trying to discipline the Supreme Court today," snarled last-ditch, Old-South-Forever Congressman Mendel Rivers of South Carolina. "They're sticking their noses into evahbody's business."

John Lindsay was immediately on his feet. He struck out at both the bill and the motivations of some of its supporters. "It's a violent and devastating proposal, hastily conceived," he charged—would Congress turn next to denying the courts jurisdiction over a long list of subjects?—"and we may wipe out the Bill of Rights."

Brooklyn's Democratic Congressman Emanuel Celler, Judiciary Committee Chairman, shared leadership in the attack. They reasoned vainly. Lindsay was joined by 34 Republican colleagues, but 122 voted with Southern Democrats to push it through, 218–175.

John Lindsay has raised his voice again and again in succeeding years to support the Supreme Court's prerogatives and, generally, the trend of its decisions. He has found in the court an invaluable part of the legislative process: "The Supreme Court frequently supplies the oil that lubricates the bogged-down machinery of the legislative branch of the federal government," he remarked. "With such lubrication the legislature is able to begin to operate its machinery."

Yet he found occasion to prod the justices. "The Supreme Court has not made the protection of the Bill of Rights grow to the same extent as constitutional grants of power to governmental complexes in other areas," he complained, "and yet the need for maximum protection of basic rights is greater today than ever before."

Over and over, in speech after speech on and off the House floor, and in paper after paper, the Congressman stood firm for the integrity of the Bill of Rights against contemporary invasions. "The bulwark of freedom is the First Amendment," he said. "Of all the personal rights and liberties stated in the Bill of Rights it is the most treasured. It restrains constituted authority from interference with the rights of individuals to speak freely, to worship freely, to assemble peaceably, and to petition against grievances.

"But the First Amendment is a dike that must continually be shored up. If neglected, it will begin to crumble and will finally burst. Rather than pressing for legislation which will further erode the First Amendment, the government ought to be seeking legislation to empower it to invoke the protection of the Amendment on behalf of individuals."

At the height of the 1964 effort to push through the so-called Becker Amendment on public prayer, John Lindsay went to the ramparts again, with the First Amendment as a lance in defense of religious liberties for the individual and for minority groups.

"This—the First Amendment—has been called the bulwark of the Republic," he contended, "and the question before us now is, 'Do we want to change the First Amendment?' It must be discussed without any suggestion that those who seriously question any change are somehow anti-God or anti-children or anti-mother. . . .

"It was that Amendment," he reminded, "that probably the founders of the country and the first immigrants fought for the hardest."

Amazingly, 111 different Congressmen submitted a total of 147 resolutions to overturn the Supreme Court's 1962–63 decisions dealing with prayers and Scripture-reading in public schools. Because it sought actually to abridge the First Amendment in order to permit religious observances in the schools, the Becker Amendment was regarded by some opponents as the most serious effort in history to alter the Bill of Rights. John Lindsay was in the first line of defense against the assault as a member of the Judiciary Committee, which held extended hearings on the proposal. Those he bucked—successfully, as it turned out—included his own party's Policy Committee in the House. Taking a partisan approach to "the God issue," the GOP Policy Committee publicly supported the Becker Amendment, angering Lindsay and many others.

As controversy swirled around the bill he helped make the Civil Rights Act of 1964, Lindsay observed, "In all the discussion about civil rights, there has been scant mention of First Amendment rights and obligations." Looking with revulsion at the violence then raging in Alabama, he added, "I find it strange to hear no mention, by anyone, of the First Amendment rights in connection with events in Birmingham.

"It is the right of individuals to invoke the protection of the First Amendment against constituted authority, whether it be the federal government, Congress, a state, or a local constabulary. . . ." As for federal ability to enforce Bill of Rights protections on behalf of individuals, he argued that it "is not a right of initiative designed to enhance any power of the federal government."

Quite the contrary, he added, "It is a negative restraint against constituted authority of every kind. It is one of our unique checks and balances designed solely for protection of the individual."

The Administration, regulatory agencies, Congress, all, he said, "seem to have forgotten First Amendment rights."

Though the Bill of Rights "marks off a protected area in which each individual may develop himself and express himself in his own way," said Lindsay, "even that delimited area can be restricted in the absence of a vigilant and vocal public opinion. I fear for the guarantee of the Bill of Rights, for I have never known a day or heard of a time when the forces of myopia or tyranny were not at work. There seems to be little concern about the subject today.

"The absence of concern—and therefore of watchfulness—is an unhealthy condition. . . . The absence of primary concern over individual rights and liberties can lead to the stagnation, and ultimately the corruption, of both government and the free system that government is supposed to represent."

This theme of the individual and his government is one to which John Lindsay returns again and again. Deploring attempts by governmental bureaus to manage the news about the public's business (specifically, a Department of Agriculture news wire and a magazine started by the Comptroller of the Currency), he complained that the taxpayer foots the bill for "direct competition with non-governmental book publishers and non-governmental services."

In his home state he assailed bills, subsequently passed with the blessing of both Governor Rockefeller and Mayor Wagner, known as the "stop-and-frisk" proposals. "More is lost than is gained" by their passage, he asserted, questioning their constitutionality. He was moved to quote William Pitt the Elder on invasion of privacy: "The poorest man in his cottage can bid defiance to all the forces of the Crown. It may be frail, its roof may shake, the wind may blow through it, the storm may enter, the rain may enter, but the King of England may not enter; all his force dares not cross the threshold of a ruined tenement."

For many months he hit hard on what he called "the right to travel" issue, though few of his colleagues could excite themselves about it. Linking it to the First and Fifth Amendments, he battled hard against legislation designed to give the State Department broad authority to refuse to issue passports. In testimony before the House Foreign Affairs Committee and the Senate Foreign Relations Committee he took issue vigorously with the State Department on the use of confidential, undisclosed information in connection with denial of a passport. He urged the committees not to report out legislation that would restrict the right of travel. His long exhortation for protection of individual citizens' rights paid off eventually, for the final legislation provided, as he told the House, "necessary safeguards for the rights and freedoms of the individual," while giving the State Department the authority it needed.

One point he employed in fighting off restrictive travel proposals also exemplifies the Lindsay approach to the whole civil liberties field: "Important as the need for vigilance is, let us not be so overcome by fear and mistrust that we lose precious ground gained in the ancient struggle for freedom."

But while maintaining vigilance against governmental incursions in the rights of free men, he cautions equally against the excesses of non-official sources of restriction and censorship. "The real danger of increasing centralism does not lie in the comparatively modest federal expenditures for the destitute, for education, or for health," he points out repeatedly, "but rather in the pervasive threat to individual liberties that stems from undue concentration of military, political, or economic powers."

In the face of complacency toward such threats, he explained, private censorship efforts fail to evoke effective "countervailing efforts by other private groups." * When efforts are made to restrict circulation of books in stores and libraries, he commented that "in most cases the motivation for censorship is moralistic, not political. In some other cases in recent years the attacks appear linked—at least in ideology—with individuals or collections of individuals who hate this group or that group or this institution or that institution. Some appear to have political goals and seek to operate within or around both major political parties. . . . Most of these hate groups are not large in number—but then, neither was the Communist Party. It doesn't take large numbers to initiate or even achieve political goals."

The personal revulsion of John V. Lindsay against undue restraints on an individual never emerged more clearly than in his strong denunciation, during his first term in Washington, of the disclaimer-affidavit requirement in the National Defense Education

* Included in the attack were those who try to erase racial references from literary classics. "I am thinking specifically of the effort to censor Mark Twain's *Huckleberry Finn* because the characterization of the Negro was found distasteful," he said. "We cannot rewrite American history."

Act. He labeled "offensive" the law requiring that a student applying for a federal education loan swear he does not advocate violent overthrow of the government.

"I rebel against this kind of requirement," he told the House. "Our history and our constitutional foundations rebel. . . ." By 1965 the prospects for repeal of the disclaimer requirement had summoned enough late-gathering support to encourage optimism. Lindsay branded the required affidavit "a form of test oath which does violence to the principles for which our forefathers fought."

And the spirit of rebellion carried him into battle after battle on and off Capitol Hill in pursuit of the ideal that the individual must be inviolate to assaults by narrow interests or by the government itself. John Lindsay has been called "The Lonely Warrior."

7

One Against the House

THE walls of the old chamber echoed with the thunder of hundreds of voices in unison: *"Aye!"*

The clerk added, almost as an afterthought, his voice trailing off in bored monotone: "Those opposed . . ."

And from the rear of the minority side a single voice replied: *"Nay!"*

The voice was that of a very junior member of the House of Representatives, who was just completing his eighth month as spokesman for the 17th District in New York.

The vote was on a bill that seemed, at quick glance, easy to support enthusiastically enough. Any member would find opposition both unusual and unpopular, for such a vote easily could be construed as a vote for sin. But such was the vote cast by John Lindsay this first day of September of 1959.

The bill was sponsored by Kathryn O'Hay Granahan.* A Phila-

* Mrs. Granahan left Congress shortly thereafter, when her District was eliminated in a reapportionment, but her name should be a familiar one, since it appears on most of our currency as Treasurer of the United States.

delphia Democrat, Mrs. Granahan headed the postal operations subcommittee; her bill had heavy bipartisan backing, voiced vigorously in Capitol Hill hearings by Postmaster General Arthur Summerfield for the Eisenhower Administration.

The bill was intended to crack down on allegedly obscene mail, first by requiring the citizen to prove in court his material should *not* be banned; second, the bill increased from twenty days to forty-five days the period in which the Post Office could impound the suspected citizen's mail.

As John Lindsay pointed out, the Granahan bill, by more than doubling the time for impounding of mail, meant that a business, guilty or not, could have its receipts cut off so long as to be virtually choked to death. Also, the bill provided for the forty-five to be extended by the court if such action were determined to be "in the public interest." The target of the impounding could receive his mail only if he could prove to the court that the Post Office was "arbitrary and capricious."

Responding to John Lindsay's lone objection, Mrs. Granahan argued that the bill was necessary to help the Post Office fight a flood of hard-core pornography. "Censorship is not involved," she maintained, adding that "only the guilty" would be affected.

Congressman after Congressman rose to praise the bill and to testify to its desirability. Majority Leader John McCormack of Massachusetts recalled that for many years no bill had received such approval.

John Lindsay unfolded himself from the chair where he was slumped. Mrs. Granahan's expression "Only the guilty" gripped him. Who would determine the guilt? Despite the unanimity of the House, he had to give voice to his own reservations. "Must we burn down the barn in order to catch the rat?" he demanded. No answer came. He recognized, of course, the need for curbing obscenity in the mails. But he added quickly that if it "shocked and amazed" him, his disquiet was matched by how the House proposed to combat it. Wouldn't the bill actually preclude the courts from passing on the basic question of obscenity? And then he struck out at the expression "in the public interest" that dwelt at the heart of the new regulation.

"We are breaking new ground with this," he exclaimed. "It is too loose, and it raises constitutional questions." Indeed, Attorney General Brownell, John Lindsay's old boss in the Justice Department, had said the "public interest" approach might well be unconstitutional. To this thought, as well, the House was as unheeding as to Lindsay's other arguments. Would it not be, he inquired, "a rather drastic new concept" to shift to the mailer the legal burden of proving his material should not be banned? Everyone, the Congressman pointed out, might not agree with the Postmaster General on what could be considered "obscene" in a given instance.*

"I am constrained to vote 'Nay,' " John Lindsay finally told the House. There was a painful silence when he finished. Then more members rose to support the bill; some referred to Supreme Court decisions upsetting certain state and federal bans on distribution of certain books, magazines, motion pictures. Michigan's Clare Hoffman even accused the court of having approved adultery.

John Lindsay's vote attracted attention, questions amazed and outraged and perhaps a few admiring ones, but no more than a few. Three days after the vote the Congressman found it prudent to enlarge his explanation. "Of course I shared the concern of my colleagues in the House over the flood of obscenity in the mails," he told his inquisitors. But he went on to list "vices" the bill embodied: placing of "censorship powers over the publishing trade" in the hands of the Postmaster General, whose decision on the question of obscenity could be final and not reviewable by any court; while the mailer would have the burden of proving capriciousness by the Postmaster General.

The whole matter is shot through with questions of constitutionality and of the individual's constitutional rights, Lindsay argued. He recognized only too well the sensitivity of his position against an otherwise unanimous House, but he was far from ready to re-

* Some three years later, objecting to a bill that sought to authorize forfeiture of property seized in connection with a violation of the District of Columbia's indecent publications law, Lindsay noted that it "set no standards; apparently any minor governmental official or policeman can set himself up as the judge." The bill passed, but President Kennedy exercised a pocket veto because of "grave constitutional and other considerations."

treat. The bill, he charged, would give the Postmaster General "greater scope to deprive persons of constitutional rights in this field than ever before accorded an administrative official."

What should have been done? he was asked. "I felt, and still feel, a far better approach to the problem could have been made," John Lindsay responded, and, he added, "one respecting the rights of all."

But the Granahan bill, for better or for worse, had cleared the House of Representatives. Senate approval could be expected next if, as John McCormack's comment indicated, no bill in years had mustered such widespread support. Lindsay's one voice against the House's roar had indeed been in a lost cause, so far.

Not a single voice had been raised before John Lindsay's. Now a few second thoughts could be heard. A newspaper in the capitol argued his position, declaring in an editorial which deplored the "scant debate and even scanter reflection" given to the bill, "censorship by official fiat cannot cure obscenity; it can only destroy freedom." It quoted the young Congressman's "sole speech made against the bill," and predicted that the bill would create "a national censor."

The Granahan bill languished in the Senate's post office and civil service committee. Six months after his forlorn stand Lindsay was asking himself and others: "What has gone wrong here? Why am I, alone of all the members of the House of Representatives, fighting this bill?" He gave his answer to a publishers' meeting in New York City: "Where the proponents of this legislation and I appear to differ is my conviction that when an abuse needs to be met, if government is to do the job, it must do it in a manner consistent with basic freedoms—or do it not at all."

Once again the Congressman paid his fullest respects to the war on "the obscenity business," declaring, "It is against the public interest, and it should be decried." He acknowledged the Postmaster General's "sincerity and good faith." But, he added, Mr. Summerfield showed "an unfortunate predilection for applying these postal bans in respect of serious attempts at creative art or literature," so that "the legitimate publishing trade has ample cause to fear the consequences of ill-considered application of a forty-five-day mail block." And as for "an ill-intentioned Postmaster General," his power to harass any publisher "without valid grounds, in advance of court determination of any kind—already great—would be immensely increased."

But John Lindsay also placed squarely at the publishers' doors much of the blame for finding themselves suddenly confronted by such an unpalatable prospect, and he proposed a publishing industry campaign "to prevent commercial distribution practices of salacious and pornographic writings and pictures," suggesting that, "If the worst offenders know that the legitimate publishers and distributors will not hesitate to report their whereabouts to public authorities, they will certainly curtail their activities; and the public authorities, in turn, ought willingly to confine their efforts to these most flagrant offenders."

John Lindsay's deeper and underlying concern for the freedom of expression showed through clearly. "The overwhelming majority of Americans deplore censorship," he said, "but the people who would curtail the freedom to publish are vociferous; they have organized well and worked hard. If those who believe, with me, that censorship is wrong, or that thinking people must learn to distinguish between what is wrong and what their government can constitutionally do—if such people would make headway, they must take the stump, too." He pointed out that before he made his speech against the Granahan bill, not one letter, not one newspaper editorial, had come to him from his District, "the heart of the nation's publishing industry," where "more people have a close, personal, everyday stake in freedom of speech and press than anywhere else in the United States."

The danger in the Granahan bill, he said in his final blast at it, was not merely in the damage "ill-advised action" could cause to a business—even to the point of bankruptcy—but rather more importantly the "damage to the interests of the public." He reiterated, "Enshrined in the First Amendment of the Bill of Rights is free and full exchange of ideas—good ideas, evil ideas, even corrupt ideas. . . . We must be constantly vigilant for incautious use of legislative restrictions," said John Lindsay that day, six months after his one-man stand on the floor of the House, ". . . so capable of wanton destruction of our liberties. We cannot afford shabby legislation, hasty legislation, unconstitutional legislation."

At the other end of the Capitol some were listening. The Granahan bill died in the Senate, never to be revived. Lindsay's stand against the whole House of Representatives had not, after all, been in vain.

Almost exactly three years later John Lindsay again rose alone to halt a bill that seemed destined to whiz through. And again the subject fell into the area of civil liberties.

Chairman Francis Walter of the House Un-American Activities Committee offered an "anti-subversive, industrial security" bill. It would have converted into law an Eisenhower Executive Order that had been issued after the Supreme Court threw out a Defense Department regulation that set up a "security risk" program for defense plant workers. Under the bill's terms, as one Congressman put it succinctly (and approvingly), the government could move against a privately employed person "for no other reason than it doesn't like the way he parts his hair."

John Lindsay's objection was immediate, when the Walter Committee sought to put it through by unanimous consent, and temporarily effective. His lone dissent in the face of the other Congressmen's approval or apathy delayed the bill, under the rules, for a fortnight. By that time he had to turn up two other like-minded Congressmen, or his objection would be for naught.

In his warning to the House, Lindsay quoted President Eisenhower's farewell address, in which he had described the danger of "the conjunction of an immense military establishment and a large arms industry" to American rights and liberties.

"We must guard against the acquisition of unwarranted influence, whether sought or unsought, by the military-industrial complex," were among words quoted by the Congressman, adding that the bill "embodies the essence of what President Eisenhower so eloquently warned us about. The danger," he went on, "is that it makes possible the forcible separation of a man from his private employment by the government, without due process.

"Scientist X or Educator Y can be denied access to his work within a company or university without confrontation, or cross-examination of evidence used against him."

Such procedures, he observed, are serious enough when used in the governmental establishment itself; "now it is extended to the general economy."

Lindsay voiced one further objection before setting out to recruit the handful of additional Congressmen who could hold the fort with him against a bill with "most serious consequences for the whole country." Citing its failure to spell out procedures for court review, he urged that review provisions be written in "and not left to the vague possibility of some non-statutory proceeding."

Acclaim for Lindsay's stand was prompt, if from relatively few sources. A *New York Post* editorial observed enthusiastically that "Lindsay has once again defied the Un-Americans in Congress—his lone voice blocked unanimous House consent to a bill for the reëstablishment of official McCarthyism in the defense industry." Too frequently, the editorial charged, Congress "looks the other way while the hardy band of nostalgic McCarthyites [the Walter Committee] tries to bring back the good old days of nameless accusation." And it concluded: "Lindsay's lonely voice redeemed the honor of the House."

Two weeks later the bill made its deferred appearance; meanwhile every Congressman received a letter from the largest association of defense contractors, urging a vote for the bill. Would Lindsay produce two more colleagues who would go along with him? He produced three—Ryan (New York), Reuss (Wisconsin), and Roosevelt (California)—all Democrats. That won further delay. The bill came off the consent calendar once more, and this time it was a full month before Walter brought it in again.

By introducing the bill on the "consent calendar," an accelerating procedure usually adopted only for non-controversial measures, Walter was gambling on unanimous approval. It was a customary tactic of his that had hitherto been unbeatable, but he had tied himself down to a rule that required him to get a two-thirds majority if it came to a vote.

Fighting against the bill, the Lindsay resistance group, now with two Republicans added, sent a letter to every Congressman, on that last summer night in 1962. They urged votes against the Walter bill in protest against the highhanded "consent" tactics of its sponsor "on a matter of such importance."

The resistance was successful. Its plea pulled 132 Congressmen into opposition, and this was enough to kill the bill under the two-thirds rule (247 were in favor). Never before had anyone mustered more than a half dozen names for an anti-Walter vote. The victory ranked as the greatest show of force ever recorded against the Walter Committee.

"Once again," Lindsay told reporters, "we have been able to mobilize enough persons who care about civil liberties to stop another attempt . . . to force through legislation to deprive individuals of their freedoms and violate fundamental precepts of due process." He was earning Murray Kempton's description of him, that he was "familiar for his solitary dissents from assaults on personal liberty."

What had he accomplished this time? Other opinion varied. The magazine *Rights* headlined the climax of Lindsay's "singlehanded" effort thus: "Brave Congressmen Block Bad Bill." William Buckley's *National Review* asked cynically: "Why did John Lindsay, whose political ambitions are vast, put himself on the line on this one? Do his sensitive political antennae tell him another anti-security brouhaha is in the making? The politicos think the answer is simpler than that. Lindsay, they say, is already bucking for Albany, and to get to Albany, he'll need hard-left votes."

The American Jewish Congress dispatched its congratulations, declaring that "the evil of the faceless informer should not be given Congressional sanction." And *The Nation* later termed Lindsay a "hero" of the session. But barely five months after he had pushed Francis Walter and the HUAC to the wall, Lindsay lost in another showdown.

In 1963, as he had in three successive Congresses, Lindsay sponsored a resolution to abolish the Walter Committee and to transfer its responsibilities to the Judiciary Committee which, he pointed out, "has a tradition of fair play." He cited the fact that Judiciary has jurisdiction over 95 per cent of the criminal code,

HUAC over 5 per cent, and that in the Senate, internal security matters are handled by a Judiciary subcommittee.

These were points that Lindsay made when he appeared before Howard Smith's Rules Committee in 1963. Chairman Smith asked if he thought his resolution would have a chance of passage, assuming that it ever came before the House.

"I do know many members of the House agree with me," Lindsay replied, "but whether they would want to go on the record to express this agreement might be another matter."

He explained that while he didn't oppose the "purposes" of HUAC, he was convinced Judiciary could do the job better, if for no other reason than the "many slips" the committee had made in the past.*

The *New York Times* commented that it was a "sound proposal," deserving the consideration of the whole House. But Rules turned away the idea by a vote of twelve to one.

* Shortly before, Lindsay was one of three New York Congressmen who joined in condemning the HUAC investigation into the nation-wide Women Strike for Peace organization, dedicated to nuclear disarmament and peace. A dozen New York City residents were subpoenaed to appear before the committee. Lindsay sent a telegram of concern to President Kennedy. Later the Congressman commented: "There were four or five Communists among this large group of women, and presumably the committee's purpose was to expose this. But what happened to First Amendment rights—the right to assemble, to speak, and to petition—in the process? Few seemed the least troubled by the point."

8

A Spear Against "The Club"

HAD John F. Kennedy lived, he might have helped to bring about a revolution in the House of Representatives, Lindsay said a fortnight after the President's assassination.

Lindsay himself has been a tireless battler for reforms, if not revolution, in House practices and procedures. He has persistently scrutinized the time-honored and timeworn machinery that inflicts inefficiencies, ineffectiveness, indecision, and incapacity on so much of the House's operations, and occasional discredit to the body or some of its members.

He had pounded away in his first five years in Congress at certain practices which the House tolerated and let accumulate under its thick carpets. He had annoyed the House about its expense-accounting practices, had worried it on conflict-of-interest, had proposed some reforms along the lines of the British Parliament, had questioned the seniority practices, had denounced some committee-system ills, had nagged about lack of meaningful debate, had wounded the Tuesday-to-Thursday legislators by showing up the shoddy habits they had led the House into, had proposed to clean up the *Congressional Record* scandals, and had tried to limit the use of the franking privilege; he had been among the band who defied the enormously powerful Rules Committee. In short, John Lindsay had been mean to the House of Representatives, had pricked its comfort and bled its convenience.*

In early December of 1963 he reflected on the future of the House and its creaking procedures as he stood before an audience at New York University. When he suggested that a Kennedy-led "revolution" in the House had not been unlikely, he characterized it as a sweeping change in the House "power structure, rules of procedure, and cast of characters."

Looking back at his five years on Capitol Hill, and farther, he saw marked deterioration. "It has come close to being totally negative, almost completely stalemated, with an incapacity to move at all."

What might President Kennedy's role have been in this? Lindsay saw it, in a melancholy glance toward a future that would never be, as the possibility that the late President might have been able to ignore his 1964 opponent and to campaign instead for a change in the entire decision-making fabric of Congress.

How likely was this prospect? The answer is only conjecture. Certainly Mr. Kennedy's successor, however able he was virtually to ignore his 1964 opponent, did not choose even to whisper about the Congressional power structure, much less to campaign for revolutionary changes.

But the Lindsay idea served to underscore his own commitment to changes in the status quo. He advocates change even when it in-

* Lindsay speaks with affectionate objectivity about the operations of Congress. He has told gatherings of students that at least one among their number will sit in such a legislative body—adding that Congress is composed of "ordinary mortals." It is, he says, like a pressure cooker on a stove, for "it produces only under pressure"; the result can be likened to "a bunch of personalities getting together and making decisions." The burden is on the individual Congressman to bring his whole experience to bear when making his decisions on legislative proposals before him, to employ all the knowledge he can cram into his head, not omitting the "hunch" factor. And when the legislator has to depart from party or other predictable elements, in favor of what he must regard as "personal principal," that private judgment ordinarily will be respected by his colleagues and his constituents.

volves the over-my-dead-body areas inhabited by laissez-faire legislators who are senior to him and so much more powerful within the Club.

Not long before the Kennedy assassination John Lindsay had outlined three specific proposals for Congressional reform. In one major aspect they drew heavily on the British system, and he recalled having once queried the government in London as to how it handled conflict-of-interest issues. The reply, he recalled, was: "Dear Mr. Lindsay: We expect our Ministers to behave like gentlemen."

Lindsay's idea for Q-and-A sessions before Congress was borrowed from the British. In many respects it would be similar to their custom of having the Ministers subjected to close questioning in Parliament. In Congress, Lindsay suggested, this would enable the members to question a President and his Cabinet members about national problems and about their policies. (Among the supporters of the idea he identified two old Oxonians, Dean Rusk and J. William Fulbright.)

Skeptical about the seniority system's values, Lindsay offered, as his second reform, a revision of the rule which assigns committee chairmanships for the longest service. He expressed preference for designating chairmen on the revolutionary basis of what they might know about the committee's subject matter.

The third reform involved establishment of a joint committee in Congress to supervise the government's intelligence agencies. Because the CIA had assumed a policy-making role, he declared, Congress would be forced to assert its right of jurisdiction.*

In another move to clean up Congressional practices Lindsay introduced a reform resolution in 1965 that would require Congressmen, and their employees, to make public all communications of any sort to government regulatory agencies, if the communication involves a matter under the agency's consideration. "Passage of the bill," he said, "would forestall many of the letters of intervention members frequently write to appease constituents, irrespective of the merits of the specific case involved. . . . The procedure would not prevent necessary and legitimate correspondence with govern-

* Lindsay's views on the CIA are discussed in Chapter 22.

ment regulatory agencies; it simply would make such correspondence public."

These themes of the parliamentary quizzing, the committee system, and the willingness of Congress to examine developments in a vital area were the crux of Lindsay's attitude about the House. Discussing the decline of debate with an interviewer, he observed that this could hardly happen in Parliament. Lindsay was just back from a trip to England and the contrast was sharp in his mind. "Every time a government spokesman opens his mouth in Parliament," he pointed out, "he's subject to immediate challenge. Of course, you get arguments in committee in Congress, but the trouble with the committee system is that it's terribly formal, and you're subject to the whims of the chairman." Then he turned to a rather favored theme of his: the Kennedy Administration's place in the matrix of give-and-take, of debate, and of disclosure.

"I don't think the Kennedys tell us enough," he said, lumping, as he did frequently, the brothers in one monolithic administrative team. "And I don't think Congress takes on itself the examination of what happens.

"In some places the debate is terribly inadequate.* There is no real examination of the guts of the thing. Sometimes it's embarrassing, how little we know. I think the press is partly to blame. I have heard some first-class professional debate, but the press has dealt almost exclusively in conclusions."

He is inclined to credit the press with snatching up a role "largely abdicated" by Congress—the shaping of issues. While Congress backed away from its responsibility, "the vital distinction between government and opposition, proponent and critic has become hopelessly blurred," he wrote.

Lindsay proposed still another experiment—adoption by Congress of the "shadow cabinet," as employed in the House of Commons. "Shadow cabinet" members are opposition leaders who would constitute the Cabinet were their party in office. In Congress, since

* "I love the give-and-take of man-to-man debate," Lindsay once told an interviewer. "After all, I'm an old trial lawyer." He offered these as his techniques in floor speeches: "Be simple. Stick to fundamentals. Be as direct and colorful as possible. A good way to empty the floor and galleries is to get involved in long, dreary debates on the technicalities."

composition of a future Cabinet cannot be determined in advance, the roles of principal questioners would be taken by appropriate members of the minority party.

The effect, Lindsay argued, would "compel both those in power and those out of power to think carefully and coherently about major issues of public policy." Advantages flowing from it could include recovering for Congress that "power to raise and define issues and to float new ideas, a power now largely passed on to the press," and "encouragement of a more vigorous and creative political opposition."

Woodrow Wilson called the Congressional committees "dim dungeons of silence" in his classic study done seventy-five years ago. The committees, with their tradition of conferring power on the men from the "safest," mostly rural and usually most conservative Districts, are inevitably among the first targets of reformers.

John Lindsay was one of eight members of the House and Senate who, in late 1962, joined in sponsoring resolutions to establish a joint committee to study how Congress might streamline its procedures. "An urgent national need" existed, they proclaimed.* Only two House members joined in the resolutions; Lindsay's companion was Henry Reuss, a Wisconsin Democrat, who had been at his side in various other fights, and would be again. Their resolution in the House died with the Eighty-seventh Congress, and as the Eighty-eighth convened early in 1963, the proposals were reintroduced. The earlier warning that "specific reforms will be urgently needed at the opening of the Eighty-eighth" was now underscored. The Eighty-eighth came and went without the reforms, though a Joint Committee on the Organization of Congress, with limited powers, was established in the Eighty-ninth Congress. But the need continues to be emphasized by more and more voices. The forward motion of such forward thinkers as Clark and Lindsay may someday provide the impetus to overcoming the inertia of the complacent Establishment. "Behind the glittering marble façade of the Capitol," Lindsay remarked, "the same old legislative machinery groans, creaks, and

* The six Senators were Democrats Humphrey, Clark, and Engle and Republicans Kuchel, Case, and Cooper. Humphrey has since left the Senate and Engle has died. Clark of Pennsylvania has written a biting scrutiny of Capitol Hill's Establishment and its methods: *Congress: The Sapless Branch.*

sometimes breaks down. . . . It needs more than oil; parts should be replaced and, in some instances, brand-new equipment should be ordered." Congressional reform, when it comes, will come from within. As one Washington observer has noted: "While the immediate success of reform is in doubt, the ultimate triumph of the reformers is not."

"For all anyone knows the member was in his office, back in his district, or sitting in a movie." John Lindsay's "speech" one day began: "Mr. Speaker, after a good deal of thought I have decided . . ." but it was not delivered; instead it was read into the *Congressional Record* as a speech delivered in the House. He pointed out midway in the "speech" that it wasn't a speech at all, but merely contrived to appear that way in the *Record*—just as many hundreds of other statements made by members each session are contrived tacitly to deceive. "Under the rules of the House," Lindsay's statement said as it appeared in the *Record,* "a member may, by leave of the House, revise or extend his remarks, putting into the *Record* matters which were never said on the floor.

"For example, these comments which I now make were inserted in the body of the *Congressional Record* by permission but were never made orally on the floor of the House of Representatives by me. I do this deliberately, in order to dramatize the point I am making."

His point was the pleasant old deception and self-deception in which Congress has indulged for so many decades. "But," said Lindsay, "an honest record of debates and other proceedings on the floor of the House of Representatives"—which was lacking under the historic arrangement—should prevail.

"I have looked with growing concern," he "declared," "on the practice of members inserting statements in the *Record* which appear to have been delivered on the floor when in fact they were not. . . . I am old-fashioned enough to believe that oral debate is still the best method of discovering the truth on any subject. . . . The floor of the House is the proper place for members to state a public position on any important matter which later appears in the *Congressional Record.*"

To abandon the fakery involved, John Lindsay pointed out to his colleagues and to those voters who read the *Record,* would not only advance the cause of basic honesty, but might well have "two collateral and highly beneficial effects." The first is rather apparent: it could reduce the unnecessary material in the *Record,* thus saving money. The second benefit cut into much more sensitive areas for too many House members: "It might stimulate greater attendance in the House of Representatives," Lindsay reminded them. "Hopefully, the new rule would make it less attractive for members to stay in their home districts on Mondays and Fridays, appearing in Washington for only three days and two nights in the middle of the week, as is the practice now of the well-known Tuesday-to-Thursday Club." This was a slap at numerous fellow members of the New York delegation, including some of the most senior members, who combine nominal effort in Washington with law practices and other private activities in New York.

"Because of greater attendance, the proposed new rule might spur the House into high gear earlier in the session, thereby sparing some of the agony and some of the blunders made possible by leaving matters until the end of the session in the hot summer or early fall."

The remedy he offered was simple enough. The Lindsay resolution on the "honest *Record*" required that, in the printing of the *Record,* a distinctive type face be employed for those items—such as his unvoiced statement—appearing in it but not actually spoken in the House. "This," as he observed, "would permit those who read the *Congressional Record* to distinguish between what has been orally stated on the floor and what has not."

The proposal made sense. Its fault undoubtedly lay in the simple fact that it made too much sense. Most members of the House ignored the resolution, preferring, it seemed, to be able to put entire speeches in the *Record* so that these appear, to the untrained reader, to have been made in Congress. They preferred to keep the arrangement whereby they can "correct" what was really said, and even rob an opponent's remarks of meaning. And they preferred the luxury of being able to slip in those good arguments which come to mind after a debate.

• • •

On another front, too, John Lindsay tried to clean up some questionably comfortable Congressional practices.

He spoke out repeatedly on the floor on the subject of franking, and he introduced legislation to back up his position, with the intention of reforming the practice of giving Congressmen a virtually blank check for their use of the mails. The "franking privilege" means that merely the signature of a Congressman on an envelope will carry it through the mails, postage-free. It is intended to enable legislators to carry on correspondence without being penalized for thus carrying out a presumably important part of the government's business. In practice, however, it is used (and abused) as a cut-rate way of carrying a heavy load of *Congressional Record* reprints, circular letters, and other mail sent for propaganda purposes, chiefly to the individual Congressman's constituents but also to blocks of special-interest voters anywhere in the nation.

Newspaper editors, for example, are deluged with franked mail from Congressmen, but this mail, at least, is directed to the individual addressee. Beginning in 1960 Congress waived this reasonable regulation, ruling that any member could get his franked mail delivered merely by having it sent to an "Occupant" at an address, a manner of address akin to the bulk mailings of soap coupons and other promotional gimmicks.

When the idea first came up for extending the Congressional frank to take in "Occupant" mail, John Lindsay was firmly opposed. "The only justification suggested is that it would equalize the difference that exists in the Congressional mailing privilege between rural areas [RFD mail] and urban areas. It is argued that members representing urban districts should also be allowed to send out franked 'Occupant mail.' I represent a solidly urban Congressional District. . . . I can assure the House that my constituents are not interested in receiving 'Occupant mail' and that I am not interested in sending it to them." *

* Since his first year in Congress, Lindsay has sent a newsletter to constituents three or four times a year. Of recent issues, about 160,000 were mailed each time. The newsletters are sent under the Congressman's frank; his office states that only individual addresses are included. The printing is paid for by Lindsay.

Terming the arrangement "diabolic," he introduced a bill two years later to repeal the "Occupant" provision. It was, of course, a highly unpopular position. "It is burdensome to the public to permit indiscriminate use of the franking privilege in this fashion. It is not only proper but important that members keep their constituents advised as to matters of state, legislation pending and passed, and the workings of Congress and the federal government as a whole," Lindsay said, "but if such reports can be sent only with the name of the addressee on the envelope, a member of Congress will be far more careful about the kind and quality of information he sends to constituents, if he is required to go through the large task of addressing the envelopes to all persons to whom the communication is intended."

But the Congressmen elected to keep their "Occupant" frank. The idea of curbing themselves was too distasteful to consider seriously.

One of John Lindsay's earliest efforts to force Congress to look closely at its own practices occurred when he was a first-termer. He called on the Administrative Committee of the House to make a thorough inquiry into members' expense accounting. His proposal came while disclosures of some Congressmen's questionable claims for travel and for other expenditures were creating unfavorable publicity and had resulted in a temporary ban on public inspection of expense vouchers.

Introducing a resolution directing a "top-to-bottom examination of practices and procedures," he declared: "The recent newspaper accounts of instances of liberal spending point to an apparent laxity and indifference in handling of public funds. This reflects on the dignity of the entire Congress—and it is terribly disturbing to me. Our function as Representatives," he reminded his colleagues, "is not only to uncover improprieties elsewhere, but to set the standard. The objective, as I see it, is to adopt clear guidelines so there need be no doubt about areas of propriety and impropriety. The most important requirement of our record-keeping should be clear and concise public disclosure. Public disclosure serves a highly useful purpose—and it usually will correct any abuse on the part of public officials."

Lindsay conceded that Congressional committee inspection tours can help legislators "broaden their views" and guard against their being "provincial in their attitudes."

"Yet," he added, "the public has a right to know whether they are performing their duties conscientiously. The time is long past for the House to put its affairs in order—and we should not have to wait for the roof to fall in on us. The House is challenged to find a solution of an age-old abuse, and we must meet that challenge now." *

Other Lindsay proposals to help Congress do its job better appeared in bills which he introduced with Missouri's Tom Curtis early in the Eighty-ninth Congress. These sought to improve Congressional and judicial procedures for handling contempt-of-Congress citations.

Lindsay was indefatigable though not discernibly successful in promoting conflict-of-interest and code-of-ethics legislation for Congress itself. But he participated in the formulation and passage of updated conflict-of-interest standards for other government employees, and it represented a major triumph for him and others associated with the bill, principally Chairman Emanuel Celler of the Judiciary Committee.

Lindsay had wet his feet in the conflict-of-interest area before he went to Congress. In 1957, when he returned to his law practice after two years in the Department of Justice, he was named to a ten-member special committee of the Bar Association of New York City to study conflicts of interest in the federal government's executive branch. After three years the committee published a book, *Conflicts of Interest and Federal Service,* and drafted a bill which Lindsay introduced in the House. In 1961 he introduced a similar bill with some improvements. The existing conflict laws, he told the House, no longer could protect the government against many subtle forms of conflict; they could, furthermore, be harmful to the nation by unreasonably deterring talented citizens from public service.

* Three years later, with Lindsay's support, the House did pass stringent regulations to curb foreign travel abuses by Congressmen. "High time," Lindsay commented.

Two "coequal themes" must be remembered, he said: ethical standards must be beyond reproach, and the government must be able to obtain the people it needs to do its job properly.

The bill that he and Celler pushed and pulled through the House was the first major legislation in modern times on conflict's complexities. Seven old laws from the mid-nineteenth century were tightened up and strengthened so that, as Lindsay said, "persons occupying a position inside government must not be allowed to": tamper with the wheels of government to their special advantage or to help any outside interest of their own; help an outside individual seeking to make the wheels move in a particular way; or use their office as a source of power or of confidential information to advance their personal economic interests.

The House accepted the complicated code by a voice vote in August, 1961, and Lindsay later testified on the bill in detail before the Senate Judiciary Committee. When the President signed the bill into law, Chairman Celler passed a major share of the credit to John Lindsay.

But that was only half of it. If there was an obligation to write laws insuring high ethical standards for government employees, there was the corresponding need to clear away unnecessary barriers to the government's recruiting of qualified people.

The Bobby Baker case and other incidents gave rise to numerous proposals for the establishment of a code of ethics for Congressmen and the Congressional staff. In 1963 Lindsay joined Senators Javits and Keating to propose a Joint Committee on Ethics which would review possible reforms and draw up an ethical code for Congress.

Early in 1965 Lindsay reintroduced his resolution for the ethics committee to "put our own house in order" and "restore to Congress the respect to which it should be entitled as the greatest legislative body in the world. The people are entitled to expect from their elected representatives . . . a standard above that of the market place," he told a Congressional committee in support of his resolution. "The line between what is ethical and what is not is often an extremely thin one, and I think it proper that Congress itself should establish guidelines giving force and meaning to a basic standard of conduct." It should include the stricture that, "no member, officer, or employee of Congress should have any interest, financial or otherwise, which is in substantial conflict with the discharge of his duties in the public interest."

The ethics code, Lindsay pointed out, would serve to guide and protect legislators (and legislative employees) where there are "possibilities of conflict in that shadowland of conduct for which guidance would be useful and healthy, but for which the criminal law is neither suited nor suitable."

Both John F. Kennedy and Lyndon B. Johnson were members of the United States Senate when John Lindsay began prodding Congress to face up to responsible action in cases of Presidential disability and of vacancies in the Vice-Presidency—"two of the greatest gaps in our constitutional system."

"Everyone agrees it is a problem," he said in a major speech to the House in the early summer of 1960, "and yet nothing is done about it." He recalled the disabilities of Wilson and other stricken Presidents in simpler times, and added, "I shudder to think of the possibility of finding ourselves confronted with a similar predicament in this present age. . . ."

Long before the sad attention Congress began to give the issue in 1964, then, Lindsay had first put in his legislative proposals for constitutional amendments to close gaps in the law, which he reintroduced in 1965.* "The consequences of letting this matter go

* Lindsay's resolution calling for a constitutional amendment provided: (1) that the Vice-President would succeed to the Presidency if the President died, resigned, or were removed; (2) the Vice-President would become *acting* President if the President declared himself, in writing, to be unable to discharge his office; (3) if the President were unwilling or unable to declare his own inability, the Vice-President could do it with the concurrence of a majority of the Cabinet; (4) if the President declared, in writing, that his disability had terminated, he would take over again with all his powers; if the Vice-President disagreed, the disagreement would be resolved by a two-thirds vote of Congress. The latter situation, Lindsay pointed out, is closely allied to the impeachment process. Legislation which in 1965 began to move toward prospective ultimate passage had principal features very similar to those of the Lindsay proposals.

Lindsay also introduced, in 1965, a bill to make the killing of a President or Vice-President a federal offense—with the penalty of death to be imposed upon conviction. (Although on other occasions, however, he has advocated abolition of capital punishment.)

unresolved are too serious to let its solution lie fallow," he said with a persistent grimness, one that for many months his colleagues, and the country, mistook for morbidness. "The nation in the present state of affairs can ill afford the uncertainties to which it has been subjected in the past," he was saying in 1960, while urging his own party's convention to pledge help toward resolving the problem. He did not, of course, address the Democrats' platform-drafters as their convention prepared to nominate Kennedy and Johnson—but his address to the House had urged both Presidential candidates "to recognize the existence of the problem. . . .

"Our form of government, more than any other, is dependent for its preservation more upon 'foresight' than upon 'gunsight,' " he had told the House in the long-ago and innocent days of 1960.

9

A Leader Arrives

JOHN LINDSAY was among the sixty-four freshman Congressmen, a third of them Republicans, who went to Washington in the first week of 1959 for the opening of the Eighty-sixth Congress. Little save his bearing, and the fact that he had beaten both a Republican and a Democrat in order to reach the Capitol, distinguished him from the other freshmen at that swearing-in ceremony.

By the next year John Lindsay had been voted by Washington correspondents as the outstanding new Congressman in his party's ranks. Even in his first year *Look* magazine had a big picture spread asking, "What makes Lindsay run?" and offering some quite superficial answers (for instance: "an ambitious politician sees lots of people"). A couple of years later *Life* counted him among the fifty most outstanding younger Americans.

A very visible part of the "outstanding" performance was his regular attendance record. Throughout the last session of the Eighty-sixth, he missed only one vote, in mid-May of 1960, when his fourth child, Johnny, was born. His voting frequency record was 98 per cent in his first term, 94 per cent in the second, 89 per cent in the third, which ended in 1964. He has frequently canceled speaking engagements in order to be present for a House vote. As candidate for Mayor of New York City in 1965, while Congress was still in session, he had to abandon the ideal of being in Washington for virtually all votes. His voting record had remained, in any event, substantially above the average for Congressmen, and even further above the record for New York City's Tuesday-to-Thursday Club delegation.

For another thing, Lindsay had spoken up early and often, and, on one occasion against the weight of the entire House of Representatives. He had shown an independence of mind that pleased neither the Halleck-Arends leadership of his party in the House nor the Eisenhower Administration, under which he had served two recent years in the Justice Department.

And his name was associated not only with dissent but with a remarkably impressive list of constructive legislation—especially for a freshman member.

He had joined Senator Javits in sponsoring a bill to provide medical assistance for the aged. He was sponsor of the Lindsay Amendment to the 1959 Housing Act, requiring advance public disclosure of financial arrangements and sponsorship of Title I (middle-income) housing. This, said Lindsay, "stripped the secrecy from the deals quietly being made between Mayor Wagner's Tammany-controlled Slum Clearance Commission and builder friends of Tammany Hall." He had labored hard, and effectively, for the 1960 Civil Rights Act.

There were, of course, disappointments and defeats—failure to head off the bill that sought to curb the Supreme Court's powers, inability to hold the line on the mutual security program funds; but principally there was the discouragement with inaction—the inability to move some proposals out of committee, where they languished in the hands of the Democratic chairman, sometimes with Republican leadership assent. And he began to realize that many good ideas were going to go exactly nowhere, getting lost in the halls or cloakrooms.

But his initiation of the bipartisan Congressional foreign affairs seminars with members of the State Department was an important coup. He introduced and fought for major legislation to reform immigration laws and the policy on refugees. He pushed legislation to create new federal judgeships, and called for a federal school-construction bill. Lindsay opened a Congressional office in mid-town Manhattan, in the heart of his District, and spent at least a day there weekly (where one reporter found him opening envelopes).* In a periodic newsletter he told the 17th's voters all about what he was up to, and occasionally sent out a pulse-taking questionnaire.

Some leaders of the Republican Party in his district responded to his independence by trying to keep him out of the New York delegation to the party's National Convention of 1960. He finally was accredited as a delegate only after lengthy discussion.

John Lindsay's experience at Republican National Conventions dates back to 1940, when he and a brother were pages at the Philadelphia sessions that nominated Wendell Willkie † (he still has the credentials, framed and hanging in his office). Twice during the Eisenhower years he had attended conventions, though not as a delegate. In 1952 he worked with Herbert Brownell, former National Chairman and a leader in the pre-nomination drive for the General. Lindsay, in his own words, served as "a legal man on the Louisiana delegate steal" for Eisenhower. At the time he was president of the New York Young Republicans, and the previous year had helped found the Youth-for-Eisenhower movement.

He found the 1960 convention to be "a creditable affair" and the

* "I find out what people are suffering from," Lindsay has said of the schedule he keeps at his midtown office. "Sometimes it's hard to do, but you find out what's bothering the world. And, what's important, this in turn can lead to a governmental result."

The office appears to have a certain link with the offices that the Lindsay-for-Mayor forces opened in scores of assembly districts throughout New York City. He projected them as potentially permanent installations (assuming he got to City Hall) to act as funnels for people's troubles that ought to concern the city government. This was based on the notion that many residents of the city lacked the opportunity to travel to City Hall, or the nerve to face the bureaucracy there—while the city, in turn, lacked the mechanics for any "meet the people" program.

† Two decades later Willkie's widow endorsed John Lindsay as "one of the best Congressmen our country has ever had."

GOP platform "the best we have yet put forward . . . strong, progressive." He would have expected, Lindsay said reflectively after the convention, difficulties on the platform, if only because of the makeup of the committee drafting it.

"Except for the few states where we have a truly open primary system," he remarked, "delegates to the national conventions are chosen by the dominant political machine in each state. The result is that the conventions are controlled by the party regulars . . . the professionals in their states."

He pointed out that, generally, they have little knowledge of federal legislative programs. Yet these platforms are designed for federal action, he said in urging that the important platform subcommittees be made up primarily of people with federal experience. He cited the absence in the 1960 civil rights committee of a single member with any substantial experience in federal civil rights legislation; on the Foreign Affairs Committee only two members had worked in that area.

It seemed questionable that the Lindsay complaint and remedy had materially affected composition of platform subcommittees of either party in 1964; in fact the inference could be drawn from some results that the anomaly might have worsened by then.

Despite the 1960 convention's run-of-the-mill speeches and contrived demonstrations, Lindsay found "an excitement and enthusiasm genuine and wholly American." He suggested two reforms: to make the convention more meaningful to television viewers, he proposed "greater access to the backstage working sessions"; and to help improve the quality of what a convention could hope to produce in platform and candidates, he urged that the method of choosing delegates be overhauled, going so far as to express the hope that future "delegates will to a greater degree reflect the interests of the people they represent." With the 1964 conventions in perspective, his sanguinity of 1960 seems barely warranted.

By election night both gloom and jubilation pervaded the Hotel Roosevelt in midtown Manhattan. On the third floor, at subdued and morose State Committee headquarters, Nixon's loss of the state by more than three times the vote by which he was losing the country became quickly apparent.

But one floor below, in the tiny and crowded Lindsay headquarters carved out of the hotel's guest-room area, was the noisy and exuberant excitement that attends a winner's camp. It was a big winner in this case, for the Congressman had won a second term by some 27,000 votes, or three to two over the Democrat, young William vanden Heuvel, who had the thankless task of trying to convince the voters he could perform John Lindsay's specialties better than John Lindsay could.

The Lindsay campaign technique, buffed in the primary and first electoral campaign two years earlier, was beginning to take on the polish that later was to become highly celebrated. As a result, the vanden Heuvel campaign never got off the ground, even though Senator John Kennedy carried the 17th by 1,000 votes.

One indication of the growing base of Lindsay's support was that he received the endorsement of every one of the city's newspapers, as he did also in 1962. In 1964 the *Daily News* position was neutralized by the Goldwater issue, but all others again supported Lindsay as "unusually qualified."

Kennedy's majority in the District, however, was a sobering reminder, despite the vote of confidence given the Congressman, that the 17th is marginal. But as a Republican spokeman put it: "That Lindsay won at all is significant. That he won in a landslide is proof that one of the party's brightest young leaders has arrived."

"Conscientious politics can also be fun if you don't mind working seven days a week," the *Look* writer had said. Another observed that, "John Lindsay seems likely to become one of New York's most outstanding and influential Congressional Representatives in many years. . . . Lindsay's electoral showing and the enthusiasm of his supporters bid well to make him an important force within his party in the coming years."

10

Quick to Sustain; Prepared to Abstain

For John Lindsay the opening of the Eighty-seventh Congress, a fortnight before the inauguration of the new Democratic President in 1961, was a time of farewells. Numerous old friends of past years were departing, including some who were retiring from the House and many from the Eisenhower days who were now turning their offices over to Kennedy appointees. Many of these were in the Department of Justice, where John Lindsay had found firm friends when he had arrived years before to serve on the Attorney General's staff.

But among those Republicans returning to Capitol Hill there were some staunch friends: Tom Curtis of Missouri, Silvio Conte of Massachusetts, Perkins Bass of New Hampshire, Seymour Halpern of New York City's Queens delegation; William Cahill and Florence Dwyer of New Jersey. John Lindsay (already well known as one of the most liberal Republicans) joined with these six in sending a letter to their 174 Republican colleagues which called for "a responsible minority and a constructive opposition" and for avoidance of "a policy of obstructionism." This, they said, would represent responsible leadership as well as good politics.

The next day they offered a resolution to the Republican caucus, asking their party to take an independent course in the Eighty-seventh; it demanded repudiation of all talk of coalition with Southern Democrats against the Administration.

The leadership promptly referred the resolution to the Policy Committee. Officially, the disappointed sponsors said that even this represented "substantial progress" in the effort to break up the obstructionist coalition, and later in the year Lindsay remarked that the real unity was between "anti-civil rights libertarians from the Democratic South and the Eastern Democrats seeking their favor."

As the lines began to form for battles that were to mark the Eighty-seventh's two years, one astute observer, Rowland Evans, warned that the Republicans' leaders, Charles Halleck and Everett Dirksen, had potential fifth columns in their ranks. The Northern big-city liberals—he identified John Lindsay as their prototype—counted a dozen adherents in the Senate, perhaps as many as two dozen in the House. Evans said they tended toward rather than against the welfare measures, the spending bills, the foreign aid proposals.

In the Eighty-seventh Congress lines were quickly drawn between the handful of Republican independents and their leadership. Speaker Sam Rayburn proposed enlarging the Rules Committee from twelve to fifteen members in an attempt to break the impasse that had stalled so much legislation at the mercies of Howard Smith and like-minded conservatives. Halleck tried to whip his Republicans into line against Rayburn, and he almost succeeded.

But John Lindsay, Tom Curtis, and a few others served notice that they intended to vote on Rayburn's side and they hoped for as many as forty votes, though ultimately their aspiration was scaled down to half that many. This put Lindsay squarely at odds with the unanimous decision of the party's Policy Committee. "Conscience and common sense compel me to oppose the committee's decision," was Lindsay's prompt rejoinder. "On the floor of the House I shall support expansion of the Rules Committee on grounds that neither the rule of seniority nor the present membership would be altered."

Declaring that in recent years the Rules Committee had "chosen to overexercise its already broad powers," he warned that his GOP colleagues were in the position of "seeming to coalesce with Southern Democrats—a posture contrary to both the principles and the best interests of the Republican Party." *

The next day John F. Kennedy, for whose benefit the Rayburn proposal had been instigated, was inaugurated. Congress then dug in for the battle. For ten days the Rules Committee fight was paramount on the Hill, but when the time came, the Republicans were allotted only thirty minutes to debate, only two minutes of which went to a dissident, Curtis. Lindsay, denied an opportunity to speak, said, "I value and will fight for my right to debate and to vote for or against measures on the floor of the House. The country has a right to expect the same."

In the dramatic countdown, the progressives barely carried the day—217–212. Their victory, which would not have been without the twenty-two votes brought by the Lindsay-Curtis forces, now shattered Howard Smith's power to withhold legislation from the floor. The Kennedy program now could move forward on its merits.

One editorial observed that John Lindsay had again "risked reprisal by the primeval leadership of his party in Congress to vote his conscience," and continued, it is "therefore quite evident why Mr. Lindsay and similar young men of integrity and ability . . .

* In his book *Obstacle Course on Capitol Hill* Robert Bendiner discusses the function of the Rules Committee in preventing many bills from reaching the floor because so many members would prefer not to have to take a public position. "Some are genuinely concerned about the moral aspects of using a Congressional agency in this shabby way," Bendiner writes, "and others are disturbed as well by the committee's inevitable misuse of such power. . . . John V. Lindsay of New York fears that the system enables the Rules Committee to 'cudgel people into line,' on penalty of being denied the intervention of Rules on some future occasion when they want it. . . . To Lindsay, as to others, 'It is a bad concept to have an institution set up as insurance against the people.' The trouble is, there are not enough others."

are being looked to by Republicans throughout the country as the future leaders of a viable, responsive, and responsible Republican Party."

The immediate picture was quite different. Lindsay was censured by the New York Young Republican Club which he had once headed. Only about 5 per cent of the club's membership actually attended the meeting at which the censure was voted; three weeks later Lindsay described the matter painstakingly and somewhat testily to the members, who declined to remove the censure. He told them they had done "a grave disservice to the cause of a revitalized and effective Republican Party," and that the issue before Congress had been, "whether the Rules Committee is to be the agent or the master of the House of Representatives."

The 1961 vote on the Rules Committee was for temporary enlargement of membership. The issue was revived in 1963, and again Lindsay's position stirred controversy among his Organization-minded House colleagues. After the vote for the permanent enlargement of the committee, which passed, 235–196, he explained his stand to a party conference: "A thin disguise for real Rules reform," he said, "but the committee should be the servant and not the master."

After the conference, Lindsay reported, he was approached by House Republican Whip Leslie Arends of Illinois, who commented that he had never seen "a man talk himself off the Foreign Affairs Committee so fast in my life." The Republican Conference named five foes of foreign aid as new members of the committee, and passed up Lindsay and Connecticut Congressman Sibal, who had reportedly been recommended by Christian Herter. Lindsay had long desired Foreign Affairs membership.

Echoes of the 1961 and 1963 battles resounded in 1965, when the House voted two changes in its rules, substantially weakening the power of the Rules Committee to block consideration of legislation. One of these was to enable committee chairmen to bring up a measure for House consideration if it had been before Rules for twenty-one days; the second nearly nullified the committee's power to prevent a bill from being sent to conference. And on a close vote

(224–201) the sixteen Republicans, including John Lindsay, provided the margin of victory.

In a separate but not unrelated move at the opening of the 1965 session, when five Mississippi Democratic Congressmen-elect were seated over protest but with the assent of the party's leadership, Lindsay and four Republican colleagues denounced the majority leadership for having "effectively condoned disenfranchisement of more than 400,000 American citizens in Mississippi and missed an opportunity to rectify the wrong."

In a real sense the more recent victories were an updating and an underscoring of the 1961 breakthrough, when the handful of Lindsay Republicans overrode the coalition.* That was the big victory of its time, and it was the one that made possible the Kennedy Administration's advance of its legislative program. It put the Kennedy forces in the debt of the handful of independent, Lindsay-minded Republicans who had obtained that all-important victory for them.

If John Lindsay had been instrumental in bringing the timeliest of support to the new Administration at its outset, what was to be his relationship with it in the longer range?

Within the Kennedy Administration's first month he was suggesting some hopeful answers. While giving Lincoln Day banquet speeches, he sounded an attitude and a policy in which he spoke for himself if not his party: "To confront the Democratic Administration with support where it is warranted—but with articulate and

* Later that same year Lindsay was indignant about one upshot of the battle. He and other Republicans voting to enlarge Rules, he said, "were giving the Democratic majority the necessary room in which to bring its proposals to the floor in orderly fashion and to provide for full debate. . . . We had a right to expect that the majority would put its legislative house in order." At the end of the session, however, the Democrats brought in a "brand-new hybrid school bill" under a limited-debate procedure, after the Education-Labor Committee had one hour to examine and vote on it. Voting against the procedure, Lindsay branded it "a crude tactic for the majority—most of whom could not even tell us what was in the last-minute bill—to resort to a clumsy, transparent maneuver designed to get them off the hook for the whole education bill fiasco, and to expect us to agree to the procedure."

coherent opposition when that Administration, in our judgment, presses unwise or ill-conceived policies or flouts the public interest." Or as a much earlier Congressman of similarly independent spirit had put it long before: "Quick to sustain; prepared to abstain."

The speech attracted wide attention, both to the policy and its advocate. One commentator observed that the strategy of the Goldwaters, the Arendses, the Byrneses, the Millers, the Dirksens, and the Hallecks of the party—with their assaults on spending, on "broken pledges," on the vanishing missile gap—hardly fitted the "progressive definition of Republican responsibility" as voiced by John Lindsay.

Later in the spring Washington was realizing that a new liberal Republican-Democratic coalition had replaced the conservative coalition which had been so effective for so long. Without consistent leadership this liberal coalition simply brought together, when the occasion called for it, individuals with a similar basic philosophy. New York was contributing on the Republican side in both House and Senate what seemed the nearest approach to a coherent leadership role—Jacob Javits in the Senate and John Lindsay in the House. Yet, as a writer put it even while these lines were shaping up, neither Javits nor Lindsay had an "organization"; neither was trying to line up votes on a measure; neither appeared to know how a given vote would turn out, though they could anticipate who, in both parties, would probably follow them. And both, as outspoken liberals, were prepared to desert party lines on an issue involving principle.

Yet if Lindsay was ready to insist on independence in voice and vote and to break clear of party discipline when he disagreed on principle, he was also ready not only to support the Democratic Administration where it was warranted but to speak out vigorously against what he saw as "unwise or ill-conceived policies."

Exactly a year and a half after the Kennedy Administration took office, the *National Observer,* noting the worsening rift between the White House and Congress, identified John Lindsay among the half dozen leaders with whom the President had to deal, along with much older and more powerful legislators—Senators Harry Byrd and Hubert Humphrey, Democrats; Senator Thomas Kuchel, Congressmen Charles Halleck and Tom Curtis of the Republicans. It was elevated company for a second-term Congressman.

II

Unpopular at the White House

John Lindsay held out an olive branch of liberal Republicanism to the Kennedy Administration in its first days, by breaking ranks with his party's leadership on the Rules Committee issue and by offering "support where it is warranted." He was soon discontented.

It is difficult to pinpoint the origin of his disillusion, but a major part must have started with the disastrous Cuba invasion attempt in March of 1961. Just forty-eight hours before the Bay of Pigs he had expressed his support for the Administration's "non-intervention" policy. "I was troubled and angered by the Cuban fiasco," he said. "I think it was a major error to get involved in that situation at all. Our action violated everything we stood for."

Lindsay felt personally betrayed within the Administration's first sixty days, for he and others like him had put their trust in the apparent candor and good faith of President Kennedy. But more significantly he felt a betrayal of the country's reputation and credibility and honor.

Lindsay felt that the drop in the Kennedy prestige after the Bay of Pigs had badly hurt his ability to prod Congress on his legislative program The drastically slashed foreign aid bill was among the worst hit. Lindsay supported it, but he found himself in a greatly reduced group, for misgivings were high.

It seems entirely likely that the Cuban debacle resulted in a disenchantment even deeper than this for John Lindsay since he discerned in the new Administration a "purely pragmatic mentality" which reversed the policies outlined in Kennedy's inaugural address.

Shortly after the invasion attempt, Lindsay observed bitterly that, "The President will now meet with Khrushchev after disavowing personal diplomacy. He will continue to dole out giveaways after calling for national sacrifice. He will now affirm both a growing economy and a healthy picture in defense after causing gloom and despair with his campaign appraisals. This kind of ambivalence demands our scrutiny. . . ."

And the Kennedy record began to receive his close personal scrutiny, by no means always unfriendly, though he maintained that "we Republicans, as a responsible opposition, must continue to inform the general public." As a matter of fact, he supported the Democratic President on key issues two times out of three in 1961–1962 and three times out of four during 1963–1964. Lindsay voted for the Peace Corps, though he was subsequently skeptical of its handling, especially in the training aspects. He criticized the President for having begun H-bomb testing before the question was brought before the UN.

He attacked the Administration most consistently, and with the greatest display of outraged vigor, in civil rights. Throughout 1961 and 1962 and much of 1963 he denounced the Kennedys for failing to make good on 1960 pledges to push quickly for new civil rights laws.*

Rather early in the Kennedy term Lindsay joined four others among the younger, independent-minded House Republicans in a series of needling jabs on governmental economy. The quintet—which included Tom Curtis of Missouri and three Easterners besides

* This record is detailed in Chapter 15. He was militant on the President's delay of many months in issuing an Executive Order to prohibit discrimination in housing programs aided by the federal government (Chapter 26).

Lindsay, Charles Mathias of Maryland, Bradford Morse of Massachusetts, and Abner Sibal of Connecticut—acted in concert over many months to sting the President on spending.

Though they were among those Republicans the press corps bracketed with the "spenders," the five urged the President to help wipe out a predicted heavy deficit in the federal budget in mid-1961, and to make use of existing economy laws and exert leadership over Congress to this end. "In all conscience, we find it difficult to vote to burden future generations with a gigantic public debt without also searching for reasonable methods of conserving federal funds through more efficient operation of federal machinery and wiser controls over federal outlays," they said in a letter to the White House.

"While you steer a majority of the Congress in voting new billions," they continued with polite sarcasm, "we respectfully suggest that you lend the same influence in implementing economy measures which would not deprive one American of social welfare, nor any foreign nation of American assistance, nor impede a single worth-while project."

After noting that the Kennedy program would involve a deficit of more than $5 billion, and that Congress had just "temporarily" raised the national debt limit by $13 billion, the Republicans outlined five major areas of economy.

To make their point that the President "can be a powerful force in eliminating this shameful abuse of the American tax dollar," they quoted to Mr. Kennedy "another great leader of your party, President Grover Cleveland," on "simplicity and prudential economies."

The President didn't ignore the Congressmen completely. His Congressional aide, Larry O'Brien, told them they would receive a reply soon concerning their proposals. Five weeks later, having received no further response, they sent another letter in which they reminded the President of the urgency of streamlining as recommended by the second Hoover Commission, and nudged him "respectfully" to heed "the basic concept of preserving our economic integrity."

Almost a full year passed before the Congressmen mailed their next letter, in what they described publicly as "the latest salvo in a running battle . . . urging the Chief Executive to act on money-saving operations he supported himself when a member of the Senate." They reënumerated their proposals for effecting economies, asking his "leadership in implementing several Hoover Commission proposals," and reminded him that his "vigorous support of these long overdue economy reforms would be heartening to every American taxpayer."

The Lindsay thrust at vulnerable Kennedy positions was persistent, most evident, perhaps most telling, in foreign relations. Midway in the Administration's first year, when the Kennedys were touring the Continent on their first diplomacy-and-glamor excursion, the Congressman remarked (and since he remarked it within earshot of a society gossip reporter, it received wide currency): "I'm for her [Jacqueline Kennedy]. She's the only foreign policy we've got."

But if he could be whimsically gallant with reference to the First Lady, both whimsy and gallantry disappeared when it came to the President's brother and foreign policy. Not long after his good-humored sally he was needling the President and the Attorney General through Secretary of State Dean Rusk. This time the needle had a malicious point. Mr. Lindsay sent Mr. Rusk a little note complimenting him on a "splendid off-the-record presentation" before the Senate-House foreign policy group,* and commenting that he increasingly liked the Secretary's brand of "quiet diplomacy." But he had noted a columnist's report of a meeting between Attorney General Kennedy and Soviet Ambassador Mikhail Menshikov—alone, and with an agenda that included Berlin and "related matters of the greatest sensitivity, possibly affecting the safety of the entire world."

If it is true, Lindsay said. "I am deeply disturbed" because "it by-passes your office and your department, and in so doing runs great risks."

The letter continued: "It appears to be part of a growing pattern

* This was the seminar that Lindsay had been responsible for initiating under the Eisenhower Administration.

—namely, the conduct of foreign relations in a casual or loose-reined *ad hoc* manner, too often involving personalities untrained in foreign policy and the art of diplomacy"; and, further, "It makes difficult for those of us who have a responsibility to our constituents and to the country to make sound evaluations which would lead to bipartisan support on foreign policy."

Did it all actually happen? Lindsay asked the Secretary. And if so, "I would like to know the circumstances surrounding it." He noted that the Attorney General was reportedly the President's representative in his conference with the Ambassador. He asked Rusk's "frank opinion as to whether this is a proper way to conduct foreign policy in general or to negotiate on the explosive question of Berlin."

The Lindsay question was, of course, "Who is running our foreign policy?" Though putting Rusk in the middle, it had the basic function of trying to strengthen Rusk's hand to run the foreign policy himself. If the President and Attorney General could be sufficiently embarrassed publicly through such gambits as the barefaced Lindsay letter, they might perhaps leave diplomacy to Rusk's department. But the hook that Lindsay hoped to lift the Secretary off proved too long. No reply came for many weeks, and when the Secretary answered, he ducked the query about the propriety and advisability of having "explosive questions" negotiated through Justice instead of State. Rusk explained only that he had talked with Robert Kennedy before the Menshikov conference and they had "discussed the topics which might be expected to come up."

Six months later Lindsay returned to the attack, again needling Rusk and again directing the jab at Robert Kennedy. Early in 1962 the Attorney General went to the Far East and Europe. "I think the Congress has a right to know the purpose of this tour and its genesis," said Lindsay in a new letter to the Secretary, "including all the facts surrounding the proposed trip to the Soviet Union [which was later canceled], plus any plans for the future along these lines. . . ."

And after referring to Republican hopes to be effective in shaping a bipartisan foreign policy, Lindsay declared, "We question whether it is necessary for you and your office to be either burdened or embarrassed by freewheeling foreign missions on the part of highly placed amateurs." He mentioned it had become "common knowledge" in Washington that some foreign embassies, "with the knowledge that the Attorney General is available for this kind of extracurricular invitation, are indulging in a kind of scramble to 'get the ear' of the Attorney General, under the notion that this means direct access to the President."

He was sure that Rusk would agree "that this can lead to all kinds of special pleading. Even worse, it can make a shambles of diplomacy, which can be embarrassing to your office and to the trained assistant secretaries and diplomats under your authority."

Twice, John Lindsay pursued the matter on the House floor, where he said that the Justice Department had plenty of "unfinished business" requiring "full-time leadership. . . . If the Attorney General wishes to educate himself on the subject of foreign policy," he said, "I would recommend that he acquaint himself with the meaning of the rule of law, a subject about which the number-one legal officer in the country should have some knowledge. Time spent on this and on the department's legislative program—civil rights, for example—would be time better spent than meddling in the area of foreign policy, hamburger fries in the great halls of the U.S. Department of Justice, and other superficial publicity gimmicks. . . ."

Rusk replied: "the Attorney General undertook this visit at my personal request and urging"—thus answering the question as to why Robert Kennedy was on the month-long trip; but it did not even pay its respects to the deeper issue raised by John Lindsay which was whether such meddling is advisable.

Lindsay had the last word. As he presented the Rusk reply to the House, he said: "If the purpose of the trip was good will, we should know it. And we should also, I think, have the Secretary's opinion as to whether this kind of Madison Avenue approach is the stuff of which foreign policy is made. Hopefully, it is not a substitute for policy. In any event, even assuming such behavior is entirely harmless, the time involved could be far better spent attending to the unfinished work of the Department of Justice here at home." *

"A strong feeling is growing in Congress," Lindsay said in the summer of 1962, "that the Kennedys are trying to shut off debate. They have made basic grabs for power that are offensive to conservatives and liberals alike. . . ." Senator Jacob Javits was saying that the situation between President and Congress was in disarray. The President had demanded much action; he was getting little.

"The trouble in Washington today is that the President has never learned how to be President," suggested John Lindsay. "He thinks he's still running. There is a difference between being a perpetual candidate and being the President of the United States. . . . The fact that he hasn't been able to get his program through his own heavily Democratic Congress indicates that the Congress recognizes more public relations than substance in the President's efforts. If we were treated to less personal image-making, and more concern about basic problems and their sensible solution, we would have better government."

Then, too, he expressed his growing concern about the Administration's disregard for personal liberties, its advocacy of bills of dubious constitutionality, and its tendency to confer arbitrary police power on the executive branch. "One is led to a conclusion that perhaps the Administration has abandoned the cause of civil liberties," Lindsay told one audience, "thereby permitting insensitive counter-pressures to have free reign."

Enumerating the inattentiveness of Congress to several issues in civil liberties, he said: "The Congress must never act on such legislation in a cavalier or indifferent fashion. It is our duty to consider such bills painstakingly. There must be a point of balance between national security and civil liberties—rapid passage of such bills

* Lindsay later defended the State Department against outside interference, this time of Secretary of Defense McNamara on Vietnam. "Positions of United States foreign policy," he said, "should be stated by the President or the State Department. . . ."

without searching debate places the Congress in a position where it seems unmindful of its responsibilities."

He added, "The Administration must likewise see to it that its influence over the course of such legislation is not wanting." While Congress was compiling a haphazard record in the field of civil liberties, he observed, "We had no word from the Administration. . . ."

The thought of anyone's "shutting off debate" was anathema to John Lindsay. He grew wary. He returned again and again to the disturbing "Why?" In turning it over in his mind, sometimes in full public view, he came increasingly to the disappointing conclusion that John F. Kennedy and his family were, *in practice,* against dissent.

For John Crosby, a columnist who found him "one of the few who dare speak up strongly" in protest even at the risk of unpopularity, John Lindsay thought aloud one day: "I blame the Kennedy family for much of it. It's gotten so that if you're against the Kennedy family, you're against progress. You can't discuss these things. The party line in the House of Representatives is that if anyone proposes a different or deeper or better approach to, say, the Kennedy civil rights program, then he's against civilization. I don't think," he added, "the Kennedys realize how much they're shutting off debate."

Crosby specifically excluded Lindsay when he observed unhappily that "everyone, Republican and Democrat alike, wants to be popular at the White House where wrath is swift and terrible."

Lindsay clearly was not afraid to be "unpopular at the White House" nor was he frightened at being so identified publicly. He took on the Kennedys, to whom he had offered and given "support where warranted," in both trivial and major matters. He kidded them tartly about the *Herald Tribune*'s disappearance from the reading room in the House of Representatives after its banishment from the White House. But he abandoned irony and sarcasm when he disputed with the President and the Attorney General on matters of state; and these occasions were increasingly frequent. John Lindsay seemed almost to work at being unpopular at the White House; he criticized the Administration over and over. He took on the Kennedys with such language as: "basic grabs for power," "personal image-making," "never learned how to be President," "disregard for personal liberties," "shutting off debate," "troubled and angered," "pragmatic mentality," "meddling in foreign policy," "freewheeling foreign missions," "highly placed amateurs," "superficial publicity gimmicks," "the Madison Avenue approach."

That Lindsay had found gaps in the Kennedy programs and flaws in the Kennedy methods undoubtedly was inevitable. That he took exception to them, and voiced this bluntly and repeatedly, perhaps attests to his appreciation of what such a socially sensitive Administration stood for, and to his aspiration, even from the ranks of the opposition, that it not compromise its commitment.

In any event, the legislative record shows clearly the extent of his acceptance of the Administration's broadest goals. More often than not, he voted to support the Kennedy program.

12

Congressman from the Constitution

"I AM becoming more and more concerned about this Administration's disregard for personal liberties," John Lindsay declared, eighteen months after John F. Kennedy took over the White House and Robert Kennedy took over the Justice Department. He had a number of ideological differences with the Kennedys and some of their legislative proposals which ended only when the Kennedy Administration ended.

Perhaps more than any other Congressman of our time, Lindsay has been consistently involved in the defense of the Constitution and the Bill of Rights and their guarantees for safeguarding the individual prerogatives of every citizen. "Personal liberties are always in danger of being invaded," he said in mid-1962, "whether it be by extremists of the left or right who have no regard for the other person's point of view or the complexities of a modern democratic civilization—or whether it be by the heavy-handedness of big government and power-seekers who believe that some ends justify any means.

"We have had to strike down (he was speaking as a Judiciary

Committee member) a number of bills pressed by this Administration that were either of doubtful constitutionality or would give so much arbitrary police power to the executive that civil libertarians —Republicans and Democrats alike—have had to come forward to object."

One occurred earlier that year when the Administration pressed an "obstruction of justice" bill. Its purpose was to make it a crime to "obstruct or impede" any "lawful" investigation by such federal agencies as the FBI, the Narcotics Bureau, or the Internal Revenue Service. But the language was much too broad, Lindsay told the committee: a "lawful" inquiry could be anything a federal agency might call lawful; and "impede" could be construed as covering any conduct.

"Under the Administration's bill," he charged, "a lawyer or any citizen could be indicted for entirely proper conduct in questioning a non-judicial federal investigation." He offered a "safer" substitute. This, he explained, "ties the offense solely to bodily harm or threat of bodily harm to another person for having co-operated with the government in the investigation of certain high crimes in the interstate field," including murder, kidnaping, narcotics traffic, and extortion.

The Judiciary Committee, heavily Democratic in composition, rejected the Kennedy proposal, and over Chairman Emanuel Celler's strong opposition, adopted the Lindsay substitute by a vote of 17 to 15.

Lindsay and Democratic Congressman Kastenmeier of Wisconsin were outflanked the following year by Robert Kennedy in his successful bid to expand coverage of the Sedition Act. They denounced the law as a "persistent intruder on the right of free speech" and called for its repeal, citing abuses since its enactment in 1917. "The abuses are so great that even a member of Congress possibly could be cited and prosecuted for verbal attacks on United States policies and action," Lindsay declared.

But he lost. The House broadened the coverage of the Sedition Act to Americans anywhere in the world. It shouted its approval after defeating, by more than 8 to 1, an effort to return the bill to Judiciary.

On the same day on which his forces took a beating on the floor of the House, Lindsay was battling futilely in the Judiciary Committee to salvage another Administration proposal. The Justice Department had submitted a "public defender program," authorizing federal judicial circuits to establish one of several alternate procedures for providing needy criminal defendants with adequate legal counsel in federal courts. It was in trouble.

Trying to rescue it, Lindsay proposed an amendment to limit "public defender" to those districts in which federal courts deal with more than a hundred indigent cases yearly—only the big cities (saying that the law would discriminate "against urban areas by preventing these areas from taking advantage of the economies to be realized from the efficient operation of the public defender system. . . ."). The strategy didn't work anyhow, and a coalition of committee Republicans and Southern Democrats voted the bill down and approved a much weaker substitute.

If the "big city" aspect of the case for the public defenders was its Achilles heel, Washington columnist William Shannon observed that the "big-city guys" frequently pose the greatest problem for the Lindsays who seek to promote the liberal cause. Lindsay's colleagues in the New York City delegation, commented Shannon, generally fall "woefully short" in espousal of liberal causes.

On other occasions John Lindsay took issue with Kennedy-backed proposals that touched on individual liberties. He sharply criticized Attorney General Robert Kennedy's proposal for legislation to permit the FBI to tap wires without court orders in cases "presenting a threat to the security of the United States."

"Wiretapping is dirty business," Lindsay retorted to this idea. "Improperly used, it is the worst kind of invasion of privacy. Modern electronic listening and eavesdropping devices have made the threat to individual rights posed by unchecked, unlimited use of this power all the more dangerous."

He also decried the Pentagon's Administration-sanctioned use of lie-detectors. Only forty Congressmen opposed a Kennedy-backed measure in 1963 which, Lindsay complained, "tossed into the ashcan any semblance of due process for accused employees of the National Security Agency. It means that any employee . . . charged by an anonymous informer of having 'wrong' opinions, associating with 'wrong' people, or doing any other vague 'wrong' thing, can be summarily dismissed and remain forever tainted in government files and records without any understanding whatever of why it happened and by whom it was caused," John Lindsay declared of this bill.

As to its effect, he noted that experience demonstrates that "gross injustices occur when the government operates in this fashion, and there is no commensurate improvement in government security." He was also critical of efforts to pass the bill without debate. "Admittedly this particular bill presented a close question because of the sensitive nature of the agency," he conceded, since the NSA handles highly secret military and Cold War operations. "But personal rights are nonetheless diminished, and full debate was called for."

Over the months, he pounded away at other excesses and deficiencies: the failure of the Administration's civil rights bill to request authority to invoke the protection of the First Amendment on behalf of individuals in no position to do so for themselves; the use of governmental leverage to induce people voluntarily to surrender some of their rights under the First and Fifth Amendments; the State Department's efforts to curb the right of Americans to travel.

He attacked unsuccessfully a proposal providing that in the District of Columbia a defendant's confession should not be held inadmissible as evidence in a court solely because of a delay in his arraignment. "Surely," he warned, "[the House] ought not to enact a bill which would so gut the presumption of innocence and so enfeeble the guarantees which our long history of criminal procedure has developed." The bill, he argued, would "deprive an accused of the cloak of innocence . . . deprive him of counsel at the time counsel is most needed . . . authorize federal law-enforcement officials to round up and arrest people on suspicion alone . . . permit detainment incommunicado . . . deprive those accused of their rights to habeas corpus. . . ."

Taking an expression directly from the legislation, he commented bitterly that " 'round up the usual suspects' is a phrase that should strike terror." The House, heedless, overwhelmingly voted down Lindsay's motion to recommit the bill.

The New Republic observed that a few votes could be regarded as indicating the readiness of Congressmen "to go beyond the requirements of practicality." * Among the House votes it cited was one in late 1961 in which Lindsay and his Manhattan Democratic colleague William Fitts Ryan stood alone, against a recorded majority of 369, against a bill to authorize the Postmaster General to send notices of Communist propaganda "alerting" the recipients to their danger. Lindsay called it "the most dangerous anti-civil-libertarian bill offered for serious consideration since I became a member of Congress," and characterized it as "mocking individual freedom" and "downgrading the intelligence of all Americans. In the name of security," he cautioned Congress, "by this bill you would make the federal government the sole judge and censor of all literature coming to the United States from abroad."

When the idea reappeared in different form early in 1962, Lindsay and Ryan again stood alone. This one, opposed by the Kennedy Administration, proposed to restrict delivery of mail coming from Communist-bloc nations; the proposal was in the form of an amendment to a postal-rate-increase bill. The President was unable to hold any of his Democrats except Ryan, even though an Executive Order the previous year had ended interception of Communist mail. Though the President pointed out that the Russians might

* The magazine commented, in language which would seem to underscore the Lindsay record: "The primary responsibility of a Congressman is the practical one of passing as much 'good' legislation and defeating as much 'bad' legislation as possible. . . . By dint of his viability, a Congressman is an educator as well as a man of affairs. As such, he may occasionally do what's right even though it will stamp him as an impractical fellow. He may do it because some inner compulsion commands, or because he believes that if there is no dissenting minority to oppose the fashion of the moment, there may eventually be no such minority outside Congress either."

retaliate by refusing to handle U.S. mail, the threat proved totally ineffective.

Drew Pearson said that, "Every member of the House except Lindsay and Ryan chickened on the constitutional right of freedom to read." More than three years later their stand was vindicated. In a unanimous decision handed down only a few days after John Lindsay had declared his candidacy for Mayor of New York City, the Supreme Court ruled the law unconstitutional.

Lawyers said this was the first time in the nation's history that a Supreme Court verdict had knocked out a Congressional statute for violating the First Amendment's guarantee of freedom of speech. Even the Post Office Department had been calling the law unworkable and a nuisance, since the government had had to spend about $250,000 annually to enforce it. The Post Office was required to intercept "Communist political propaganda" and notify the addressee who had to return a card affirming that he wanted his mail; if he failed to do so, it would be destroyed. The Supreme Court decided that the law's provisions violated the First Amendment and added tersely: ". . . an addressee is likely to feel some inhibition in sending for literature which federal officials have condemned as 'Communist political propaganda.' " The court continued: "The regimen of this act is at war with the uninhibited, robust, and wide-open debate and discussion that are contemplated by the First Amendment." One justice added that ". . . inhibition, as well as prohibition, against the exercise of precious First Amendment rights is a power denied to government."

Drew Pearson suggested that the decision "should give more backbone to politicians in both parties when it comes to standing up against witch-hunting."

A declaration by Justice Oliver Wendell Holmes on the mail system appears to have motivated John Lindsay's reactions to the several bills on which he has dissented so vigorously over the years. "The United States may give up the Post Office when it sees fit, but while it carries it on, the use of the mails is almost as much a part of free speech as the right to use our tongues," Holmes wrote. Lindsay quoted Justice Holmes in a fiery speech to the House immediately after returning from the 1964 Republican National Convention.

This time the subject was a bill to keep "morally offensive" mail from being delivered to homes. If any person or his child received mail that in his opinion was morally offensive, he would have the right to ask the Postmaster General to notify the source to send no more unsolicited mail. The Post Office would then direct a halt to the mail, and the Attorney General could seek a court order to force compliance. Under the bill's terms, Lindsay charged, the Post Office would be required to act at the behest of a single person without due process of law. "Does the House realize this bill means the Post Office must perforce act as a mail censor at the request of a single person?" he demanded. "Does the House realize this is a plain invasion of First Amendment rights?"

The speculation in the House may have been that the Senate would not get around to the measure during the session, so without much fear that immediate legislative action would follow, Congressmen could avoid being publicly "soft on obscenity" in an election year. In any case, only eighteen Congressmen joined John Lindsay in voting against making censors out of householders. On the other side were 325 members, not-soft-on-obscenity but soft on the constitutional questions raised by the Attorney General, by the Post Office, and by Congressman Lindsay. As predicted, the bill later died in the Senate.

In addressing Congress on the 1960 civil rights bill, Lindsay made much of the constitutional base, referring to the never-ending struggle to publicize the "wide gap between the great American promise of our Constitution and its practical application. Basic rights repeatedly are being denied," he asserted. "A denial of these rights to one is a denial to the nation as a whole." To Congressmen in doubt about the legislative responsibility, he advised: "Read the Constitution. You will be reminded that the Constitution is not self-executing; that it stands in danger always of becoming a meaningless piece of paper enshrined in glass in the Archives, unless we take the necessary steps to keep it alive and meaningful." He recalled that the Fourteenth and Fifteenth Amendments state, "in very certain language, 'the Congress shall have power to enforce by appropriate legislation the provisions of this article.' "

In the civil rights legislation he saw "very fundamental constitutional principles involved . . . [that] we seek now to implement. . . . Denials of constitutionally protected rights of course involve the nation as a whole. If the idea of government by consent is the essence of our Republic, the right to vote and the equal protection of laws must be secured and protected. Otherwise, we have no right to the claim that our Republic was 'conceived in liberty and dedicated to the proposition that all men are created equal.' "

The Lindsay approach to civil liberties was never better illustrated than in his remarks about a bill amending the 1950 Subversive Activities Control Act. It concerned employment on an American merchant vessel or waterfront facility. Aimed at anyone who was alleged to have answered falsely, or had failed to answer, a federal agency's questions about suspected subversive activities or connections, it provided no hearing for the accused and no notice of charges. "A mere refusal to answer questions before any tribunal for whatever reason would be enough," Lindsay pointed out, "to deprive any individual of his choice of a means of livelihood. It is difficult to imagine a procedure more at variance with the rule of law," charged Lindsay, "than that one which relieves the government [of the necessity] of proving its case before depriving a person of any rights. . . ."

And he voiced a stern warning that, "The appeal to considerations of current public policy and political necessity" (as in the need to prevent a subversive infiltration of the merchant fleet) "must not obscure the fact that legislation of such moment is apt to be treacherous to all of us. Security which may demand so much may endanger what it claims to secure."

Congress, he cautioned, should never look at such "security," treacherous security, with indifference, but should always examine legislation painstakingly to find the "point of balance between national security interests and civil liberties."

Lindsay has often spoken about the subject generally: "Constitutional precepts are as alive, and as controversial, today as at the framing of the document. The Constitution, its meaning and its application, is the heart, head, and pulse of the American legislative process. Not a day passes that some new proposal is not propounded, or assailed, in the name of the Constitution. . . . The decision-making power which the Constitution vests in each citizen will be safeguarded to us only so long as the Constitution is recognized for what it is—the embodiment of a birthright of immeasurable value that, as men, we will keep or lose as we choose. . . ."

In another speech Lindsay expressed a revealing, and touching, note as an "admonition to myself, as well as to you":

"Our constitutional guarantees must be scrupulously observed at all times. Unequivocal loyalty to the principles of equal protection of the laws and due process is the only true ingredient to inspire loyalty to our nation. In such a manner we can maintain confidence in ourselves and gain the confidence of those others in the world who seek comparable freedoms. In the final call, vigilance to the Constitution as we know it must always be a matter of conscience with us."

Lindsay's record led James Wechsler to write that he had "occupied distinguished, distinctive ground in his tenacious and lonely allegiance to the Bill of Rights," and added that even though his positions "contain only political liabilities . . . it is also through such unpopular endeavors that profiles in courage are drawn."

13

The Magic Moment

FIVE minutes one July night in 1964, when John Lindsay stood defiantly before an angry Republican National Convention, could be said to be both the climax of his long battle in the civil rights cause and a beginning as well.

Beginnings are always difficult to isolate. When, in the recesses of his mind, does a man turn from innocuous and platitudinous pleasantries that have marked his public utterances to the words of a social rebel destined to found a new era? When does a man realize that he must take a stand amid the nation's travail and shun the past's ambiguities? When does a man become a reformer, a professional politician in inner spirit? When did the young attorney with a social conscience become a convinced crusader, vocal and persistent, for other people's dignity and protection? The exact moment is totally unnameable.

For John Lindsay the moment of truth must have come at some time in 1955 or 1956, as he found himself forced to think unromantically and pragmatically about what America today euphemistically has labeled "civil rights."

This is hardly to suggest that until age thirty-five John Lindsay had not thought about "civil rights," about whether people he would never see could cast a ballot, could pursue an education in order to achieve their goals, could walk in the streets without fear. But it is certain that at some moment he was forced to focus, to examine, to make a commitment. When?

It was in the mid-fifties when the young lawyer with a pleasant blend of political idealism, ambition, and curiosity had left the familiar comforts of the law office to respond to Herbert Brownell's bidding to do a stint in Washington; had found himself enmeshed in the uppermost thinking of the Department of Justice.

The nation itself was beginning to think about "civil rights." The May, 1954, verdict of the United States Supreme Court, overturning decades of easygoing adherence to the "separate but equal" doctrine for a people's education, was forcing the most agonizing of self-appraisals. Montgomery and Clinton, Faubus and King were unfamiliar names to the American people.

In Washington the men who could be the progenitors of a lawful and ordered growth began to understand and then to act. The imperative for finding the lawful and ordered way was coming into focus. Increasingly the men in Washington accepted the challenge and made their commitment. In this period, too, the young Manhattan lawyer was required to think, constructively and with conviction, about that disquieting thing called "civil rights"—to think of all its moral implications, to give these the most immediate and practical of applications, to realize that he and many other people would have to make individual commitments if the lawful and ordered was to foreclose on the lawless and uncontrolled.

The statutes that were to become known as the Civil Rights Act of 1957 were beginning to take shape, far from Montgomery and Clinton. And assigned to work on the drafting of these germinal landmarks was that émigré from a Manhattan law office, John Lindsay.

The laborious efforts of Lindsay and other Justice Department lawyers were to be worried over, sniffed and snapped at, chewed on for sixty-three days by Capitol hounds before the legal entity of a Civil Rights Act would emerge. But emerge it did—the first of its kind in eighty-seven years. By the time the worriers and harriers of the United States Congress had finished with it, the young draftsman—soon to be a Congressman himself—had left Washington and returned to Manhattan. But he took with him a focus, a conviction, a commitment. The hour when these appeared cannot be isolated; but it did come to pass, very possibly in some midnight scrutiny of a statute which grew into a scrutiny of self that in turn gave direction to the Congressman who, in his first week in office, produced a bill to shore up the bland and timid Act of 1957; the same Congressman who wrote and fought for meaningful portions of the Act of 1960, who badgered the Kennedy Administration for two and a half years to realize its own commitment, who was to play a unique role in winning a Civil Rights Act of 1964; who, that tense night in San Francisco, stood before the nation and bade his party honor its heritage.

❦ ❦ 14 ❦ ❦

A Good Fight, Well Fought

By the time the Eighty-fifth Congress had finished carving up the modest provisions of the civil rights legislation it had considered for so many weeks in 1957, some essential bone and sinew had gone back to the kitchen. One of the deleted provisions, Title III, would have given the Justice Department injunctive powers against violations of constitutional civil rights, a provision written in by the Justice Department while John Lindsay worked there on drafting the bill.

The first year of the law's application revealed some of its many inadequacies. In mid-January of 1959 the new Eighty-sixth Congress received a stronger proposal which included restoration of the missing Title III. In the Senate the new bill's sponsors were New York Senators Jacob Javits and Kenneth Keating, Pennsylvania's Hugh Scott, New Jersey's Clifford Case; in the House, the sponsors were two New Yorkers—Seymour Halpern and John V. Lindsay.

This was the first big legislative foray for the 17th District's new Congressman, who went to work with a will. The deleted section, he charged, possessed "equal or even greater importance" compared with the actual achievements of the 1957 law. "The bill does not ask for new and untried powers," Lindsay explained, "nor does it seek any extension of federal jurisdiction in civil rights cases. The rights now sought to be insured . . . are rights protected by the Constitution. When they are violated, the government may not act under existing criminal law. This legislation would permit the federal government to take civil remedial action, instead of having to depend solely upon criminal procedures; to meet intelligently our responsibilities and to preserve the constitutional rights of all Americans."

Lindsay later argued to retain Title III, which would empower the Attorney General to begin action without waiting for someone else to go to court, if equal use of public facilities, including schools, was denied. But these provisions were not destined even to see the light of floor debate in the House. By an overwhelming vote the Judiciary Committee, to which John Lindsay had just been appointed in recognition of his two years in the Justice Department, killed Title III once more.

Calling its rejection "a great shame," Lindsay later pleaded for Title III on the floor, where he hoped the principle would receive the Eisenhower Administration's backing (it did not). Then, in a burst of partisan candor, he noted that the Title III provisions were also conspicuously absent from a bill introduced in the Senate by Lyndon B. Johnson.

Johnson advocated an anti-bombing provision, as did Eisenhower, but John Lindsay viewed the anti-bombing proposal as the "least controversial" item. "All this does," he contended, "is supply the necessary jurisdiction for the federal government to come immediately into one of these hate-bombing cases." But even this provision was not to become law in 1959, for neither enough interest nor urgency could be mobilized to overcome the inertia and apathy dominating Congress and so much of the nation on that bothersome matter of "civil rights."

Even though it lacked Title III and other strength he had hoped for, Lindsay termed the ultimate bill a good one. He agreed with most of the Administration's "well-thought-out and well-balanced" proposals. The Civil Rights Commission was extended through 1961; Lindsay had supported it as "reasonable and moderate in its approach, yet firm. . . . [The Commission]," he noted, "has covered the North and it has covered the South, but it has barely scratched the surface. A great deal more is to be done. . . ." He applauded the Commission's holding of hearings in Northern states, declaring: ". . . in the North . . . none of us are without fault in this regard; we have problems. We must recognize them and stand up to them. The fact is that if progress is to be made in this field of civil rights," said John Lindsay during this intermediate period, "it must be made at the seat of government in Washington."

The fact was also that this new Congressman, launching his civil rights activities on Capitol Hill so aggressively and outspokenly, was already well ahead of both the Republican Eisenhower Administration and the Democratic leadership under Lyndon Johnson.

"Few Republicans are eager enough to see a civil rights bill passed to risk the displeasure of the [Republican] leadership," noted the *Baltimore Sun* early in 1960, adding that one eager leader was John V. Lindsay.

Eager John Lindsay was urging fellow Republicans in the House to "exercise a leadership role" in civil rights. "This is not a subject we can play politics with," he declared, "so let us take whatever step is necessary to give us a bill." Later, in debate, he asked bitterly, "What is this cry of 'election-year politics' that I keep hearing? It is meaningless. It ignores our history. It ignores, too, the movement of history the whole world over. What we do here today and tomorrow is part of the current that sweeps the world. . . . If people want to call it politics, let them call it that. I prefer to call it our democratic process."

This "political" year of 1960, the Presidential-election year, was a year of sit-ins at lunch counters and other public places throughout the South; of occasional violence and a growing, grudging attention to the civil rights arena; of slow steps toward integration of schools; of platform demands by the parties for legislative action; of tentative moves (in spite of a record-breaking Senate filibuster) by the nation's legislators toward new laws to protect Negroes' rights.

The year opened with efforts to force the 1959 civil rights bill out of the Rules Committee so the House could consider it. It was, in effect, a preview of events of exactly one year later when the twelve-member committee was enlarged to fifteen to avoid just such an impasse.*

Rules was split between four Republicans, four Northern Democrats, and four Southerners following the chairman, Howard Smith of Virginia. Many programs of the Eisenhower Administration and of Congressmen outside the ultraconservative Southern-dominated coalition, Republicans and Democrats alike, were frustrated here.

Republicans awaited word from the Vice-President on whether to sign a petition to force the bill out of Rules. "I would be delighted if the Vice-President would urge the members to act," said John Lindsay; but no sign was forthcoming from Richard Nixon. The Republican Party's House leadership had been tepid on the petition, and Democrat Emanuel Celler, Chairman of Judiciary, had charged the payoff on an "unholy alliance" with Southern Democrats.

On the same day that the *Baltimore Sun* quoted John Lindsay as urging Republicans to sign, Charles Halleck in Washington was reporting, after an hour-long conference with those same Republicans, that he had refused to advise them to sign. And another high-placed Republican was forecasting difficulty in persuading as many as sixty to sign, even though they might favor the bill (ultimately, thirty including Lindsay, of course, did sign). Even as Halleck was denying Celler's charges of a deal, his position seemed to give substance to the allegation—at least, it produced the effect the Southerners wanted.

Then the freshman Republican and the Democratic thirty-five-year veteran of Congressional fencing, Emanuel Celler, locked in a radio debate. Lindsay minimized the potential role of the "very small, tiny, little" minority in prying loose the bill from Rules. "If the Democratic leadership wants a civil rights bill to come out on the floor, they could get it out on the floor," he contended, by

* See Chapter 11.

"applying some real leadership. We [Republicans] don't control any of the committees; we don't have any chairmanships; we don't control any of the machinery at all," Lindsay noted wryly, "but we are given credit for preventing a two-to-one majority from bringing very important legislation to the floor."

Celler, scornful of the four Republicans in Rules for failing to vote the bill out, derided the Republican delegation for withholding names from the petition. He even urged Lindsay, "with your perspicacity and your powers of leadership and your dedication to a good cause," to strong-arm his colleagues. They found two points of agreement—support of the bill itself and an accurate prediction that the House would approve the bill if ever it could be forced out of committee.

The Lindsays of the GOP were trying, in effect, to overcome the inertia of their leadership, not merely in Congress but in the White House as well. The President, in a conference with Halleck and Dirksen, had nothing to say about the petition. Dirksen quoted Eisenhower: "I sent my recommendations to the first session of the Eighty-sixth Congress [in 1959]. That represents my sentiments and my viewpoint." As *The Sun*'s account put it, "Few Republicans are eager enough . . . to risk the displeasure of their leadership. . . ."

By February of election year, legislation was finally afoot. The Eisenhower Administration came up with a package and Lyndon Johnson forced its consideration in the Senate with a masterpiece of maneuvering, though a record filibuster ensued. In that same month John Lindsay introduced two bills aimed at strengthening the 1957 Civil Rights Act and insuring the right to vote. His first bill, embodying proposals offered by Eisenhower's Attorney General, provided for appointment by the federal courts of "voting referees"; the second, proposed by the Civil Rights Commission, provided for temporary federal registrars for voting.

By early March, however, Lindsay joined other members of the Judiciary Committee in reporting out still another bill, which he called "balanced and moderate." But he warned that he would support amendments to strengthen its safeguards of voting rights.

As debate opened he rose on the floor to urge Congress "to take a leadership position in the never-ending struggle to demonstrate that the United States Constitution means what it says." For more than twenty minutes he spoke vigorously, calling voting rights "the key to the solution of all other civil rights problems." Civil rights in this area have "retrogressed, not progressed," he added, scorning the opposing argument that "progress is being made . . . and [that] therefore we need no new legislation." And he detailed some of the miserable statistics from Southern states.*

After enumerating the "balanced, moderate" provisions of the bill, he returned to its omissions—those hanging over from 1959, including the now fabled Title III proposal. He urged several amendments and promised to propose an amendment that would provide for voting referees.

John Lindsay was a principal participant in the debate, which was chiefly on the amendments. It continued for a fortnight, until the House, by nearly three to one, approved a five-point bill that included a voting-referee plan. As it moved to the Senate massive obstruction efforts launched by the Southern Democrat-Conservative Republican coalition were frustrated in part by Johnsonian maneuvering. Nevertheless, what finally emerged in April was hardly the "balanced, moderate" bill Lindsay had praised in March. Among other things, the voting-referee proposal was gone; one of the fiery Northern Democrats snorted, in fact, that virtually nothing was left.

Now the House had to agree to these amendments and in an effort to establish legislative intent in case of a court test, Lindsay joined a senior Republican, McCulloch of Ohio, and two Democrats, including Chairman Celler, in a deliberate colloquy on the House floor.

They passed this conversation for the record, while some Southern Congressmen interrupted repeatedly with objections:

"A Negro seeking help under the referee plan must have tried to register within the time period established by state law. . . .

"The only exception to this would be if a court finding of a pat-

* The 1956 figure on potential Negro voters registered showed 23 per cent for eleven states; Alabama's percentage was 9.9, Mississippi's 4.1.

tern or practice of discrimination were handed down after the state registration period were ended. . . .

"Yes, the judge could then waive state registration time requirements.

"The judge would decide, also, if the applicant was qualified under state law and should be allowed to vote provisionally on the basis of the applicant's sworn statement and the report of the referee.

"And there'd be no need for full-dress proceedings. . . ."

In case the bill were to be harassed by constant court cases, this brief conversation would help to establish the will of Congress in passing it.

John Lindsay was pleased that something, even this little, had been accomplished, but restive that it proved so scant. The new act, he said, was the "major accomplishment of the Eighty-sixth Congress"; in fact, little competition for the distinction could be found, and he called it a good law, an historic one for which, "as one of the drafters of the legislation, I was pleased to have had a major share of the responsibility for securing passage. . . .

"Nevertheless, as is true in all measures in this civil rights field, the battle must go on." He promised to "press for the further expansion of civil rights," and later in the year he was true to his word. As the time of the Republican National Convention approached, he explained his views to the committee drafting the 1960 platform. He urged them to draft a "constructive and comprehensive" program with a nine-point plank which would: Affirm the Supreme Court's school decision and urge a speed-up of desegregation; support legislation to prevent discrimination in employment; recognize the sit-in movement as in accord with moral principles and American traditions; * call for an Executive Order requiring non-discriminatory policies in federally assisted housing; back new legislation in other areas—to prevent a denial by

* He signed a statement which a few other House members also signed in those days when the sit-in movement was relatively novel and highly controversial: "We believe that the opening of lunch counters and restaurants to all persons, regardless of race, is overdue."

states or localities of any constitutionally guaranteed rights, to prevent the use of federal funds for segregated facilities, to require the NLRB to refuse certification to any union operating on a segregated basis, to outlaw state poll taxes in federal elections, and to enact a federal anti-lynch law.

The platform ended up with some strenuous gestures in these directions, but clearly John Lindsay was ahead of his party. If the 1960 legislative proposals were mild, the GOP's position was almost equally so. Though a delegate, Lindsay understandably had a much lesser role in the platform's civil rights aspects than he was destined to share in the febrile San Francisco sessions four years later.

Back in session after the conventions, Congress found itself still stalemated on further civil rights proposals, despite the professions in both party platforms. Lindsay introduced a bill to end discrimination in voting, housing, schools, and employment. His bill provided for technical assistance to communities making efforts to comply with the law under the Supreme Court's desegregation ruling; for the creation of a Commission on Equal Job Opportunities on Government Contracts; for authorization of the Attorney General to bring actions for school desegregation when threats deterred private individuals from going to court for their rights. In a new proposal, he added an item from the GOP platform which would establish a sixth-grade education as conclusive evidence of literacy for voting.

"Congress should deliver on the promises of the Democratic and Republican civil rights planks," he asserted, "and I see no better time to begin than now." The parties' planks "provide ample evidence that these past efforts are far from complete," he pointed out. "The legislative setbacks suffered in the past can be overcome in an atmosphere for meaningful action."

He reminded the Democrats, headed by nominees Kennedy and Johnson, of their "large promises about delivery on their legislative proposals in this wind-up session of the Congress," and added, "In the area of civil rights, I shall hold them to their promises."

But that summer there was to be little holding of the leadership or of Congress itself to any promises. As the members hurried through unfinished business, they were reminded by Lindsay that, "Among the items of unfinished business is civil rights. . . . Most of what I now propose was rejected by the Congress before the political conventions. However, at the conventions both parties pledged performance on each of these points. Therefore, how can we now avoid our responsibility to finish the job? We heard many promises in the recent party conventions on civil rights legislation. We have the promises; now let's have performance."

But more than a week later he still was asking Congress to stay on until it completed its unfinished business, especially on civil rights.

Congress went home to campaign that same day, leaving much "unfinished business," including all the new civil rights proposals. The civil rights year, 1960, had seen a modest advance—an intermediate stage between the lethargy of so many past years and the momentum of the years to come.

For John Lindsay it had been a year of driving activity, frequently in opposition or contradistinction to his party's leadership in Congress, in the White House, or in the assembled convention. He had fought to release a bill from the committee where the conservative coalition was holding it. He had introduced bills of his own to strengthen existing laws. He had participated in drafting the Administration's plan, had become recognized in the House not only as its advocate but as an authority, and he had helped steer it through to approval. He had urged on his own party a stronger course and a commitment to specific progressive legislation for the future; and then he had sought to translate that future into the present. In some respects success and recognition had rewarded his efforts—"I direct my question to the gentleman from New York, Mr. Lindsay"—and in others the result was at least temporary defeat and disappointment.

But in any event, the nation now had a 1960 Civil Rights Law —"the major accomplishment of the Eighty-sixth Congress"—for which Lindsay could, if he wished, claim much credit. It was credit which many others were willing to extend. The American Jewish

Committee addressed Lindsay with these words: "During the entire debate, your leadership role, especially in repelling the efforts of foes and even more dangerous 'lukewarm' friends of civil rights, carried the day. Yours was a good fight, well fought."

15

Surprised, Troubled, Profoundly Disappointed

"THE greatest disappointment in this Congress," said John Lindsay in mid-1961, "is the deliberate failure of the Kennedy Administration to submit a civil rights program." This theme was one to which he was to return with vehement persistence, yet with a real sadness in his "disappointment," again and again during the next thirty months.

In a major speech on the House floor, he recalled his 1961 Lincoln Day promise to go along with the Democratic Administration "unstintingly when support is warranted," but also to offer "coherent and constructive criticism when criticism is warranted."

Now it was the first week of May, and Lindsay felt the time was long overdue to confront the four-and-a-half-month-old Administration on civil rights. He related at length the 1960 Democratic platform and the campaign speeches in which Candidate Kennedy had promised that submission of a civil rights bill would be "among the first orders of business when a new Congress meets in January."

"It is now May," he observed, "but still we have received no legislative proposals on civil rights from the Administration." He twitted those Democrats who had termed the 1960 Civil Rights Act inadequate. "Not a single omnibus civil rights bill embodying the Democratic platform" had been introduced by Democrats.* "Political platforms and campaign promises sometimes have a way of fading after the votes have been delivered, the election won, and the jobs parceled out," Lindsay commented in one of his relatively rare excursions into cynicism. "I have vainly looked for a Presidential message on the subject of civil rights, and I am surprised, troubled, and profoundly disappointed. . . .

"Can it be that for some obscure political reason," he inquired suggestively, "the Administration has lost its ardor for civil rights legislation? Prompt and resolute action by Congress is necessary: the legislative process is slow and painstaking and it is never too early to begin. Let us, therefore, begin."

Lindsay urged Congressmen to "ask anyone who has lived and worked with civil rights, and he will assure you that legislation is what we need. We cannot do the job merely by occasional executive orders, still less by Presidential pronouncements that have no teeth—that do not have the force of law behind them."

And then Lindsay ticked off the items on which "the time is ripe, indeed long overdue": A federal law on fair employment practices with respect to concerns operating in interstate commerce; laws to prevent discrimination in employment policies of government agencies and private industries holding government contracts; legislation to prevent denial by state and local authorities of any constitutionally guaranteed rights (a revival of Title III); assistance to states that had attempted to comply with court orders by instituting programs of transition from segregated to integrated schools; anti-lynch legislation and anti-poll-tax laws.

"Where, one must ask, are the Administration's proposals on

* With some poetic license Lindsay quoted "a former mayor of my city," Jimmy Walker, as having asked the people of New York, "Will you love me in November as you did in May?" Lindsay then went on to wonder whether some voters might not now plaintively inquire, "Do you love me this May as you so ardently professed to love me last November?" He missed the point somewhat: Jimmy Walker, as lyricist rather than politician, was expressing the sentiments of a love song, and the month he mentioned was December, not November.

Congressman John V. Lindsay, with Mrs. Lindsay and their four children (left to right): Anne, John Jr., Katherine and Margaret.

Congressman Lindsay in Central Park with Johnny, Margie and Anne.

Congressman John V. Lindsay at the Judiciary Committee, House of Representatives.

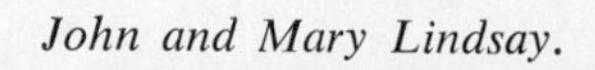

John and Mary Lindsay.

these subjects?" the Congressman asked, and he suggested further areas for scrutiny: "widespread discrimination in labor unions, aided and abetted by management"; "implications for civil rights of existing federal grant-in-aid programs"; the relation of an anti-segregation amendment to federal-aid-to-education bills.

Noting that "the President lays great stress on the vigorous use of the powers of his office," Lindsay challenged President Kennedy to ask the Attorney General to rule on certain questions of law and constitutionality involved in withholding federal funds from segregated facilities. "He did not hesitate to do this in the case of the constitutional question of the separation of church and state," Lindsay reminded the House. Then he chided Robert Kennedy: "I have looked in vain for vigorous action on the part of the Department of Justice in the area of civil rights," though "in at least four Southern states not a single school has been desegregated and in the rest only token integration has begun . . . our preoccupation with missile gaps and with unemployment gaps should not blind us to the existence of a legislative gap in the field of civil rights.

"Congress has a job to do and it is not doing it—nor is the Administration suggesting that it should."

He enumerated five of his own bills which needed support, "especially from those whose eloquent pronouncements in the past have evidenced a most sincere dedication to the cause of civil rights. With the backing of the Administration, so conspicuously lacking when set against the pledges of its electoral platform and campaign," he challenged the Democrats, "the battle for individual freedom can be continued and ultimately won.

"With the President's enthusiastic support," he challenged Kennedy, "we can close the broad gap between the promise of the Constitution and the firm application of its principles."

He described recent gains: a twelvefold increase in Negro voting registrations in the Southern states within two decades; "slow but measureable progress in integrating schools and other facilities; laws in 1957 and 1960 that were significant, "though inadequate in proportion to existing needs and injustices. Our satisfaction with these advances must be greatly tempered by shame that they were so long overdue," he commented.

John Lindsay closed his long and thoughtful review of the civil rights dilemma with these words: "The history of injustice and neglect that preceded these gains must be duly recognized lest we judge progress only in relative terms. In terms of the broad gap that remains between the promise of our Constitution and the realization of its principles, the task is barely begun."

Though his final words were sobering, John Lindsay's most telling remarks were directed toward the President and his Administration: "Now I find it incumbent upon myself to be sharply critical of a serious omission on the part of the Democratic Administration [which is] the deliberate failure, contrary to campaign and platform pledges, to submit to the Congress a civil rights program."

The language and the charge were strong medicine for such men as the Kennedys. Five days later a series of civil rights bills were introduced for the Democrats by Congressman Celler and Senator Clark, and initially backed by the President. But Mr. Kennedy's subsequent intimations that no new legislation was necessary that year proved disastrous to the Democratic proposals which resembled Lindsay's.

The day after the bills were submitted Lindsay was back on the floor of the House accusing the President of breaking faith with the public by failing to submit a message that would have put the Administration explicitly behind the bills. "I take it this is a flat repudiation of a campaign pledge by Mr. Kennedy and the Democratic platform," said Lindsay. "By refraining from submitting a Presidential message to Congress on civil rights, a campaign pledge was broken. Now the Administration, by disassociating itself from the legislation introduced not in January but in May, has compounded the breach of faith with the public. This isn't even standing still," he added. "It's moving backward."

Federal marshals were dispatched into Alabama in late May when Freedom Riders, there to test segregation barriers in interstate bus terminals, were attacked by mobs.

"No other choice could be made," said Lindsay of the President's order. "State and local authorities were apparently unwilling or unable to protect the rights of citizens to travel freely and without harm. I stand firmly in support of the action taken by the federal government to meet this disgraceful situation. . . . But it is now doubly clear," he added, "that we must have new legislation arming the Attorney General with the legal tools necessary to initiate court actions where civil rights have been violated . . . to prevent and to punish willful denials of the right of peaceful assembly, or of free and equal access to publicly supported institutions, or other constitutionally protected rights not necessarily tied to interstate commerce.

"There must be no doubt or equivocation, as there is now," he said, "about the authority of the federal government with respect to all constitutionally protected rights. . . . Legislation is long overdue, and we have a right to expect that the Administration will support it, consistent with its platform."

During the summer Lindsay played a losing hand in an effort to make the Civil Rights Commission permanent; * he used the discussion as another occasion to rebuke the Administration and its "deliberate scuttling of campaign and platform pledges for meaningful civil rights legislation." The President and Attorney General, he contended, could have averted defeat within the Judiciary Committee of the proposed permanent status for the Commission. With another Republican, Cahill of New Jersey, he outlined the additional difficulties the Commission would face because of its temporary nature, and charged that the Judiciary majority, by extending it for only two years, had played directly into the hands of those who would slow its work, pursue delaying tactics, and discourage recruitment of top-grade staff. We regret the failure of the President and Attorney General to press for a better bill," they said. "Such failure made the difference between the success or defeat of the Lindsay-Cahill amendment" which would have made the Commission permanent.

When the two-year extension of the Commission's life reached the House with Judiciary's blessing, Lindsay reiterated the desir-

* In 1963 Lindsay again noted the Administration's failure to make the Commission permanent. "Wholesale resignations of good men from the Commission have occurred," he said, "because of its impermanent nature and the cavalier way in which it has been treated by the Administration."

ability of permanent status. Slugging away again at the Administration, his comment keynoted his simmering feud with the Kennedys: "Perhaps the greatest disappointment we have had in this Congress is the deliberate failure of the Administration to submit to Congress a civil rights program."

When the Commission brought in an extensive report to Congress in the late summer * Lindsay noted that it advocated "broader measures" than were passed in 1957 and 1960. He fired at both the White House and the Congressional leadership: "This session of Congress is closing and yet no Presidential message on the subject of civil rights has been received. In view of all the promises of the campaign—and now the impact of this report—this is inexcusable. As a result, the Judiciary Committee of the House has not even called hearings or scheduled the subject for discussion. . . ."

"I share the disappointment of millions," the President of the United States read in a letter as he ended the first year of his Administration, "to whom it has become apparent that no Executive Order ending racial discrimination in federally assisted housing in the United States will be forthcoming. . . ."

The letter was from John Lindsay. Whereas during 1961 he had told Congress and audiences around the nation of his disappointment in John F. Kennedy's record on civil rights, he began 1962 by telling the President himself, as directly as a letter, shortly made public by the Congressman, could.

A few days earlier he had told reporters, as Senator Javits had also, that President Kennedy's annual message lacked major new proposals in the rights field. Now he deplored the "abandonment of solemn pledges" and urged an immediate Executive Order on housing. The single most significant aspect of the President's failure to exercise executive powers is related to housing discrimination, said the Lindsay letter. He recalled that in 1960 the Presidential candidate had "said as much," and added, "You said further that, if

* Lindsay pointed out that most of the Commission's recommendations in the legislative field "are included in the omnibus civil rights bill I introduced shortly after the Congress convened and which I have pressed for ever since." The Lindsay bill, with seven principal points, embraced chiefly the main points he had urged upon the GOP platform committee a year earlier, and he had enumerated them as necessary legislation in his May speech.

elected, you would have the courage to move on this front by 'a stroke of the pen.' The climate is right," said John Lindsay, "for the immediate issuance of a truly effective Executive Order barring discrimination in all housing programs which are aided in any way by the federal government. . . . I respectfully urge you to live up to your promise and execute such an order promptly."

He nudged the President once again on his "continued refusal to submit a legislative program on civil rights," and commented that the two omissions "compounded the failure."

No answer came, and neither was there action until the year was almost spent. Civil rights legislation lay on a fallow field those months; * on August 27 the House completed Congressional action on a proposed Constitutional Amendment outlawing the poll tax, but even this was an object of Lindsay derision. He drew cheers from the Republican side by decrying the proposed amendment as "legislative gamesmanship." Again accusing the Kennedy Administration of breaking its 1960 pledges, Lindsay criticized the amendment, which was limited to national elections, for failure to cover the state and local situation. The greatest need, he contended, was for the South's Negroes to acquire a voice in local politics.

"If we're going to have a Constitutional Amendment," he told the House, "let's have a meaningful one." He argued that the poll tax could have been banned by a simple statute rather than an amendment, and snorted, "This is using a sledgehammer, a giant cannon, to kill a gnat. If you can do it [amend the Constitution] as easily as we do here today, . . . just think of what can occur in the future in the event the extreme right should be in the ascendancy."

The amendment had finally come to the House floor, despite Rules Committee roadblocks, through a limited-debate arrangement that allowed no changes in its wording on the floor. Lindsay denounced this way of bringing it up, for it meant that it had to be

* In the Judiciary Committee, Lindsay demanded that Chairman Celler call early hearings on civil rights proposals. The venerable chairman leaned back and quoted what he called "an old Turkish saying," to this effect: "Don't roll up your pants until you come to the river." It was forty-eight hours later before Lindsay found a chance to retort: "The chairman is not always able to walk on water, but I've never seen him fail to try."

swallowed whole, and the amendment that was proposed, he charged, "prevents us from even trying to apply this to all elections, not just federal elections."

The measure's history was stormy. Several times in previous years the House had passed statutory poll-tax bans, only to see them fail in the Senate. This time the Senate had acted first, giving its approval to the amendment five months earlier than the House, after a two-week filibuster. In the House, Howard Smith held it up for more than two months in his Rules Committee before it finally was forced out by the Rules suspension and limited-debate technique.

"It offends me very deeply," Lindsay commented. The efforts of the Democratic leadership to get a rule to permit amendments were, in his view, just "a mock battle" which played into the hands of the Rules chairman. The Democratic strategy, he suggested, was part of a "deal with the Southerners by the Attorney General and the Democrats [in the House leadership]."

Once more he was in sharp conflict with the Kennedys, for not only did Robert Kennedy figure in the purported deal, but the measure itself was one that John F. Kennedy had urged upon Congress. This was a major difference between the Administration and the Lindsay activists.

Chairman Celler, the amendment's principal sponsor, ridiculed the Lindsay views as "a lot of baloney." At length, after certain Southern Congressmen had forced five roll calls that took nearly four hours, the amendment was passed, 294–86. Lindsay was, nonetheless, among those voting "Yea"—along with 131 other Republicans. (Only fifteen GOP members were opposed; the measure was considered to place the Congressmen either "For" or "Against" civil rights.)

Even though he had voted for the amendment Lindsay continued his opposition to the way approval was won. He cited the 1961 report of the Civil Rights Commission which suggested that it was only in Alabama and Mississippi that the poll tax discriminated against Negroes, and that poll taxes were levied in only three other states.

"Under this kind of gag procedure," charged John Lindsay, the

Democratic leaders "casually and cynically tinker with the United States Constitution, for political reasons, to get off the hook on civil rights. The Constitution is entitled to more respect."

1962 was a year of relative inaction on the legislative front, but civil rights forces were active elsewhere. As autumn began the nation's attention was riveted on Oxford, Mississippi, where violence erupted around the last-ditch efforts to prevent enrollment of a Negro, James Meredith, at the state university.

When the situation got out of hand, Kennedy ordered in federal troops, but the delay drew Lindsay's fire: "President Kennedy should have sent federal troops as soon as federal marshals were rebuffed the first time." He contrasted the delay with President Eisenhower's action "with dispatch" at Little Rock five years earlier. The Administration had "drifted too long," said Lindsay, alleging "political reasons," and suggesting that the President hadn't wanted to "ruffle the Southern public."

Of the situation that had flared, he said, "Lawlessness and chaos . . . cannot be tolerated. . . . The United States is a government of laws and not of men, and each state which is a part of the United States is subject to the laws of the whole. . . ."

Early in 1963, shortly after the Eighty-eighth Congress convened, Lindsay and other Republicans in the Judiciary Committee introduced a new civil rights bill which with one important exception restated the 1960 Republican platform proposal. As the bill's principal spokesman, Lindsay once again assailed the Administration for proposing only minor rights legislation in two years. He described Congressman Celler's occasional bills as intended more for public-relations effect than for passage. Indeed, in this respect some Congressmen saw a similarity to the Republicans whose largest purpose was to embarrass the Kennedys.

The bill now sponsored by Lindsay and other Republicans of Judiciary had a single new proposal which added this significant feature: the Census Bureau was directed to determine how many minority-group citizens in each state were qualified but didn't vote. Carried to its logical end, this could be used to reduce the representation of some states in the House, since the Fourteenth Amendment requires a state's Congressional representation to be cut when qualified citizens are denied the right to vote.

Otherwise the bill was fairly familiar, ranging from a proposal making the Civil Rights Commission permanent and giving it added investigative authority, to proposing authority for the Attorney General to institute suits for citizens denied admittance to public schools.

The first bill just sat there. The year's second Republican civil rights bill came four months later. The House Republicans were still awaiting an Administration plan, and their new bill beat the muscle-bound Democrats to the draw again.

The new Republican plan focused on a ban on segregation in any state-licensed facility. It was a tough proposal that would have outlawed, as a violation of the Fourteenth Amendment, discrimination in stores, restaurants, and other public places. The Republican position was this: If the Administration lacked legal weapons to protect citizens from rifle butts and dogs' teeth (violence was flaring in Birmingham and other Southern cities), why had the Kennedys not asked for broader authority? This foot-dragging is irreconcilable, they said, with the temper of the times, which demands immediate action.

The band of thirty pushing the proposal was led by Cahill of New Jersey, MacGregor of Minnesota, Mathias of Maryland, and John Lindsay. Lindsay summed up their position: "We're committed to getting a bill through Congress. We think this is the better bill, but if we receive no support for our route" (the Fourteenth Amendment's protections), "I am sure Republicans will support the interstate commerce route." The latter was believed to be the Democrats' preference; though no legislation had been forthcoming, the Administration was now working feverishly to whip something together.

Meanwhile, the Lindsay barrage against the Kennedys' record continued. He told a Judiciary subcommittee hearing that the President had failed to exercise all his authority in connection with police brutality in Alabama which was obstructing the "legitimate goals" of American citizens. Because the brutality had occurred in connection with voting rights, he averred, executive power to act was implicit. Lindsay recommended action on the Civil Rights Commission report calling on the President to consider withholding federal funds from Mississippi.*

As a summer approached that was, indeed, to prove long and hot, Lindsay deplored the President's trip to Berlin, Ireland, and other points, on the "eve of a possible explosion . . . such as this country has not seen in decades," and spoke of a "cynical abandonment" of legislative needs. The next day the Kennedy program finally was unveiled.

On the whole, said John Lindsay after reading it, the Administration's program turned out to be "fairly good." But, he added, "85 to 90 per cent is exactly what I and others" supported and advocated for many months. "It won't meet the pressures in the country," he warned them, "but will do something" toward helping to ameliorate civil rights problems.

As for what lay ahead in Congress, he forecast accurately that the civil rights battle would make the session the longest in Congressional history. He characterized the mood of Congress as "churlish and unpredictable."

His analyses were uncommonly true. But now, at least, the way was opened for the real battle to achieve a new civil rights law for the country. It was to be a battle fought on many fronts, with numerous campaigns and engagements, skirmishes, maneuvers, some victims and victories.

* In Judiciary sessions Lindsay even challenged his own colleagues. He urged the committee to hold civil rights hearings in Birmingham, and declared: "The trouble is, the committee doesn't want to get involved. When you get involved, you get things thrown at you and you get picketed. It's nice and comfortable here in Washington." Presumably his committee-mates agreed with his last observation—for there was no support for moving hearings from Washington to Birmingham.

16

While the Country Burns

"LET'S be frank about this," said the Congressman in a sharp-edged tone. John V. Lindsay looked steadily at Robert F. Kennedy hunched forward in the witness chair before the Judiciary Committee in the House of Representatives' big hearing room in June, 1963. "There are rumors in the cloakrooms all over Capitol Hill that the Administration and the leaders have made a deal. . . ."

The Attorney General flushed, started to speak.

". . . a deal to scuttle public accommodations."

His reference was to the provision in the Administration's 1963 civil rights bill which would authorize the Attorney General himself to institute suits to curb discrimination in public accommodations where interstate commerce might be a factor.

Robert Kennedy had come to Capitol Hill to win friends for the Administration's week-old, two-year-incubated civil rights bill. But his manner was combative and his attitude seemed unreceptive to ideas outside the limits of his own bill. Besides, he had fallen into the trap of quarreling, and as he testified his main antagonist was John Lindsay. Now the Attorney General bristled and shot back to the Congressman: "I am surprised that you would come out in open hearings and say you've heard rumors in the cloakrooms without any further substantiation. Neither the President nor I," continued the President's brother, "have to defend our good faith to you or anyone else."

Yet in a sense he was there, in part, to do just that. The Kennedy Administration had been dilatory in submitting major legislative proposals. Congress, the nation, and the leaders and beneficiaries of the civil rights cause had waited for nearly thirty months for something stronger than messages.* The House Judiciary Committee, of which Lindsay was a member, had been holding hearings for more than six weeks; the Attorney General had canceled four scheduled appearances before the Committee in order to give his Justice Department more time to pull together some specific legislative proposals. Meanwhile, the Republican-sponsored proposals, at least as strong as those Kennedy now offered and in some respects stronger, were on the table.

John Lindsay now asked the Attorney General about the public accommodations section of the Republican bill. This provision was conceded to be the most controversial since it forbade discrimination by race in such places as restaurants and hotels. Opponents might, and did, contend that the constitutional rights of private property would be impaired.

"Have you read the section?" John Lindsay asked Robert Kennedy, referring to the Republicans' bill.

The Attorney General didn't bother to be polite. No, he said, he hadn't read the bill, and he implied he was much too busy to waste time reading Republican legislation.

Now John Lindsay, too, was angered. He pointed out that he

* The first Kennedy civil rights message, sent to Congress at the end of February, had resulted within the next few weeks in bills in both houses that restated or resurrected previous bills: basing literacy for voting on a sixth-grade education, providing voting referees, expediting such suits in federal courts, and extending the life of the Civil Rights Commission. When, later in the year, the House voted a one-year extension for the Commission, Congressman Lindsay defended it against Southerners' charges that it stirred up demonstrations and unrest. "The Negro revolution," he said, "would be ten times stronger, and the unrest more acute, were it not for the small steps Congress has taken on civil rights in recent years."

and dozens of other Republicans had introduced bills in January and he was disturbed, he added, that the Attorney General apparently had not even considered them.

The quarrel moved on to a basic difference in approach. Lindsay held the view that the Fourteenth Amendment provided a basis for executive action to protect the individual citizen. Kennedy was vociferous for the interstate commerce clause and rejected the Lindsay view entirely. He cited as the "law of the land" an 1883 Supreme Court decision supporting the Administration's argument that only accommodations involved to a "substantial" degree in interstate commerce could be subjected to federal controls.

"I don't know whether you can get it through Congress based on the commerce laws," Lindsay told Kennedy. He conceded, however, that he would probably vote for an Administration bill, if it reached the floor, instead of one based on the Fourteenth Amendment. Their exchange was alternately harsh and respectful of differences: "We'll need everybody's help to get by," the Attorney General insisted. "Yes, it has to be bipartisan," agreed the Congressman. Now it was Kennedy who conceded a point. The Supreme Court, he said, might possibly uphold the Lindsay approach, via the Fourteenth Amendment, despite that 1883 decision, but he thought not.

The Attorney General shifted back to the offensive. It didn't make sense, he commented, to argue which powers should be employed; there would be difficulty enough getting the bill through Congress. Prodded as to whether the Administration would or would not accept the Fourteenth Amendment argument to get a bill passed, the Attorney General fell back on the 1883 court case.

Finally, Lindsay again expressed his own doubts as to the Administration's sincerity; he asked the Attorney General: "Do you really want a public-accommodations section?"

Robert Kennedy was the big witness, but ninety-two others were heard over twenty-one days before the Judiciary Committee appointed a subcommittee to pull together legislation that would ultimately go to the full House. Meanwhile, strategy thinking was very much in flux—Lindsay's arguments for the Fourteenth Amendment were giving the Kennedys second thoughts, and in an hour-long debate within Judiciary itself he all but converted Chairman Celler, who began to concede that the bill's future might well be safer if it employed *both* concepts. As for the viability of that 1883 decision, Lindsay reminded Celler, later decisions already had "half reversed" it.

During the summer of 1963 a good-will cruise on the White House yacht carried a small party down the Potomac. Among those aboard were Republicans John Lindsay and his senior, Ohio Congressman William McCulloch, the ranking GOP member of Judiciary, with whom the New Yorker was developing an increasingly close working relationship. Playing the Administration's cards were Larry O'Brien, White House emissary to Capitol Hill, and Deputy Attorney General Nicholas deB. Katzenbach. Whatever genial arm twisting or moral suasion occurred, on either side, may never be known, but the occasion was timely—the eleven-member Judiciary subcommittee was starting work on its huge problem, the evolution of a civil rights package able to win strong bipartisan support in the thirty-five-member full committee. Though not a member of the subcommittee, John Lindsay was sitting in on the drafting of the package. When an interviewer asked what the prospects were, he forecast that a bill would pass despite "terrible difficulties in the House and a filibuster in the Senate."

"Any petition for legislative activity is good," said John Lindsay, after attending the multi-sponsored civil rights demonstration at the Lincoln Memorial which climaxed the August 28 March on Washington.

"And the March," he continued, "will have assisted the legislative process. It certainly did not hurt it."

"There is a very deep moral base to the passions that have swept the country," Lindsay observed another time, "and they will not be calmed until the American promise of equal treatment under law becomes a reality for all Americans.

"Legislation is only part of the answer, but it is an important part and must be supported. Education and job opportunities in the long run are the areas that need the greatest attention." Later he commented that "fulfillment has to be brought about by citizen engagement."

Speaking of the philosophy behind the March, Lindsay expressed troubled feelings that "such scant attention is paid to the First Amendment to the Constitution, which unequivocally and absolutely established 'the right of the people peaceably to assemble, and to petition the government for a redress of grievances.' To those who are in opposition to the March and to orderly demonstrations," he added, "I would urge a rereading of the First Amendment. There is no doubt as to the absolute nature of the protection given by this most basic of all liberties safeguarded by the Constitution."

It may well have been an incident far from Washington's sweltering streets and chilled hearing rooms that finally changed a lot of things. In mid-September a bomb's fragments killed four little girls in a Birmingham church, and the impatient and weary conscience of John Lindsay cried out: "I call upon the Congress to act on legislation and to stop fiddling while the country burns."

The bombing, he said, "ought to shake the conscience of America to its root-pins. Nothing that we legislators in Washington can say or do will bring these children back," he told Congress. "But we as legislators can do our appointed task with fresh determination and conviction: that task is to draft a proper civil rights bill nation-wide in scope and calling upon all Americans, through our constituted federal government, to respect the equal protection of the laws and the full mandate of the Thirteenth, Fourteenth, and Fifteenth Amendments to the Constitution. We have done little enough in this Congress; let us at least, in this area of primary importance, accomplish what we have set out to do. . . ."

And he said he hoped there could be a new bill within the week which would go beyond the Kennedy Administration's proposals.

Only hours later the Judiciary subcommittee working out the bipartisan "package" rejected an amendment he had proposed and adopted a Democrat's, almost identical. (The Lindsay amendment, which would ban discrimination in accommodations, was supported by the Civil Rights Leadership Conference, which represented forty organizations.) Committee Republicans protested that rejection of Lindsay's plan in favor of a Democrat's betrayed the Administration's pledge on bipartisanship. But an ironic twist could be seen in the incident, for it was John Lindsay and a Democrat, Robert Kastenmeier of Wisconsin, who shortly joined forces and emerged as leaders of the drive to obtain a stronger bill than the Kennedys had proposed.

In mid-October there began a subplot that was complicated and sophisticated. But if the plot was thick, the plotting which accompanied it was melodramatic to boot. There were heavies and heroes, but it was sometimes difficult to tell them apart.

Downstage and *sotto voce* were the diehards who wanted no bill at all, but who would support the most liberal bill in committee in order to help assure its ultimate death on the floor. In the wings were the cautious conservatives, tending in sympathy to play along with the diehards. At center stage were the sincere moderates, hoping for a down-the-middle bill that would have the best chance of enactment and at the same time be sufficient to enable the disappointed Negro leaders to keep their own extremists in line. Upstage was the Administration camp, seeking legislation that would be enacted, in any event, and, if possible, build the Kennedys' reputations as moderates in civil rights.

And all over the stage were the swashbuckling liberals, very much *en garde,* distinguishable from each other only by the degrees of their intransigency. Lindsay and Kastenmeier played their roles with these liberals. All were from the North, many, though not all, were from urban centers, and they were from both parties.

And in this early fall season the aggressive and militant liberals seized and held the initiative. Dominant in the drafting subcommittee, they were able to write a bill that exceeded the aspirations of the Kennedy strategists and almost everyone else. Their measure called for a Fair Employment Practices Commission, and a broad, clear-cut public-accommodations clause, and gave the Justice Department clear new powers to act on behalf of any Negro whose rights were violated by police or other public body.

The result was general dismay; many thought these features might make the bill generally unacceptable. The Administration called for dilatory tactics in Judiciary while alternatives were sought.

Congressman Kastenmeier claimed his side could produce a majority of nineteen votes for the bill from Judiciary's thirty-five members.

Lindsay contended that the strong bill could pass the House where, he predicted, at least a hundred Republicans would swing behind it. Chairman Celler, the subcommittee's chief, under pressure, joined McCulloch, the top Republican in Judiciary, in seeking compromise. The President told Northern Democrats in Judiciary that the subcommittee's bill was probably unconstitutional.

Apprehension ran high on all sides. Liberals suspected that maneuvering within the power structure would produce too many concessions and yet another toothless bill. Moderates feared that if too strong a bill were reported out, it would be defeated on the House floor because not enough men of good will could find common ground. The last-ditchers alone, perhaps, could be complacent. Though they resisted any legislation they saw in the wrangling between moderates and liberals a chance to stick in their own knives and kill all chance for any bill.

Meanwhile, the Lindsay position was under assault from both extremes. An East Seventy-second Street apartment house in Manhattan where he had lived (he had moved away months earlier) was picketed by demonstrators pressuring him to fight for the strongest bill. From the other side columnist Joseph Alsop attacked Lindsay and some other Republican and Democratic liberals (Kastenmeier was the only one named) for their "vain, empty, impractical, competitive posturing" which was indicative, he said, of the "endemic disease of liberalism." Their "fatal fondness" for noble attitudes," he charged, "directly imperiled the chances for any civil rights bill at all."

Lindsay fired back immediately: "The subcommittee bill for the most part is sound legislation," but he added, "All of us who support it in principle understand the need for three or four tightening amendments.

"Title III, for example, can be brought back into proper shape with a single amendment to make it identical to the Title III provision which I and other Republicans introduced last January and which the Attorney General went out of his way to say he had never bothered to read. Title II on public accommodations can be narrowed slightly to be more acceptable to a wider group. These amendments are prepared and can be offered as committee amendments on the floor of the House. . . . Line-by-line rewriting of the bill in the full Judiciary Committee will take weeks, and in seeking to achieve these amendments, we will probably lose all of public accommodations, most of the voting provisions, and all provisions on job opportunities."

He struck hard at the critics. "Some of the disparaging comments, most especially those that question the bill's constitutionality, may come back to haunt those who make them, when a near-like bill is before the House for debate. They will then be for a strong bill, but they will not have assisted its passage."

Such attacks, Lindsay charged, "aided and abetted by members of the press," were not helping "the quiet diplomacy which some of us have been trying to carry on [which could] lead in the next few days to a compromise bill not too far removed from the subcommittee bill."

To a Manhattan audience he added, "If we, as legislators, fall down on this issue, we will have made a bed of thorns for ourselves and others for many, many years to come." He pointed out that compromise was necessary, but warned that it must not be so great as to discredit the whole civil rights legislation.

Within a day Judiciary had voted for a compromise bill which retained the greater part of both Administration and "liberal" thinking. The committee's vote for the compromise was 23 to 11, with Lindsay joining the majority. In opposition were eight Southerners, two conservative Republicans, and five Democratic liberals —Kastenmeier and four others.

Where did compromise come from? A weekend of laborious conferences with Administration representatives and committee Republicans, led by McCulloch and Lindsay, did it. His prediction that "the next few days" might see a workable, supportable compromise had been understated. "Getting the bill out of committee —that was the real miracle," Lindsay said later, "and it was when most of the hard spadework was done." He described "a couple of long four-day weekends with Nicholas Katzenbach and Burke Marshall of Justice. We, that is Mr. Celler, Mr. McCulloch, and Jim Corman [a California Democrat], faced an almost impossible deadlock. Somehow, I guess we'll never really know how, we got it resolved."

Now the wails of the detractors were drowned in the general acclaim for what had been achieved and also for the statecraft that broke the deadlock. Columnist Roscoe Drummond commented, "McCulloch and Lindsay salvaged civil rights from hopeless deadlock by negotiating the terms of a strong bill capable of winning decisive bipartisan support." This bill, Drummond pointed out, had finally attracted the indispensable support of Minority Leader Charles Halleck. And the *New York Herald Tribune* credited Lindsay and McCulloch with the major roles in achieving a workable compromise. Though Lindsay had been among Republicans hoping for a more liberal bill than the Administration presented, "his concession was a real one, and in the general interest—this was the work of the constructive center."

Congressman McCulloch, with whom John Lindsay was to be closely allied in fighting the bill through the House, paid an unusual tribute to the younger Republican. Lindsay was, he said, "most helpful," not only in the shirtsleeve work through long weekends in drafting the bipartisan bill, but in bringing other young Republicans along in its support.

And important lessons could be found in the whole period of conflict and compromise, noted the *New York Post*. Though the Lindsay liberal group had suffered denunciation for seeking a tougher bill than the Administration proposed, they had finally worked out a strengthened bill that won both Republican and Democratic official blessing. "There should be orchids for the liberals who refused to give up, and a dunce cap for their detractors." The lesson of the episode, the newspaper suggested, might be: "Faint heart rarely prevails on Capitol Hill."

And now on November 20, Chairman Celler sent the Judiciary bill along to last-ditcher Howard Smith of Rules with a request for speedy hearings. Capitol Hill speculation suggested Smith would insist on exhaustive hearings in order to delay the bill as long as possible.

But before the week's end, the President of the United States was dead. The forthcoming battle would be fought under new and unexpected circumstances.

❦ ❦ 17 ❦ ❦

The Rights of All People

THERE was much uncertainty on Capitol Hill, as there was in so many other places the morning after President Kennedy's funeral. Republican leaders advised Congress to go home quickly. But Lindsay and Javits were urging that this was the time to press for civil rights legislation, "as a tribute to the President." Chairman Celler of Judiciary said he would push for quick action by the Rules Committee, where the civil rights bill now rested, and a number of insistent voices were demanding Rules clearance before Christmas. Lindsay joined seven of the fourteen Republicans on Judiciary in announcing plans to write a separate, supporting report.

But Howard Smith was not to be hurried; the bill remained in Rules's care for weeks. In mid-December a petition was circulated to force the bill out, but this was a Democratic strategy that nearly backfired. As a Washington correspondent noted, such Republicans as Lindsay, needed in important strategy conferences, were shunted aside. Sixty Republican signatures were needed but were not forthcoming. Even Lindsay, who did sign, complained that not one of his party was consulted on the discharge plan; he contrasted this with the "delicate coalition" formed in October.

"Where is the good faith?" he asked. "Why is it necessary now to go in separate directions? Many majority members have been charged in the past with preferring an issue to a bill. They should take care lest they give further credence to the charge." John Lindsay, writing to constituents near the year's end, branded the delay "another indication of the needlessly slow pace of Congress and the inadequacies of the Congressional power structure." And, he added, "the road ahead is still long, arduous, and full of roadblocks—not the least of which is a certain Senate filibuster."

It was on January 31, one year to the day since the Republicans had put in their principal proposal of 1963, that the compromise finally reached the floor of the House. It was enacted ten days later. What happened in that time was a masterpiece of strategy and co-ordination.*

On the fifth day of debate Lindsay, as one of the floor managers in the bipartisan effort, was able to declare the Conservative Republican-Southern Democratic coalition "broken!" The vote to reject the Southerners' first amendment was 176 to 125. A close vote on some sections appeared possible, said Lindsay, coming off the floor after a long day of dogging key members. "We'll have to keep all of our people on the floor for every vote," he said with a somewhat grim confidence. And keep "all of our people on the floor" was what the floor managers did. The next day two more efforts to amend were defeated, the first by more than a hundred votes, the second by about forty.

The strategy was varied. For the debate on Title VII (dealing with fair employment practices), for example, the strategists yielded to the committee on education and labor, into whose province much of it fell. "What we had to do here," Lindsay explained, "especially on the floor when that issue was under debate, was to defer

* An editorial in a New York City newspaper commented that acceptance by the House was "due in no small measure to the yeoman work" of Lindsay, who had "distinguished himself both in planning and execution—it was a hard job well done."

to members of that committee whose support was vital, because we knew that the opposition would capitalize on the slightest trace of disunity. So we planned our strategy pretty carefully three days beforehand. . . . Then, when a question arose during debate on amendments, say, that was really in their ball park, we would yield to them immediately. It worked very smoothly, really, but I can't overemphasize how much hard planning went into it."

Planning, Lindsay observed, is in a sense "even more important than what happens on the floor, though that's terribly important, too; you've got to be on your toes all the time, because debate can get pretty confusing sometimes, even when nobody's deliberately out to confuse."

Lindsay and his senior Judiciary colleague McCulloch were telling audiences that the bill was "largely a Republican measure." *

Some liberal Republicans feared that the Johnson Administration might participate in a retreat from some of the bill's stronger provisions. As the first week of debate ended, their fears seemed confirmed. Arkansas Democrat Oren Harris suddenly presented an amendment to cut back Title VI—the section requiring an end to discrimination in all federally financed programs. Harris sought to go back to an earlier proposal that had been discarded as too weak, by the Kennedy forces.

And at this point Democratic Whip Hale Boggs, a close friend of the President and a key man in the party's overall thinking, came in to support the Harris amendment. He termed it far preferable to the "sweeping authority" the existing Title VI could employ to cut off federal funds.

No one had known the Harris amendment was imminent or that Boggs, in his first entry into the debate, would support it. Of all the Republican strategy team, only John Lindsay was on the floor, where confusion had immediately flared. To alert civil rightists of both parties to the amendment's import and to impress the Democrats that no deal would be endured (since none had objected to the

* Later in the year they parted company on the platform issue at San Francisco, where McCulloch was a spokesman for the Goldwater "soft" plank on rights.

amendment), Lindsay demanded: "Do members realize what is being attempted here? I am appalled that this is being supported in the well of the House by the Majority Whip, who takes the floor and asks us to throw into the ashcan Title VI of this bill. Does this mean there is a 'cave-in' on this important title?"

Congressman McCulloch, hurrying back to the floor, angrily declared that if the amendment passed, he could no longer support the bill itself. Under this pressure, Chairman Celler finally announced that he too opposed the amendment. It went down to defeat, 126 to 80.

The thumb-in-the-dike act by John Lindsay had saved the day, for the influence of Boggs, together with the sudden inertia of Democratic strategists, had been ominous. "It turned out there was no deal," said Lindsay later, "but you have to be ready for anything."

In retrospect, Lindsay saw the House passage of the bill as "a genuine bipartisan effort—excluding the Southern Democrats, of course. I think we got a good, strong enforceable bill, which is what I wanted because I feel so strongly about civil rights," he said, after the bill went through. "We got it for several reasons, in addition to comprehensive planning. First, of course, was the mood of the country. Then, too, many Republicans, even conservative Republicans, were sick to death about the so-called conservative coalition between them and Southern Democrats. The fact is, the coalition in recent years has rarely coalesced; the Southerners are pretty shrewd, and in reality the Republicans rarely got their votes on financial matters. And in the main, the Republicans are for civil rights."

As the House-approved version made its tortuous way through the Senate, Lindsay complained that even allowing for the need of Congress, "as a deliberative body, to set aside reasonable time for discussion of the issues before it, in order to reach rational decisions," he considered "the open-end Senate filibuster" an obstructionist tactic, not a reasonable discussion. The filibuster was not only delaying the final enactment of the new law, but was irksome and confusing to the entire country.

"This," Lindsay said in a message to the people of the 17th District, "is a time for faith in the principles for which this civil rights measure stands."

Meanwhile, he pointed out, "distorted interpretations are being broadcast across the country and have resulted in a great deal of misunderstanding about what is in the measure and what is not in it. . . . Too often people fail to read the legislation itself; instead, they read inaccurate interpretations of it."

More than four months after receiving the bill from the House the Senate passed it, after adding some amendments whose emphasis was first to seek voluntary compliance and rely initially on state and local anti-discrimination laws. "Some of these improved the bill," Lindsay remarked, "but changes made in the job opportunities section . . . weakened the House bill." He explained that the strategy of the rights leaders in the House was to take up the Senate's amendments directly and approve them, thus avoiding a conference which would produce compromise versions that would be sent back to the Senate. The possibility of new filibusters might have resulted in "inordinate delay, if not defeat."

Within a fortnight, the House had approved the Senate's version, as Lindsay attacked some contentions, including those of Barry Goldwater, that the bill was unconstitutional. "We who are lawyers," he exclaimed, "restate our conviction that the bill is constitutional in all respects."

Within hours President Johnson signed the bill. John Lindsay, who had exhorted the people of America a year earlier not to betray their heritage by rejecting a strong civil rights act, stood now in the White House and watched the final step in the creation of the most sweeping law of its kind since Reconstruction—outlawing discrimination in schools, in voting, in use of federal funds and in places of public accommodation.

To Lindsay and to a few dozen other Congressmen, Senators, Justice officials, and civil rights activists, the President gave pens he used in signing the law. To a much smaller group—among them Senators Humphrey, Dirksen, and Kuchel and Representatives Celler, McCulloch, Halleck, and Lindsay—went his thanks for having steered through an enactable version of the country's will. Columnist Roscoe Drummond linked them with the United States

Supreme Court, Martin Luther King, Roy Wilkins, John F. Kennedy, and Lyndon Johnson as sharing the greatest credit for enactment of the law.

John Lindsay's 17th Congressional District is nearly 90 per cent white. Only one voter in fourteen is Negro (which is below the national average) and 4 per cent are Puerto Ricans. A New York City Negro newspaper noted, during the civil rights struggle, that though the District includes many wealthy Republicans, its Congressman is "anything but a spokesman for the rich and mighty. He's built most of his reputation," said the newspaper, "as a fighter for the rights of all people, rich and poor, black and white."

At the same time, the *World-Telegram* was making the point that every important provision of the civil rights bill already could be found as law in New York. The bill's passage, therefore, would accomplish nothing in Lindsay's home district and city and state, "except provide a moral lift." Lindsay, too, had pointed this out to his own constituents. "It took political guts to do this," the newspaper commented. He risked disenchanting "the comfortable middle-class liberals [in the District] who feel they are dispensing with their civic chores by backing civil rights in Congress." And, in fact, the Congressman had been at pains to tell those very constituents, in one of his periodic newsletters, that neither he nor they were heroes—not only was the law "neither extreme nor unreasonable," but "a majority of the states, including New York, have long had this legislation on the books."

The law was hardly without its application, however, to a city like New York, Lindsay pointed out, since it is designed "to create a rule of law under which men will live peaceably and through which their grievances will be settled, at the conference table and in the courts, not in the streets. . . . It is a large step forward in the safeguarding of individual rights and should ease tensions, not intensify them." His remark was in response to people who had written opposing the bill because of terrorism in the subways, the streets, and the parks of New York City. "Their rightful outrage is clearly understandable," said Lindsay, "but the target [the bill] is wrong."

The Congressman put the burden for action on the city administration which, he said, "has an immediate obligation to intensify police patrols in all public areas in order to enforce the rule of law and to protect every person from danger or threat of danger." This was in the early summer of 1964. He had declared himself earlier on civil rights demonstrations: "They were bound to happen." He contended that "It's good for these groups to bring their grievances to the surface, providing they don't become violent and disruptive. People will give vent to their feelings. But at the same time, I wish the press would give equal attention to the positive things being done to bring justice to all Americans. . . . We need to talk about the good as well as the bad."

And the alternative for the nation, for the South, for the metropolitan areas everywhere, if Congress had rejected the civil rights bill? "The moderates in the leadership would have been discredited," in Lindsay's analysis, "and their places taken by others who favor extremist tactics."

Exactly a week after the President signed the Civil Rights Act, Lindsay was in San Francisco appealing for its endorsement by the committee drafting the Republican platform.

He cited planks in previous party platforms, going back to 1856 and including 1960, which had demanded full exercise of federal powers to guarantee civil rights to all citizens. The 1964 platform, he urged, should state "unequivocally our belief that the bill is in all respects within both the purview and the command of the Constitution. We Republican members of the House Judiciary Committee," Lindsay told the platform drafters, "ten out of fourteen, would not have reported to the House of Representatives the bill which was ultimately passed by the House, and for which more than 80 per cent of Republicans voted affirmatively, had we not been thoroughly convinced of its constitutionality in all respects. Nor would we have recommended acceptance, by the House, of the Senate amendments had we not been assured of their constitutionality."

Five days later John Lindsay's voice was among those shouted down in the Cow Palace as the Goldwater-dominated convention angrily insisted on the Senator's version of a civil rights plank.

"Somehow," said Lindsay after his fruitless midnight appearance before the convention to advocate a strong plank, "they were able to feel that they could afford to ignore an issue which had quickened a generation and redefined fundamental American words like 'equality' and 'justice.' "

18

Young and Old in Crisis

"YOU *do* something with your education!" John Lindsay exclaimed as he contemplated his own schooling as the basis for a career in public service.

His was, by any standards, an advantaged education. And though his education did not include a single year in a public school, he has been consistently one of the most insistent and determined advocates for steps that would build stronger public school systems. "Poor education," he has said, "is at the root of most social problems."

"Educate people and that's half the battle. It shows them how to help themselves—it opens vistas to people. The area of worst unemployment is always the same as the most poorly educated area."

City schools, he maintains, "have not given our children a fair break. We need more and better schools, more pay for more teachers. We need to make our schools the beginning and not the end of a child's career. We need their brainpower and their manpower —we cannot afford to waste this precious asset."

And to young people themselves he has directed this counsel in closing one of his Congressional newsletter reports: "Education will be the most important asset in your lives, and it will never stop yielding values. For those of you who find it a struggle—stay with it! The rewards will be many times worth your efforts."

Pushing for an education bill in 1965, he declared that, "If anything is going to help solve the problem of our seriously disadvantaged city areas, it is improved primary and secondary public education. . . ." The bill was particularly keyed to the needs of city schools; he noted with approval that New York would receive the largest share of funds freed by it. "This is as it should be, for New York has the biggest problem in some of its pressure areas. Good strong public schools at early ages are essential to more jobs and less welfare, more leadership and less indolence, more responsibility and less crime, more abundance and less poverty."

Lindsay has frequently cited the inadequacy of too many school systems which because they are "slow in receiving wide public attention . . . has received inadequate public action." To help meet the problem he has urged federal action—"massive aid to build better schools and to pay the teachers for them." In 1960 he supported a plan for federal assistance to school construction, calling education "the most critical domestic problem before the United States. I doubt," he told Congress, that any member "would deny the importance of proper public education for our children— and yet in the Congress few issues have provoked such controversy. We agree as to the problem, but we battle over its solution." Over the years Lindsay has expressed disappointment about the unwillingness on Capitol Hill to grapple with this problem. "As usual, this area [primary education] remains untouched by Congress," he noted with frustration. When Congress failed to enact an education bill in 1960, he termed the result a disaster and declared that Congress "had a solemn responsibility to complete its work on this measure."

One of his principal approaches has been a proposal to create a National Advisory Council, a "permanent, high-level group which can help bridge the gap between what we know and what we need to accomplish, and thus improve the quality of our education, bolster its national prestige, and instill in the country a sense of urgency which is sadly lacking."

Noting the confusion that has prevailed in Washington with each successive approach to the national question of what to do about educational standards, and especially the role of the federal government, Lindsay commented pointedly: "We need only look around us and observe the bickering that has accompanied the introduction of each bill . . . to realize the depths of uncertainty that surround the problems of education in the United States today. Our nation's failure to fix priorities can only mean that we are unable to see clearly what they are."

The National Advisory Council, he contended, would help to find the answers to the questions as to which programs—ranging from adult illiteracy to school lunches, from college aid to teachers' salaries—are the most important, which are of the highest national significance, which should receive priorities. "The subject of the federal role in education has become a source of bewilderment and dismay to the American people. It has been caught up in a series of political and religious crossfires which have divided the nation, and confused by a plethora of proposals that have compounded the problem of establishing meaningful priorities," Lindsay said, as he proposed establishment of a fifteen-member Presidentially-appointed Council to "make an annual assessment of the goals, progress, and deficiencies of education and submit its findings to the President and the Congress." In addition to providing the President with distinguished consultation on means of improving education, the Council would focus attention on the basic need for high standards in education and then help establish priorities.

The Council bill received little attention in Congress for three years after Lindsay introduced it, but in 1965 an education bill that included the notion of a National Advisory Council was moving through the legislative machinery.

Lindsay, ranking education as one of the "two major domestic challenges" (the other being automation), called it one of "the priority goals of governmental activity affecting the domestic economy."

He contrasted it (and such other priority items as retraining in fundamental skills and vocations, incentive to invest, and the removal of bureaucracy and other artificial and discriminatory barriers and practices in the industrial complex) with Kennedy Administration proposals for a Youth Employment Opportunities Act and a Domestic Peace Corps. "Whatever the individual merits of these proposals," he said, "they are being paraded as basic solutions to basic problems—which they are not."

Throughout his term in Washington, Lindsay has expressed great concern for the elderly. Early in his first term he joined Senator Jacob Javits in advocating a plan for health insurance for the aged which would assist states to establish and administer plans for voluntary participation in insurance plans.

Inadequate medical care for the elderly "cries out for action," Lindsay declared at the time, urging his party to support such a proposal. "This nation has long since passed the day when a segment of the population is to be denied adequate medical care because of individual financial inability to pay for it."

Over the years he has plugged away at this theme, introducing bill after bill. In 1962 he offered a plan which would provide medical care through Social Security but incorporating an option under which persons might elect to receive federal cash payments for as long as they were covered by private lifetime renewable policies with overall benefits at least equivalent in value to those provided by the government. His bill also established a separate health care fund in the Social Security system and provided a way for people over sixty-five who are not covered by Social Security to be brought into the federal program.*

But the Lindsay bill, along with all the variations on it proposed by so many legislators throughout the early sixties, made little headway against inertia, indecisiveness, and AMA opposition. "One of the principal failures of the Eighty-seventh Congress," Lindsay declared late in 1962, after watching one more of his bills go down the drain, "has been its inability to enact a reasonable program to provide a measure of medical care for persons over sixty-five."

By 1964 he offered "a new model" of the previous bill, still with

* Lindsay has long urged an amendment to the Social Security Act that would raise to $2,400 or $2,500 the outside earnings permitted to beneficiaries.

Social Security financing, which offered the individual a choice between a private and a government plan. And by 1965, the year in which enactment of a health care plan was at last a realistic possibility, Lindsay offered still another bill. He hoped it would make possible a breakthrough in the Congressional impasse. This bill provided for 180 days of hospital care yearly, 180 days of nursing home care, or 240 nursing visits at home for people age sixty-five or over.

At one stage in his fencing for "a plan" Lindsay made the point that his own proposal would not "interfere in any way with doctors or the medical profession—it attacks only the problem of hospital and nursing care costs." Throughout the long battle, he had stood, nonetheless, with the forces that wanted action on a "domestic issue of highest magnitude," as he himself put it, against the bitter-end opposition of the AMA and other foes.

19

A Hope of Government

"In him there is a hope of government. . . ." It was spoken of the future Edward V in Act II of *Richard the Third;* it is inscribed on a plaque presented to John Lindsay by the Broadway Show League. The League was expressing its appreciation to the Congressman, whose territory includes virtually the entire theater district,* for his efforts to aid the drama. John Lindsay, according to *Show* magazine, is "the theatre's foremost champion in Congress."

A semi-frustrated Thespian, Lindsay has appeared in various productions over the years, and during one Congressional season he came up from Washington on weekends to read the narrator's part in *John Brown's Body* at the Martinique Theater.

He has suggested, half-seriously in fact, that "the theatrical aspects of politics" probably drew him into that career. Politics and

* Lindsay's 17th District is regarded as the cultural center of the U.S. It includes many of the on- and off-Broadway areas, and takes in many of the city's major museums, library branches, art galleries, communications centers, and publishing houses (including the publisher of this book).

the theater often have a lot in common—ham. And he admits happily to possessing a hammy streak.

Prior to politician, which quickly enough became his favorite role, his favorite part was the Devil in Shaw's *The Devil's Disciple,* which he played in his last year at St. Paul's School. He recalls reveling in the opportunity to be diabolical all evening, while his brother was stuck with a good-guy's part. At Yale's Jonathan Edwards College, he participated with great relish in Gilbert and Sullivan operettas. But if he never quite achieved fulfillment on the stage, he lives it vicariously as a tireless first-nighter and backstage visitor.

Among his favorite works are Giraudoux's *Tiger at the Gates* and Ionesco's *Rhinoceros; West Side Story,* with its story of young people from the same area of Manhattan in which he himself was born, moves him greatly.

For six years, as if to make most graphic his concern for the theater and other lively or refined arts, John Lindsay worked to get Congress to adopt a bill, co-sponsored by Frank Thompson, a New Jersey Democrat, to establish a National Arts Council. When he first proposed the Council, soon after arriving in Congress, it was defeated "on the grounds that the arts and their general condition are no business of any government." But Lindsay concludes that since then something has happened to the politicians—such as hearing from the housewives back home who "are beginning to get as excited about the condition of the local drama society as they are about the price of butter."

What does the Council hope to do? John Lindsay thinks it should "mark the end of government's general indifference to the arts. Through it, the federal government may be able to solve a few of the problems, some of which it created itself, which face the arts—the most pressing being financial instability. . . ."

But he sees some pitfalls, for the Council someday will have to decide on government involvement in subsidizing the arts, and may have to work out a way to enable the arts to receive federal aid with no strings.

But if federal interference, along with grants, was viewed as a villain in the wings, censorship is seen as equally threatening. "The

Council has a duty to prevent exercise, on the local level, of artistic judgments by bureaucracies in deciding which organizations are most worthy of receiving federal subsidies. Censorship and personal prejudice would inevitably confuse the best bureaucratic good will."

The Arts Council is far from the only evidence of Lindsay's affair with the drama, or the opera, or almost any creative presentation. For years he plugged a bill of his own to repeal the 10-per-cent federal tax on admissions which would lower ticket prices, but, as Lindsay noted drily, "the legitimate stage, shooting galleries, dog races, and flea circuses are all the same in the eyes of the Treasury's taxmasters." We still await the tax relief.*

Another Lindsay bill would extend to authors, playwrights, and composers the same capital gains tax treatment for their creations which inventors receive for theirs. He has argued persuasively that the tax law discriminates unfairly against the creative artist whose income is likely to fluctuate from year to year, with earnings sometimes concentrated in a relatively short period though completion of the work may have required several years. In 1964 the tax bill contained a limited "averaging out" provision for the benefit of such artists—"a good step in the right direction."

His deep sense of involvement, in addition to being personal, springs from his identity with his city as well—"one of the world's great centers for literature, music, drama, and the creative arts; these enrich and energize the city." He made the point in a statement advocating a revision of the nation's copyright laws in 1965. "It is essential to bring about a fair balance between the private economic interests of the creative individual, and the public interest in the product of his work," Lindsay testified.

Among the problems he pointed out was that of the songwriter whose songs were played 128 times on neighborhood juke boxes, which netted him absolutely nothing though the juke-box operator made $12.80. Another problem was that the rate of payment to the songwriter from phonograph recordings had remained where it was fixed in 1909. Yet another was broader protection for the unique

* Lindsay has also advocated, unsuccessfully so far, repeal of New York City's admissions tax and other "steps to prevent the decline" of the live theater.

work of choreographers and stage directors. Lindsay finds himself very much sentimentally as well as politically involved.*

John Lindsay wears his almost boundless enthusiasm for the theater and other creative arts on his sleeve, and sometimes it even runs away with him. In 1963, in a long speech in the House on the federal government and the arts, he remarked grandly, "Let us hypothesize that in a given year Congress were to appropriate $5 million to aid in the production of plays, operas, concerts, and so on. . . ." A year earlier he had published a magazine article on the same subject, using some of the same language, though it had been even grander: "Let us hypothesize that in a given year Congress were to appropriate $10 million. . . ."

The Lindsay affair with the theater has led him into odd crannies of the legislative industry. He may take along leading Broadway producers and introduce them to the Ways and Means Committee, where they can argue about the federal admissions tax. Then he will write, for one of the nation's leading book reviews, a commentary on playwright Gore Vidal's book of criticisms, an undertaking few of Lindsay's House colleagues would have considered, in any circumstances.

He worries that no Broadway theaters have been built in years, that wages are "indecently low" for stage hands, dancers, and orchestras, especially in comparison with soaring costs; that three quarters of Broadway productions can't make money and their number has dwindled by more than half in a generation.

John Lindsay loves the theater and theater people, the arts and artists, and they return his love with equal ardor. They form committees to insure his election and turn their apartments into sites for very genteel rallies for their lion.

* It is important to note, however, despite John Lindsay's identification with the theater and the arts, and his affinity for them, a sharp distinction exists between him and the recent movement within the California Republican Party. The tendency there is to retread old actors and fit them out with political accents. Entirely apart from the degree to which his own philosophy departs from the much more conservatively oriented views of George Murphy and Ronald Reagan, Lindsay never has been other than a professional in politics and an amateur on stage, rather than the other way around. The distinction has basic significance.

Harold Prince, one of a pair of Broadway producers introduced by Lindsay to the House Ways and Means Committee to support his arguments against the federal admissions tax on theater tickets, resigned his post as president of the League of New York Theaters in order to organize a show-business campaign for the Lindsay mayoralty bid; Tom Bosley, the actor who portrayed Mayor La-Guardia in *Fiorello!,* was enlisted in the campaign effort.

John Lindsay does not remember ever having the opportunity to take a role in *Richard the Third,* but somewhere he earned the right to that plaque and its inscription, "In him there is a hope of government. . . ." *

* In his immensely successful 1964 campaign for re-election much of Congressman Lindsay's publicity literature bore the slogan contrived by his campaign staff: "The District's Pride—The Nation's Hope."

20

Politician in Paris

ITALIANS, Greeks, and Turks rarely take the same side of an issue. But it was Italians, Greeks, and Turks who banded to spearhead a pro-Lindsay move on a November day in Paris and give the Manhattan Republican one of his most interesting, and perhaps most significant, political victories.

Lindsay was fresh from what was then the major victory of his domestic political career—he had just been elected to the United States House of Representatives for the fourth time in an overwhelming triumph over two opponents.

Now, for the fourth consecutive fall, he was spending a brief post-election period in Paris as an official delegate from the House of Representatives to the annual conferences of the NATO Parliamentarians.

Since he was first named as one of the eight House delegates (eight Senators also go), Lindsay had served on the political committee of the Parliamentarians' sessions. He was its executive secretary or *"rapporteur,"* as it is officially called. With the committee's chairman, Lord Ogmore of England, he had helped to prepare position papers and recommendations designed to persuade American and European legislators to strengthen the Atlantic alliance. And now, at the end of Lindsay's fourth year, Lord Ogmore was vacating the chairmanship and the political committee found itself faced with the selection of a new chairman. The head of the delegation from the U.S. House of Representatives, a Democrat, proposed a slate that provided for no American representation in any of the committee's three offices; even Lindsay's executive secretaryship was to be taken over by a European.

It was at this stage that the Italians, the Greeks, the Turks, and some other Parliamentarians revolted and nominated John Lindsay for the chairmanship. In the ensuing election, Lindsay won by a three-to-one margin.*

If this was a pleasantly reassuring personal victory for the Manhattan Congressman, it had deeper and more significant implications, for John Lindsay had won renown as a principal advocate of the creation of an Atlantic Parliamentary Assembly. The same Paris conference, in fact, endorsed establishment of a consultative Atlantic parliamentary body.

"In the face of some disintegrating factors at work in the alliance, this is good," Lindsay commented. "It is new and hopeful . . . it goes beyond NATO." Here was a forward step to which his enthusiastic and effective support would be given in the future, looking to a meeting at which key American and European legislators could prepare a draft charter for submission to all the parliaments of the Atlantic countries.

John Lindsay had actually found the NATO Parliamentarians' meetings vital and creative. "Men who run for elective office are much the same the world over," he observed, pointing out the

* Six months later John Lindsay's candidacy for Mayor of New York captivated the European press and public. A London correspondent, within weeks of his announcement, found that "an affable American, in these days when to so many foreigners we seem so ugly, has broken through abroad in the image of a handsome reformer—young, indefatigable, and glamorous. . . . Lindsay has already made an impression over here, where votes may not count for us, but subjective feelings do in the long run. . . . On the Continent, he has become a popular personality." One observer, looking at a collection of Continental newspapers with their stories and features about Lindsay, commented, "You'd think he was running for President of North America."

common ground he shares with legislators from fourteen other nations. "They have more in common than they have differences. And the longer I am a part of representative government, a parliamentarian, the more I become aware of the enormous value of parliamentarians from all free countries working together in common endeavor. Men and women who live by the ballot box, who represent constituencies, and who are constantly subject to the will of the people, have something in common that no non-elected 'statesman'—the minister, the cabinet officer—can possibly have. There's something intangible about the understanding that exists between elected 'politicians.' As professionals, they immediately respect each other."

And talking politics in human terms is a subject that John Lindsay quickly warms to: "Those of us who meet at the Parliamentarians' conference have to run for office at home. We have to have the support of our constituents before we go to Paris, and we have to be ready to go back home and seek the support of our constituents. Thus we form a much more freeswinging, frank, and representative body than the NATO Council, which must act under instruction from its chiefs of state or foreign offices. This is as it should be. Unlike the usual appointed diplomats, we have a nicely developed talent for quick friendships based on the common need for votes. The plenary sessions, committees, and corridors are filled with working politicians establishing quick rapport in several languages."

John Lindsay waxes reminiscent as he reflects that, "as in all parliamentary bodies, much of the conference's work is accomplished off stage, in the cloakrooms and over, in this case, good French coffee. Politics is politics, and politicians are politicians in democracies the world over. In French and English, work is conducted with a minimum of ceremony. And we do work; the conference is no place for junketeers."

Lindsay finds all the "great many members of parliaments" that he knows around the world subject to the same pressures and hazards: "We quickly discover we have mutual problems, common aspirations, and shared techniques. There's an understanding, a frankness, and a respect that one never seems to discover among the statesmen and ministers in their diplomatic dealings with each other."

They recognize the need for discussion and debate, for compromise, for ways out of impossible situations—and for new discoveries and common agreements for the future. "Being working politicians," he explains, the NATO Parliamentarians can get agreement and results in a hurry.* "Resolutions worked out in draft and debate in the five committees are submitted to the entire conference for what may be strenuous debating there." The debate, he finds, is not unlike that in the House of Representatives, "and not without a certain amount of blarney emitted for home-town consumption."

His political committee of the conference meets intermittently. For example, they were in session in London early in 1965, two months after the yearly Parliamentarians' meeting in Paris. Members of Parliament of a half dozen other nations—Belgium, Italy, Germany, France, the Netherlands, the United Kingdom—also serve on the committee. That session followed a three-day conference on "Britain and the U.S. after the Elections," in which Lindsay and thirteen other members of the Senate and House participated, together with members of the British Parliament. The site was Ditchley, near Oxford, Winston Churchill's World War II retreat; on the same trip Lindsay attended the funeral of Churchill, "a man I have admired perhaps more than any other in public life in modern times; Sir Winston in his long life was the embodiment of the parliamentary system."

John Lindsay and J. W. Fulbright, chairman of the Senate delegation to the Parliamentarians' conference, have become the principal spokesmen for the proposed Atlantic Parliamentary Assembly. Its representatives would come from both the fifteen NATO countries and the twenty-nation Organization for Economic Cooperation and Development.

* It was in NATO Parliamentarians' sessions that the Organization for Economic Cooperation and Development was conceived as a parallel, in the economic sphere, to NATO in Western military strength. The conferences also previewed the Atlantic Institute, of which Henry Cabot Lodge became the first secretary-general.

A consultative Atlantic Assembly, Lindsay explains, would have many functions, including its primary one as a common meeting place for parliamentarians of all free Atlantic countries. Though lacking power to force policy in executive-branch institutions, public impact of new policy statements would be "enormous," he suggests. Further, it could soften the blows and tensions that develop in international views between friends.

21

The Bridge at Andau

"MANY an early dawn," recalls John Lindsay, "I stood on the Austrian side of the bridge at Andau that autumn of 1956, walked the Hungarian border, and saw courageous freedom fighters, women, and children, come over the freezing swamps and canals. It was a sight and an experience I shall never forget. . . ."

In 1956, the year he worked at drafting the Eisenhower Administration's civil rights program and thereby did so much to shape his subsequent career, John Lindsay took on another challenging assignment for the Attorney General of the United States.

As the Hungarian revolts broke out, and Central Europe alternated between hope and despair, the problem of the desperate people fighting against oppression became inescapable. What could the United States, compassionate and charitable, do for them? Could there be a home, could there be hope of a haven for these latest victims of man's inhumanity?

To learn what might be most expeditiously and wisely done in the name of man's humanity President Eisenhower turned to his Justice Department. And there the burden fell very considerably on the shoulders of the young lawyer, some of whose forebears had sought refuge in America under very much the same conditions that have lured so many millions of others toward the land of promise.

As the Attorney General's representative that fall, he made two trips to Austria and West Germany to set up the machinery to bring almost forty thousand refugees of the Communist tyranny in Hungary to the United States.

A quick device was found whereby the refugees were "paroled" within the U.S. under terms of an obscure provision of the immigration law. The clause had been intended to take care of such cases as persons who had lost their passports; but in this emergency it was broadened into a gaping hole through which forty thousand people could walk.

Hungary was a moving and a vital experience for Lindsay. "Anyone who has witnessed the chaos, the fear, the suffering of human beings in mass flight from their homeland can never again think of the plight of uprooted peoples as anything less than an urgent and compelling demand on individual conscience and human compassion," he remarked later.

The plight of the refugee, and his cause, have been a consistent concern of Lindsay's ever since. A national magazine named him and two Senators as the legislators with the closest and most effective continuing concern for the friendless. In Congress, he has advocated legislation in every session since he first went to Washington, to improve the nation's performance on immigration generally, and specifically to extend a helping hand to the refugee.

When he reintroduced his immigration bill in 1965, he branded the present laws "antiquated, demeaning, and prejudicial," and in need of reform to insure "a fair and honest administration of the existing levels of admission. We adhere to a blatantly discriminatory immigration policy that evaluates human beings not on the basis of what they are, but where they were born. It is one thing to say to the thousands of people who wish to become U.S. citizens: 'We are sorry, but we have no more room.' It is something altogether different to say: 'We are sorry, but we have no more room for Italians.' "

He noted that Ireland's quota is more than twice as large as that for all of Asia and Africa combined, yet Ireland uses less than 50 per cent of its quota, and the law makes no provision for use of these numbers by countries with backlogs of applicants. "I can see no reason whatever for the national origins policy," Lindsay contended in an unusually long statement to the House. "It vitiates our heritage; it undermines our foreign relations. It presents to the world a totally wrong image of the American character."

The desperate problem of refugees in other situations where migration to this country is not possible or contemplated, but where enlightened aid is essential to the relief of incredible human misery, has long attracted Lindsay's efforts. He has focused his inquiry into refugee problems on three points of wretchedness: Arab refugees in the lands around Israel, Tibetans in India, and Chinese in Hong Kong. Among the Arabs he found "thousands of children and adults living without hope, without the barest material comforts, and, above all, without the conditions of human dignity that we Americans have come to accept as our birthright."

It is the children who suffer most, he points out in such words as these: "Try to look at a ration card belonging to a wide-eyed ten-year-old girl waiting in line for her 'supplemental' feeding in a refugee camp in the Jordan Valley. She has learned to accept the loss of her home—the hut in which her family lived was washed away in a flood; she still clings to the doll she carefully pieced together with rags and bits of cloth, but she can survive the loss of this, too. But reach for that grimy, half-torn ration card, and the panic-stricken expression that spreads over her pinched but lovely dark face is one that you will not soon forget." *

Such a background makes the problem of refugees, individually and by the millions, real for Lindsay, and it is intimately connected with much legislation he has introduced and advocated. "Whenever refugees take flight across an international frontier," he has said, "the issue immediately becomes an international problem for two reasons: the human plight is one to which the civilized

* In the political aspect, he noted, "permanent solution will come only when the Arab States accept the fact of Israel as a nation, when Israel makes serious efforts to conciliate her neighbors, and when both sides cease to use the refugees as pawns of power politics. In the meantime, it is the duty of the entire world community to do what it can to assuage the misery and hopelessness that blight a million lives."

international community cannot in conscience turn its back, and no country of asylum can, in justice, be expected to bear the burden by itself. Further, a refugee situation is usually the product of international tensions or conflict, and so the world community is bound to concern itself with the political issues involved."

American response, Lindsay has specified, should be prompt and within two broad lines of action: first, we should take the leadership in encouraging a world-wide co-ordinated program of relief and rehabilitation under UN auspices; second, we and the other free nations should adopt substantial measures of liberalization of national immigration policies. "Our own refugee laws are very restrictive," he has said. "Our response to the refugee question has offered piecemeal temporary solutions to permanent, festering problems. The refugee problem should be considered as an integral and essential facet of overall immigration policy." His own legislative proposals, Lindsay feels, seek "to make some headway toward meeting this world tragedy, moving away from the piecemeal approaches of the past."

He has suggested three categories of general reform: drastic overhaul of the national origins immigration quota, which would raise the annual quota to about 300,000 instead of about half that; a quota pool for unused quota numbers, to remove existing inequities and institute a truly non-discriminatory immigration policy; selective qualitative immigration that would seek individuals with specific skills and talents.

Lindsay's immigration-refugee bill defines "refugee" primarily as any alien who because of persecution, or fear of persecution, on account of race, religion, or political opinion has fled any Communist territory or a country of the Middle East. It would empower the President, in emergencies such as the Hungarian revolt, to parole into the United States ten thousand refugees. These ultimately could become eligible to apply for permanent residence. His proposals also offer other alleviations to the problems involved in finding homes for the homeless.

Lindsay's bill, introduced first in the spring of 1964, later attracted a number of similar or identical bills. He reintroduced it on the first day of the 1965 session and declared his intent to pursue it, contending that, "Our country can scarcely press other countries for meaningful solutions to world refugee problems without offering to accept a fair share itself. Some of these unsolved refugee concentrations are explosive, and it's to our own interest to remove the fuse. We have an obligation, in advancing an overall resettlement plan, to participate in such a plan by offering refuge within our own country to at least a reasonable number of refugees. By so doing, we will let the world know of our desire to bring this problem closer to a solution—and we will be giving notice that America's belief in freedom and humanity remains an enduring tenet of our democratic credo."

Hope or help for ten million refugees is only part of the nation's need to resolve its conscience and its response to all people beyond its borders, Lindsay argues, as he frequently deplores the "sad and ironic comment on our national ideals" reflected in the immigration laws.

Though "all aspects of our national life were molded by the greatest folk migration in history," he says, "our immigration policies are restrictive and discriminatory, neither sensible nor becoming." Our basic immigration statute, dating from the period immediately after World War I (though modified and codified in the McCarran-Walter Act of 1952) shows a built-in bias against southern and eastern Europeans, and non-whites from Africa and Asia. But he adds that a "return to the massive, unrestricted policy of pre-World War I is out of the question. American immigration policy cannot solve the problem of world overpopulation. Chronic unemployment would be aggravated by a return to the immigration policies of a less complicated age."

When introducing one of his bills designed to accomplish the reforms he envisions, John Lindsay said, "The need for prompt and effective action in the area of immigration policy appeals to our conscience and to common sense. Yet few seem willing to press for positive reform. It is time we had it. . . . It is incumbent that we take the lead. We are the leader of the community of free nations. It is our responsibility in all world problems to point the way by example and by persuasion toward workable solutions. Neither individuals nor nations," he conceded, "are disposed to act on problems, however critical, that do not present themselves with tangible and dramatic urgency.

"For my own part, I need only recall that frightened little girl, clutching desperately at her ration card, to see the plight of the world's refugees for what it is: an urgent problem of human suffering in which the seeds of political tension and conflict find fertile soil. . . . And so the need for prompt and effective action appeals most urgently to our wisdom and our consciences."

22

Flexible Lines and Harsh Realities

"A POSITION of flexibility . . . by not calling our shots in advance."

With those words, in a letter to the *New York Times* in the final days of the 1960 campaign, John Lindsay placed himself squarely between the two Presidential candidates on the day's hottest international issue, U.S. policy on Quemoy and Matsu. He deemed the original positions of both Vice-President Richard Nixon and Senator John Kennedy "extreme ones, perhaps under the pressure of debate," and added, "Fortunately, both now seem to have moderated their position." Some of his other observations are still timely.

"It seems clear to me," he wrote, "that it is unwise to draw hard and fixed lines which will commit our government to a single future course of action. . . . A flat statement that we will, on all accounts, defend a position which we might not wish to defend, or be in a position to defend, can be dangerous. Geographically fixed lines can be as troublesome in any given situation as can be deadlines. . . . It is best to maintain a position of flexibility by not calling our shots in advance. . . ."

If this could be called the nucleus of a Lindsay Foreign Policy, it would be because foreign affairs have occupied a substantial though not dominant portion of his interest in Congress; and because he has maintained "a position of flexibility" between the foreign policy positions of two parties. At various times he has strongly supported, or vigorously denounced, policies of both parties, demonstrating his thoughtfulness in the entire area of foreign affairs.

In his first term he was sharply critical of the Eisenhower Administration's handling of the U-2 affair, conflicting statements and all. "We have a right to expect that such blunders shall not occur," Lindsay snapped. "I urge the officials of government to take every precaution against this kind of mismanagement in the future."

A few months later he was bitterly critical of G. Mennen Williams, the Kennedy Administration's African specialist, for his open-mouth policy in Africa which, among other things, was raising howls from Britain. "Where is quiet diplomacy?" Lindsay asked.

The New York Young Republicans commended three hundred Congressmen for signing a statement opposing recognition of the Peking government or seating its representatives at the UN. The resolution specifically noted that the group's former president, John Lindsay, was not among the three hundred. The Congressman retorted: "I do not intend to sign any statement that seeks to tie the hands of the President where he might need freedom of action." The President whose freedom he valued so highly was John F. Kennedy.

A month after Lyndon Johnson took office Lindsay was one of only two Republican Congressmen who voted for the President's position on a measure that removed an anti-wheat-deal rider from a $3-billion foreign aid money bill. Twice defeated earlier in the House, the measure was successful this time by a thirty-one-vote margin.

He voted for the 1962 Kennedy trade bill, which Eisenhower and Herter supported, though only a handful of House Republicans went along. The bill gave the President broad tariff-cutting powers. (A month earlier Lindsay's questionnaire, polling sentiment in his district, had found the voters there five to two in favor of such tariff-cutting powers.)

Lindsay voted with forty-two other Republicans against a Republican-sponsored measure offered as a substitute for the Kennedy trade proposal.

He was one of seven Republicans in the House who voted against the Saund amendment of 1961 that sought to limit a key section of President Kennedy's first foreign aid bill. The amendment would have sapped the measure's strength by handcuffing funds to Congressional controls. Similarly, he supported Walter Judd, in 1962, in opposing any handcuffs on the President in his conduct of foreign policy. This was in answer to a proposal in the House to spell out those nations which could not receive U.S. aid.

He expressed support for "the integrity of the World Court at least until the contrary is proved," in urging repeal of the so-called Connally Reservation limiting U.S. participation in the court. "If we cannot settle international legal problems by rules of law," he declared as he urged such a policy on his party, "there is no hope in this day and age except their eventual settlement by force."

He was among the Republicans in Congress who were angered by a report turned in by a special committee of the party under Congressman Hosmer of California which attacked the Kennedy Administration's position on a test-ban treaty as dangerous to the national security. The Lindsay group of Republicans felt that the Hosmer committee's report unfairly identified their party as "a war party." Four years earlier, soon after he entered Congress, Lindsay had commented that, "The day may never come when everyone concerned with international security can be satisfied that an absolutely airtight system has been achieved, but it is far more important to reach an agreement on a test ban than to await a 100-per-cent-foolproof, airtight means of inspection."

He supported the Kennedy Administration's recommendation for an independent disarmament agency, telling the House that the agency was needed so that U.S. arms control negotiators could operate "in this dangerous and complex area" with "a total knowledge of the techniques and scientific language that accompany the problems of arms control."

He berated the Kennedy Administration for having "brought about an era of disaster in Cuba and created tremors and disgrace in Laos and South Korea."

He chided Kennedy for meeting with Khruschchev "after disavowing personal diplomacy" and "continuing to dole out giveaways after calling for national sacrifice."

Expressing the "full backing of Congress to the President on a policy of firmness in Berlin" at a time of crisis, he said this was "one subject on which there is no disagreement between Republicans and Democrats."

Lindsay sharply criticized President Johnson's inaugural address for virtually ignoring foreign policy and deplored "the curious silence of the Administration on matters affecting our most vital interests." He underscored "an obligation on the part of Congress to insist that the government tell us what policy is and who is making it. . . . I wish to serve notice that I am going to insist as just one member of Congress . . . that the government define the future course of foreign policy in this country . . . to make decisions it probably would rather not make. . . . Sometimes it is very difficult to have to make up your mind as to what your position is on a given subject, but in a free system it is expected that you do."

While pledging adherence to the principle of Vandenberg bipartisanship, he warned the Johnson Administration and the Democrats in Congress that "Bipartisanship does not mean that we can or should ignore our obligation to the country to discover what our policy is. . . . If the government wants bipartisan support, which we [in the minority] will give as far as we can, it must be honest with us, consult with us, and tell us its program. And it is not enough to receive a chunk of boilerplate marked 'Special' and 'Confidential,' all of which has appeared in fuller form in the newspapers a month earlier, and which still says nothing."

In Vietnam, he said, "policy has been made by the Department of Defense, not the Department of State, so far as we can discover. . . . As near as I could make out, operations were making policy and snowballing into policy, instead of policy governing operations. . . . It seemed there was no policy in Vietnam. And now we are frozen into a hopeless position into which we should not have fallen."

He scored the State Department under President Johnson for failure to resist boycotts organized by some of the Arab nations. "When an attempt is made to blackmail American companies into participating in such a boycott, it is time for us to do something. . . . We must strengthen the hands of those companies by prohibiting them from engaging in such practices [agreements with the effect of furthering an Arab boycott of Israel]." Lindsay introduced a bill to put Congress on record as opposing boycotts by foreign countries against nations friendly to the U.S.

Lindsay's conviction that the UN must be maintained and strengthened as an international organization, and its peace-keeping functions preserved, was the basis for his stand on a UN bond bill before the House in the fall of 1962.* Lindsay urged support of the UN through the purchase of such bonds to "serve notice to the General Assembly that the UN should pursue to the fullest measure its efforts toward achieving a permanent solution to the financing of the world organization." The House later accepted a Lindsay amendment to instruct the Department of State "to submit to the Congress, not later than January 31, 1963, a report on steps taken in the seventeenth session of the General Assembly on long-term financing of the UN." The amendment was aimed at gaining support for the bond bill and heading off possible crippling amendments. Secretary Rusk later recognized Lindsay's "dedicated efforts" which "contributed greatly to the passage of the bill."

Much of Congressman John Lindsay's involvement in foreign affairs has found an outlet in the NATO Parliamentarians' conferences, where he has served as one of eight House of Representatives delegates for four years, and is now chairman of its political committee. (See Chapter 20.)

* The UN's financial crisis was, and still is, largely a result of the refusal of Russia and France to pay for peace-keeping operations in the Suez crisis and the Congo which were undertaken by the General Assembly under the "Uniting for Peace" resolution.

He has made ventures into other foreign affairs areas. At the end of his first year in Congress, he prevailed upon Secretary of State Christian Herter to arrange for systematic meetings between State Department representatives and interested members of Congress. In his bid to State for the briefings Lindsay told Herter he had the impression that during the debate on mutual security many Congressmen had cast their votes on the basis of "absence of information rather than on the basis of knowledge." The nonpartisan arrangement begun under the Eisenhower Administration has continued under Presidents Kennedy and Johnson. In an extension and enlargement of that project, Lindsay has urged a major change in Rules so that the Congressmen could have question-and-answer periods on the House floor with the Secretary of State. In the spring of 1965, he led a dozen Republican members in introducing a resolution to permit the change which would yield the following benefits: the Administration could expound its foreign policy to the public advantageously, and simultaneously the State Department would "benefit from a sense of liability to prompt and public explanation"; members of Congress could obtain and consider "prompt and authoritative information on America's foreign relations"; for its part, the public could have "the utmost confidence in the government by facilitating the flow of information. . . ."

Lindsay has made the idea of a watchdog for the CIA one of his major goals in Washington. He has presented a careful analysis of the CIA's record (as best it could be pieced together in view of the super-secret activities) and has introduced a resolution proposing a Joint Committee on Foreign Information and Intelligence.

He told the House that the CIA's operations in Iran, Guatemala, Hungary, and East Germany, "unless carefully supervised and controlled by responsible political officers, could unwittingly involve the U.S. in a major international crisis, possibly in war. If this was not clear before the Bay of Pigs, it ought to be clear now." Intelligence agencies, he charged, often "blundered seriously," with the result that the U.S. has "paid a heavy price."

The proposed watchdog committee would be along the lines of the Joint Committee on Atomic Energy; it would have its own staff and funds, and four main lines of inquiry: the relationship between the CIA and the State Department; the link between intelligence-gathering and special operations; selection and training of intelligence personnel (Lindsay thinks the CIA overdoes its use of refugees and retired military men); and "the whole question of intelligence evaluation." He denied that the CIA's secrecy would be breached, citing the Atomic Energy Committee as an impeccable example of secret-keeping by a committee; he charged that the CIA makes policy instead of merely carrying out the decisions of others; and he effectively refuted the contention that the CIA is already subject to Congressional scrutiny in existing committee operations. "I abhor government secrecy," Lindsay told the House. "I regard it as alien to our way of life, a threat to our fundamental liberties. Things are done to us and in our name which we know nothing of. The American people have at stake not merely their liberties but their lives."

Later Lindsay examined the CIA and his proposed committee in a long article in the March, 1964, *Esquire* and reiterated some of his earlier arguments, declaring, "The shaping and implementation by secret processes of some part of foreign policy is an extremely serious matter in a free society."

As a supporter of foreign aid in principle, Lindsay has found numerous occasions to suggest improvements in its practice. One of these, during his second term, was a successful proposal to amend the foreign aid bill to require that, whenever possible, people administering it abroad have "special competence, such as appropriate language and practical experience." Only a small fraction of U.S. officials then administering the aid program had any proficiency in the languages of countries in which they were working.

In also urging the State Department to place greater emphasis on language proficiency, he has underscored repeatedly the need for ambassadors to have a working knowledge of the appropriate languages.

In House debate John Lindsay has described himself as "one of the strongest supporters of foreign aid." Early in his Congressional career, he advocated an increased emphasis on a lending program for long-term development rather than on grants-in-aid, and he opposed Congressional cuts in President Eisenhower's overall foreign aid requests. But in arguing for the principle of foreign aid, in the Kennedy Administration's first year, he criticized the President's statement that "foreign aid should be supported because it is right."

"Not that philanthropy is bad," Lindsay commented, "but it most certainly should not be the basis for a relatively revolutionary long-term commitment. Foreign aid is an integral part of our foreign policy and . . . should be regarded as an instrument of long-range strategy." He argued for loans which, he said, "being on a more businesslike basis, tend to engender more respect and more economy" rather than grants which "tend to induce a disrespect for the donor and extravagance in use."

He delivered a long, thoughtful, and positive speech on behalf of "the long-range hope of the free world," but in it he revealed insights and misgivings which have later emerged in his subsequent foreign aid positions.* By 1963 he was warning the Foreign Affairs Committee, then considering another aid bill, that general public discontent with the assistance program was growing and that steps should be taken to improve confidence in it to combat mounting disillusion. And in the spring of 1965 he delivered another major address in the House. In it he proposed a major shift in handling of aid: "Seldom in the history of international relations has an instrument of policy been either more productive or more abused," he observed, "than the American foreign aid program. For twenty years the American people have provided assistance ranging from the reconstruction of the European economies left shattered by World War II, to the introduction of basic health and educational facilities in countries that are just beginning the long process of development. . . . It is true that foreign aid has not fulfilled the hopes with which we undertook it, but that has more to do with the extravagance of our hopes than with the failure of our aid. . . . The

* The Congressman gave credit during his talk to an incipient "brain trust" he had pulled together on foreign policy. "My thinking has been profoundly influenced," he told the House, "by long-range study completed by a group of young experts in New York, whom I brought together early in the year and asked to assist me on this subject." He expressed gratitude to them for their help.

program has contributed to impressive economic progress of which both recipients and donor may well be proud. . . . Foreign aid has not, by any means, achieved all that we had hoped, but it has achieved a great deal and can, if properly reformed, achieve much more. . . ."

And though the reform John Lindsay offered was, as he said, far from a major departure in American foreign policy, it was a substantial change in organization.

He called for a shift in the U.S. foreign development aid program to the hands of international organizations, such as the World Bank's International Development Association, as "a logical transition in the United States' ventures in world order." The threefold benefits he described as: establishment of economic development as an essential objective in itself, to be promoted by an agency with no political goals except development of the world's poorer nations; removal of aid from "the mounting pressure of our own domestic politics"; and conversion of assistance "from separate acts of generosity to something closer to a community responsibility."

Lindsay told the House that "internationalization will advance the ultimate political objectives of our aid, which are to build a world community in which freedom is secure and prosperity is at least a realistic hope for all men.*

"Having taken the lead over the last twenty years in efforts to build an international security community, it is now time for the United States to take the lead in building a no less important community for social and economic development. The concept that our aid to underdeveloped nations is a temporary obligation is illusory and should be discarded. We should align our foreign aid program with the world's needs and aspirations throughout the century. Far from having run its course, one form or another of foreign aid remains a necessity, if development is to continue in the world's poorer nations." He called, then, for U.S. commitment to "the idea of a development century," and to our own long-term interest in making it a success.

* Some three years earlier Lindsay had put the general idea a little less elegantly. In a radio talk he advised the U.S. to give up its "Donating Daddy" role, and become a financier or banker in helping the developing nations.

But if a long-term aid program, covering that "development century," was a goal that deserved attention, that same spring there were issues that demanded even more immediate attention. Lindsay devoted another major speech in the spring of 1965 to one of these. For the most burning of all the problems then on the nation's agenda, he called for "new policies to meet the harsh realities of Vietnam." The search for a solution there, he said, should concentrate on creation of an international commission to negotiate a settlement, supervise free elections, oversee an orderly transition of government. The concept of a single Vietnam, the probable "key to a peaceful settlement," is on the list of "harsh realities" to which Americans should begin to reconcile themselves.

His remarks were reminiscent of his declaration, early in his Congressional career, during a Radio Free Europe interview: "What we have in our country is simply the principle of government by the consent of the governed. It means only that people must have the right to choose their own leaders. And this," he added, "is the principle which must eventually be achieved in every country of the world, if there is to be ultimate peace."

In another instance Lindsay challenged before his colleagues the Administration's justification for the escalation in Vietnam. "The President must define our policy," he said. "We need not be taken for fools in accepting further explanation that widening American bloodshed, and the confusion of military buildup and meaningless inspections, are permitted in the name of 'stability.' I'm not suggesting that we pick up and walk out of Vietnam tomorrow morning. . . . I do suggest, however, that the heads of state display some willingness to communicate . . . in order to prevent this miserable war from unnecessarily enmeshing the entire globe in a conflict of arms. The initiative, including a definitive report to the Congress and the country, must come from the President of the United States."

In May of 1965 Lindsay again expressed only partial approval of the U.S. role in the conflict, refusing to endorse large-scale buildup "without allies and without the exercise of great diplomacy."

He was defending, with these reservations, a resolution to appropriate supplemental funds for Vietnam to the Defense Department. "I hope the President will recognize that many of us who vote for this resolution do so in the hope it will contribute, not to the widening of an unwarranted war, but to the pursuit of an honorable peace."

Again speaking in troubled tones of the American dilemma in Vietnam, Lindsay concluded that "We are fighting what is probably the most unwanted war in this country's history. . . . A debate has been lacking, and I find the silence disturbing," he said on one of the many days when the news was all bad. "It is essential to the nature of a democracy that its leaders state their policies and explain their actions. If no questions are asked and no dissent is heard, we may have but a single viewpoint of limited knowledge and understanding on which to form judgments. The American people should know our role in the perspective of history and in the prospective of the next century, and how that role is to be derived from our fundamental policy after World War II—that no nation in the atomic age can afford to go it alone. A national debate will help us determine that role, for it is from the conflicting opinions of free men that the truth emerges."

23

'61: A Prescient Postscript

"LINDSAY for Mayor!" or at least "Lindsay for Mayor?" was heard on the sidewalks of New York for almost six years before The Man himself said "Yes."

In mid-spring of 1959, not long after he went to Washington as a Congressman and only a year after his political debut—the successful primary fight for the 17th District nomination—speculative comment began to link Lindsay and City Hall. It had to do with the 1961 mayoralty campaign which was more than two years away, but Lindsay was sounded out, frequently, by rumor-chasing reporters. He wasn't interested, he said, and furthermore, he was "inclined to say 'No' to a draft."

No one seemed particularly interested in initiating a draft, but in the absence of other determined candidacies, Lindsay's name stayed on the lists. Early in 1960 City Councilman Stanley Isaacs mentioned Lindsay as a possible fusion candidate, and the new Republican County Chairman, Bernard Newman, did the same a little later. The columnists were counting him in—or at least they were not counting him out.

By 1961, the year of the municipal election, Lindsay, pressed to the point, finally said, "I want to be a Congressman, and that's it." He predicted that the Republicans would nominate an "independent."

In the spring of that year, however, a "Broadway Committee to Draft Lindsay" was formed. Some hopeful party leaders were talking of a drive to nominate either Senator Javits or Lindsay, and Bernard Newman was working on both men. The *Times* observed that Congressman Lindsay possessed the qualifications for City Hall, but the decision to go with Attorney General Louis J. Lefkowitz was in fact shaping up. In the Capitol, Lindsay was assuring reporters he had taken no part in discussions of the mayoralty, nor had he been pressured to run, and that he preferred "national affairs" as his arena. A Republican journal commented that mere mention of him as a potential candidate showed how far he had come in only about two years.

The idea of fusion as a way to victory in the city still demanded attention, however, and in the summer of 1961 the Congressman wrote that fusion, "offers the best prospect for victory and the best prospect for good government in New York City, a greater chance to overthrow the entrenched machine." But, he added, success would not depend on a mere formula; the prospects would rise or fall, depending on the skill, vigor, persistence, and resourcefulness of highly qualified candidates of integrity and experience who would campaign with vigor and enthusiasm. They would have to "appeal to the social conscience" of the city's electorate.

He named no one, but there were some who thought he had, presumably quite unconsciously, painted a word portrait of himself and the kind of campaign he would expect to conduct if or when he might be a candidate for city office.

Later in the year, as the Lefkowitz campaign * dribbled toward collapse at the polls, there was speculation about how other candidates might have done against Wagner. One newspaper reported that the Democrats' polls indicated Lefkowitz would lose by

* The campaign manager-of-record was John Lindsay, who turned out to have little time for the task because of the Congressional session.

400,000 (the figure turned out to be very nearly accurate); and hypothesized that Javits would have lost by 250,000, whereas Lindsay would not have run even as well as Lefkowitz.

In any event, Wagner was returned in November to try again during a third and, it turned out, final term. Viewing the "New York malaise" at the time, the *Times*' James Reston found that many factors compounded it, but suggested that one significant contribution was that younger men like John Lindsay might not get the nomination for mayor, while seasoned men like Senator Javits, "stricken by Potomac fever," would not take it.

When it was all over, Lindsay added a postscript. He addressed some remarks to fellow Republicans which he was still able to voice almost unchanged four years later: "Mr. Wagner pretends to 'reform' the system. He promises a few superficial changes at the top, but meanwhile consolidates his position at the level where it counts. The solution is to start anew with builders who have a blueprint for a better New York. It is time to clean out the mess and to put into office men of high caliber who think in terms of the general welfare of all, rather than the insatiable appetites of a few special friends."

His post-mortem on the 1961 failure was in a sense a keynote address for the campaign he was to wage four years later, but despite his reference to builders with blueprints, he was offering none at that time. The blueprint stage was many, many months in the future. Meanwhile he had urgent business in the Capitol.

There were two more elections to Congress before another city election and it was impossible to see then that he would continue to multiply his amazing majorities and, by 1965, become a logical if not inevitable candidate to speak for New Yorkers who continued to look for a man with blueprints.

Lindsay's preceding victory, over an NYU professor named Martin Dworkis, was almost staggering. Winning better than two to one by some 53,000 votes, Lindsay almost doubled his impressive 1960 record. His margin was more than one tenth the size of Governor Rockefeller's statewide majority, though the 17th District contains only about a fortieth of the people. But the triumph lacked the impact of his first victory in 1958; it had little of the suspense of 1960 when he had finished his first successful term in Congress; and it had none of the complexities of the 1964 race "without reference to" Goldwater, fought against two opponents and receiving an overwhelming vote of confidence. Yet among the things which 1962 did indicate was the readiness of voters to support a Republican who stood frequently independent of both his own party's House leadership and the opposition-held White House. In 1962, as in the other Congressional races, Lindsay's opponents also had the Liberal Party's nomination. His capture of the party's nomination for mayor in 1965 was the first time he had sought or obtained a Liberal designation.

24

Is It Really Alabaster?

Is a city the size, complexity and diversity of New York ungovernable? There are many students, writers, political scientists, politicians and pessimists who think so.

Robert F. Wagner, who has been its mayor for twelve years, calls his the second most demanding public job in the nation, second only to the Presidency, and has a melancholy fondness for relating the physical strain and drain. The city's budget of nearly $4 billion and its payroll of 240,000 people are considerably larger than those of New York State, which has twice as many residents and a territory 130 times larger.* More than half a century ago William

* The common plaint is that the city is incompatible with the fifty-seven upstate counties, and that the continuing struggle to wheedle or blackmail the state government into providing more money to the city is typical of their conflicting interests. Lindsay has consistently taken an opposite point of view. "Problems and issues" of city and upstate are "more common than people think," he has said repeatedly, naming among them, "unemployment, urbanization, and stresses and strains of expanding population."

With some accuracy, he warned an upstate Republican audience in the late spring of 1964, even before the Goldwater nomination helped it to come true months later, that Republicans should not take for granted that upstate would always go Republican, or that New York City would inevitably vote Demo-

Jay Gaynor scoffed at the governorship as inferior in stature to his own office. Even the playboy mayor, James J. Walker, found the demands of office taxing enough to require his many "much needed" rests, and Fiorello LaGuardia, a symbol of indefatigable resilience, died exhausted only months after leaving office.

And what is the role of the residents themselves? What does city-dwelling hold for the eight million—for Spanish-speaking Puerto Ricans or starry-eyed college girls from the Midwest, each sure that New York is the land of beckoning opportunity? And where is the true New York? Is it in the crusty dirt of the subways or the shining towers of the financial district, in the teeming streets of Harlem or the tree-lined streets of a Queens community? Is there an answer or answers that would supply the clues and make New York a governable and governed city rather than a fretwork of autonomous, anarchic tributaries lacking common cause?

"Give me your tired, your poor . . . the wretched refuse," says Emma Lazarus' verse at the feet of the Statue of Liberty. Though it refers to America, the spirit is most particularly that of the city which received the huddled masses for so many decades. Is New York really a golden door for them and their descendants or is it really a dream, a phantasmagoria that shines from across the sea or across the Hudson but dissolves into a world as chaotic as it is unreal? How is it to be governed—this city of small armies of police who seem to be fighting a losing battle against the muggers and the hoods, of sanitation workers who seem never to catch up with the problem of cleaning up, of striking teachers who are sometimes outnumbered by striking students, picketing parents, truants and educational bureaucrats?

Is there a common denominator for the migrant from Arecibo Province and Washington County alike; or a formula that can

---

cratic. "Without fresh effort and attention, upstate can be lost," he warned. In the November election of that year, every county in the state went Democratic on the Presidential line for the first time ever, and the overturn sent a Democratic legislature to Albany for the first time in three decades. Some of the most prominent Republican names in the state went down to defeat.

But the Lindsay forecast also included the prophesy that "with fresh effort in every block, New York City can be won" from the Democrats. A year later he was engaged in such an effort.

restore this as one of the gleaming alabaster cities—The City of the American Dream?

John Lindsay is no transient in the city. He is a native son * who admits to a lifelong love affair with his city, denies that it is ungovernable, but admits that the citizens and their government are alienated from each other. So does his ally, Senator Jacob Javits, who has described the idea that New York City is "ungovernable" as a myth "perpetuated by barren leadership," with resulting low morale but high levels of frustration and hopelessness. Javits called the typical American a metropolitan resident, harassed, inconvenienced, demoralized, and troubled. "One of the most significant aspects" of the Lindsay candidacy in New York, said Javits, "is that it will focus public attention on the long-neglected crisis in our cities. . . . John Lindsay believes New York City is governable, and . . . he is out to lift the morale of the city, to give it a new spirit of youth, vigor, determination, and creativity. If he succeeds in this mission, John Lindsay will restore the faith of Americans in cities, and he will give the metropolitan man, not only in New York City but all over the country, a much-needed shot in the arm."

Lindsay recalls that a friend, one of his constituents, commented to him, "There's such a tortuous road between a man and his government these days." He saw in the remark "a feeling somewhat like the one you might get from watching a huge machine operate at a distance. . . .

"How many of us, I wonder, have this same sense of standing a great distance off from our government? Is there reason to feel this way? I've often thought about it. Think of the intense human problems in which almost everyone feels a sense of involvement—civil rights, for example, or the fight against poverty's ravages. These hit very close to many hearts and homes; and government, at any level, has a right and duty to involve itself in these issues—to help people facing such social problems.

"But the planning, I fear, the proposals, the legislation by gov-

* He was born three weeks after the re-election of John F. Hylan as ninety-sixth mayor, an office in which he served so effectively in one way only: to make his successor, Jimmy Walker, seem a relief at first.

ernment will go no farther than 'good intentions,' if, in the end, it can still be said that a 'tortuous road' runs between a citizen and his government. Most of all, we need a realistic, man-to-man approach that brings trained, dedicated people into constant contact with the marrow of these problems and the people who are being hurt by them.

"What we must do increasingly in this modern day of big power complexes, like government, is to humanize government. I find it dismaying, if not wholly surprising, to find the people and their government so far apart. The task of the future is to find better ways and means of bringing government and its services closer to home."

Plato observed in *The Republic,* "They have filled the city with harbors and docks and buildings and all that, and left no room for reason or justice. . . ." And John Lindsay, troubled citizen of a city filled with docks, buildings, and all that, quotes Plato and adds: "I discover more and more, in the midst of all this machinery and concrete, that Plato was right when he pleaded for more room for reason and justice. Human beings must be treated like human beings, not like cogs in the big machine. I'm looking for a little bit more reason and justice and I hope I'll find it. . . ."

At other moments, Lindsay has found much cause for optimism in tabulating the city's assets: "We have everything here," he said, "the most people, the brightest minds, the tallest buildings, the smartest businessmen, the finest museums, the longest ships." He termed the city "the storehouse for the continent's superlatives," and continued: "The city is always moving; there's always lots going on," he has said. This is the home of the movers, the shakers, the people who get things done in the most demanding and rewarding city on earth."

Specific needs, "among other things, are brains, talent, absence of bias and prejudice, more money, people willing to serve, the experience of other cities, and more money still. . . .

"I don't think they are going to cover the entire earth with concrete, but they are coming close," John Lindsay has said. "The big question is, What do we do with the ghetto?" After what he calls "a generation and a half of neglect," Lindsay declares that in some parts of New York City "the rats and mice have all but taken over, and it's too late for steel wool and Scotch tape." He likens big cities to a man who hasn't seen a dentist for ten years: "The decay is so massive that the experts, the professionals, are not quite sure whether to plunge in with total extraction and removal, assuming it can be afforded, or whether to patch . . . and, in any event, whether to withstand the political heat that comes with any decision.

"One thing is certain—and that is that the people will not stand for no action at all—policies of no policy, of neglect and increasing decay. People don't stand for inadequate education and inadequate housing and *de facto* segregation, and all the elements that go into the vicious cycle of the ghetto, but will eventually vent their frustrations in extralegal ways if the community turns its back too long on community problems."

Here again Lindsay touches on the "humanizing" of government: "What does his government mean to the individual citizen?" And from where should come the inspiration, the genius, and the objectivity that can spur government on to better performance? John Lindsay sees "enormous resources of unused human talent" in New York.

"The city," he points out, "has a great many men and women who are well qualified in various aspects of municipal affairs and whose talents could readily be made available to a municipal "shadow cabinet." He has already advocated such a "shadow cabinet" to operate between the Congress and the Cabinet (see Chapter 8). A city "shadow cabinet" could study, criticize, and propose a whole range of public affairs, from housing, schools, and taxes to parks, pollution, and police.

"Municipal government," Lindsay said early in 1965, at a time when he had withdrawn from consideration for the mayoralty, "like national government, functions well only when it is held to account by a vigorous, responsible, and creative opposition—one which does not hesitate to criticize, but at least suggests alternative lines of action, and extends its proposals to future opportunities as well as present necessities."

In New York, a "shadow opposition," in the Lindsay view, would consist principally of people not generally connected with the regular organization of the opposition party. At the time he wrote this, of course, the Republicans were the "opposition," as they had been for so many years, having been out of City Hall for two decades (or vastly longer, depending on how one construes Fiorello La-Guardia's Republicanism) and having only one fifth of the City Council's members and less than a tenth of the Board of Estimate's votes. Presumably he would seek to have the Democrats form a "shadow cabinet" of their own if he reaches City Hall.

He was directing his comment to the Republicans, the traditional "outs" in the city, when he criticized the lack of a vigorous and creative opposition.

In any event, the organization of "shadow cabinets" would enable the party to act "in full consonance with its own best traditions," he believes, these traditions being "wisdom and effectiveness in power, and responsibility and creativity in opposition."

25

The Cries of the Cities

SINCE he was born in an apartment house on West End Avenue, John Lindsay has never had a permanent home off Manhattan island. He is a city boy, and he has very close to his heart the special problems of his own town and of the other metropolitan areas that share many of its problems. "Why," he exclaims in wonder, "we spend more money to provide and maintain storage accommodations for wheat that we can't use, than we do for housing homeless citizens.*

In supporting 1965 legislation which closely paralleled his 1960 bill, Lindsay told Congress again that "the troubles of the cities are increasingly susceptible to national solutions. . . . The federal

* Though hardly a farmer, his votes on agriculture bills won him a rating of 82 (out of a possible 100) from the American Farm Bureau Federation. The National Farmers Union, whose positions usually are toward a larger governmental role, scores him at 50. Commenting on his vote against a wheat subsidy bill, he noted that it "not only would have increased the cost of the program but probably would have aggravated surplus problems in other crops. . . . These high crop supports, paid for by the taxpayer, directly relate to the high cost of food in our city."

obligation in the affairs of our cities is most apparent along the Atlantic coast, where we already are witnessing the creation of a huge super-city, spreading irregularly from Boston to Norfolk.

"New York City, which I represent, will be at the center of this formidable complex of power and, we hope, prestige. Perhaps our most urgent responsibility is to plan the growth of our city complexes so that expansion is properly channeled. An urban outburst of the kind already under way cannot be properly directed by isolated, parochial committees and studies. The need is for comprehensiveness, and it should logically develop from the highest level of our government."

Noting that the five years which had elapsed had intensified rather than lessened the need for legislation, Lindsay supported the 1965 proposal as "a giant step toward the effective consolidation of federal functions concerning the nation's cities and suburbs." But he added that it omitted one important provision of his own bill—establishment of a federal Urban Affairs Council to advise on the new department's programs and policies.

Creation of the federal department, Lindsay argued, would contribute substantially to making it possible for "all Americans to take pride in all our cities.

"We have a Department of Agriculture to take care of the needs of twenty million farmers, a Department of Labor to concern itself with twenty million organized workers, and a Department of the Interior to nurse along the interests of our Western states," Lindsay commented when he presented his proposal for creation of a Department of Urban Affairs.

Housing, transportation, sewage disposal, water supply, airports—these are among the cities' problems that he cited during his first term in Congress when he pointed out that, "We spend twenty to thirty times as much on farm housing research as we spend on urban housing research and we spend more money on research about potatoes than we do on urban economics." All this adds up to "more than justification for the inclusion of our cities at the Cabinet level. . . . Right now, the cries of the cities produce only the faintest of echoes in the highest of chambers."

And he forecast with melancholy, "Alas, the introduction of a new bill, such as the one I have introduced [this was in 1960], does not mean we shall have immediate action. I have not been around the Congress long, but long enough to know some of the problems we face in matters of this sort."

He told the Congressional subcommittee that the inescapable conclusion to be drawn from the nation's urbanizing trend is that "We can no longer be satisfied with a Scotch-tape job on our urban problems. Our rapidly expanding cities need housing and access and clean air and light," he said. "But, instead, slums and urban decay race ahead of progress."

While local responsibility is paramount for finding long-range solutions, he contended, the federal government, the government of all the people, must assume as its concern the problems created by changes in the face of the nation. "If we allow further deterioration of our urban centers and fail to promote their dynamic growth, we will be guilty of permitting erosion of the base of our economy," he told Congressional colleagues in 1961, while testifying in support of his bill. His proposal, as he pointed out, "is not new; others have suggested it, now and in the past; others will arrive at the same conclusion."

Among those who reached the same conclusion was the Kennedy Administration which proposed an Urban Affairs Department the next year. Lindsay contended that his bill, which had gone nowhere, was better than the Administration's, but he supported the latter because "the concept is the same." At the same time he was critical of what he called "President Kennedy's shameful injection of a racial issue into the subject of a Department of Urban Affairs," by his "unprecedented" prior designation of Robert C. Weaver to head the not yet established department. Lindsay said Weaver would be "an excellent choice" if such a department were created, but that the President's statement did a disservice to him since it implied that the choice was made "because Mr. Weaver is a Negro, not because he is necessarily the best man." The department was not created during the Kennedy Administration but became a fact in 1965, with Weaver still foremost in speculation as to its chief.

Though the salvaging of the cities ordinarily evokes this kind of seriousness, Lindsay wrote more lightly on the question for an architectural magazine. He described the frustrations of a tour by "Mayor Jones of Urbanville" through the federal establishment in search of information and guidance on a whole range of problems from urban renewal to school, highway, airport, and water needs. Faced with a multitude of problems, "Mayor Jones packs his bag and goes to Washington," Lindsay commented, adding that this at least has the advantage of getting him out of town for a while.

"The Mayor is not quite sure where to begin in Washington.* His Congressman is a member of the opposition party and has called him a boob, so he decides to figure it out for himself. . . ." Tracing the Mayor's adventures in an almost endless series of agencies, most of which he had never heard of before, Lindsay concluded that after a week he would go home, his suitcase heavy with regulations, forms, telephone numbers, and maps, and his heart heavy as well. "Mayor Jones is not alone with his troubles . . . all mayors have the same troubles." And these, he concluded, could be lessened by a federal department that would gather all those endless agencies under a single roof.

Though his whimsy might qualify as one of the lighter attempts to add a small human touch to the massive problems of Megalopolis, author Lindsay failed even to hint at whether or not Urbanville was his own home town and whether its mayor could be expected to be as naïvely unsure of himself in his wanderings through the Washington maze.

* In calling for a committee to investigate problems of urban areas in 1961, for instance, Lindsay pointed out that the responsibility for housing legislation and inquiring into the effectiveness of urban renewal programs is in a subcommittee of the committee on banking and currency.

❦ ❦ 26 ❦ ❦

The Roof Is Falling In . . .

JOHN LINDSAY has called housing the most pressing problem of New York City and of other urban areas. In 1960 he organized the Lindsay Corps, a housing team, which has grown to include about fifty volunteers who "help people who are in trouble and don't know where to turn." The young men and women in the Corps contribute their time and energy to aid 17th District residents—the people, says Lindsay, "who are being choked by the rent squeeze, who are caught up in the tangle of landlords, lawyers, and local rent administrators, who are being forcibly relocated in the name of urban renewal and who have no one to turn to for help."

The Corps members, even more graphically, "spend their nights and weekends traveling the streets, climbing darkened stairways to give a helping hand to people who are frightened, who live in apartments where the roof is falling in, or the rats won't leave, or the rent is so high they can't eat, or the Social Security is inadequate."

The Corps handles every kind of housing hardship imaginable. Every day the Congressman's midtown office receives a flood of requests for help from people who want to get into public housing; but, as Lindsay has found, though "these are often sad and desperate cases and need help, there is never enough room." Providing enough decent housing at suitable prices is a preëminent concern.

What his housing team has uncovered is, he believes, "the gap between governmental programs and the people who sometimes need help the most"; and, "existing programs don't seem to be available to a great many people who need help." *

For years Congress has heard Lindsay's warnings that "the most critical" problem is middle-income housing, where shortages are driving young couples with growing families out of the city, and where older people with fixed incomes can't afford the rents. Many thousands of middle-income families, he has said over and over, have left New York City because housing programs have failed to meet the need. The prices are simply too high.

New residents who replace the displaced have a much lower income, he points out, and "this significant change bears heavily upon the city's need to provide special services and facilities and, of course, affects our general economy." He argues that although it's only partially true, as a much repeated remark has it, that "New York is becoming a city of the very rich and the very poor," the city must take suitable steps to hold the middle-income resident who is caught in a construction-cost, tight-housing-market vise.

"I have spent endless hours cruising the streets and avenues," Lindsay said one day in the House of Representatives, "examining the new construction wave that has demolished a sizable portion of the city, talking with families who are being displaced, and with dis-

* Early in his 1965 campaign for mayor he pledged a "war on slums" if elected; one such comment was made after a visit to a city-owned tenement in the Bedford-Stuyvesant section of Brooklyn. He noted signs of deterioration, and called the building "a monument to inaction and indifference." Such conditions as he found in the building "cannot be permitted to exist."

A New York City newspaper commented, "Unfortunately, the people trapped in these slums have been hearing similar declarations of war for many years, from the political ins as well as the outs," and added, "This is the challenge facing Lindsay—not merely to denounce slums, or even to come up with a program of workable antidotes, but to convince promise-weary New Yorkers—especially those directly affected—that this isn't just the old refrain again." The Lindsay record in Washington indicates the likelihood of his doing that.

traught parents looking for a place to live that is both within their means and large enough. Weekend after weekend I have listened to the frightening, oft-repeated tale of people who bear the burden and hardship of inadequate housing."

He described the facilities and prices in the "new, high-rise apartment buildings, usually red brick in color, rapidly built, dull looking," with a small room and a half or two rooms in each cramped apartment. The rentals, which were then sometimes as high as $150 a month for a room and a half, rose to $200 or $250 for a two-room apartment. Some apartments with two bedrooms had minimum rents of $315.

"Many," he explained, "are occupied by childless couples where both husband and wife work. No space is available for families; these apartments are not built for children. There can hardly be room for more than one at best.

"Between half and three quarters of the family income goes into rent. . . . People find they have overcommitted themselves for the rent. The result is a huge turnover, with a great many families moving out in less than a year. And high residency turnover," he added, "does not promote sound community relations. If the exodus becomes extreme, it creates widespread dislocation, which, of course, is one of the prime breeders of slums, delinquency, and crime. . . ."

"Just ask the neighborhood merchants and shopkeepers," Lindsay said after one of his tours of the city. "They will tell you so much money has gone into rent that no cash is left over for spending. An electrical repair man, a specialist in kitchen appliances, told me that as he goes into kitchen after kitchen in these new buildings, he finds the refrigerators empty except for three eggs, a little salami, two cans of beer, and a quarter-pound of butter. The cash is not there for a family to load up with a full larder. The grocers confirm this."

Then, looking at the bulldozers which push down old neighborhoods to make room for high-rise apartments, Lindsay expressed concern for "families who have lived in the neighborhood for decades, some for two or three generations. Living conditions aren't good; the buildings are old; too often, an unsympathetic landlord; the city's administration has patently neglected enforcing housing and building code violations. But at least they have had homes in neighborhoods which are their neighborhoods, in which they grew up, and when their building comes down, there is neither sufficient space in the new one nor sufficient income to pay the high rent. . . . There was a neighborhood quality in the block before the bulldozers came in. That quality does not exist now. And good people who live in the new buildings find themselves in a worse squeeze than their predecessors."

Because John Lindsay tends to see "housing problems" in human terms, he has offered solutions which he himself has occasionally termed "drastic." *

"I was once severely criticized," he has commented with some asperity, "for saying that housing in a city like New York should be regarded as a public utility. Real estate men said this was a socialistic statement. I'm the first to admit that I'm not always right—but how can it be argued that housing in the City of New York is not a public trust?"

Lindsay thinks that "excessive federal" participation should be held to a minimum, but we must recognize that governmental programs are vital: tax concessions and long-term, low-interest loans as well as direct grants-in-aid; and adequate procedures written into the housing programs to insure the protection of taxpayers' money, since "quasi-public facilities, like public facilities, always need protection against plunder." Without government aid, "the needs cannot be met, for the private system cannot do it alone."

Further, the city administration in New York should provide a relocation program that would require private builders to make

* Lindsay's readiness to welcome the drastic or unusual in approaches to housing and renewal problems was dramatized in a letter that he sent to *Harper's* late in 1961. "There has grown up a kind of orthodoxy about housing and urban renewal in cities. Some of the leaders in this field fail now to recognize that it is time for new thought. It is important to have people . . . who have the brains and courage to point out that the 'king is wearing no clothes.' . . . This has enraged many housing people who perhaps feel that existing governmental programs somehow will be impaired.

"Not at all," the Congressman concluded. "If such programs are not redirected, they may not be saved at all."

available comparable housing space. The rental charges would be the same as before for similar space, with no more than a 15-per-cent increase allowable, spread out over the first three years of occupancy. Not only would his solution be "drastic"; it also would set "arbitrary standards," Lindsay conceded. But he challenged "anyone to propose a standard or procedure less arbitrary."

The action would be taken by the city, he said, since there would be no federal money involved and therefore no federal jurisdiction. He also backed a bill intended to deal with the problem when federal jurisdiction is involved.

In the absence of such action, Lindsay warned, "we can look forward only to a compounding of the evils that now exist—mass destruction of existing properties and the creation of high-rent buildings that only a few can afford . . . with a continued exodus from the city by young families with children, the future strength of the city."

Much of his attention was directed, of course, at the problems peculiar to New York City, but he spoke in principle of all great cities when he pointed out that their problems, "particularly those concerned with the most basic essential of all, adequate shelter, cannot be neglected, and no public officer can pretend that they do not exist.

"My job is to help find the best solutions for the greatest number, and that I am pledged to do."

Wherever housing is inadequate to the needs, Lindsay pointed out, the effect is felt in conditions of health and safety, with resulting growth of delinquency and narcotics use. "Slums breed crime, and crime breeds crime. The slum conditions must be eliminated by proper housing policies and programs" and, he added, in New York City "it is the mayor's chief responsibility to see that this is done."

As an example of how untended housing problems can fester, he describes the conditions that he found on West Sixty-fifth Street, typical of many others. Housing deterioration there, he says, has led to vandalism, open narcotics peddling and usage, mugging, prostitution, and race tensions. "My investigation established total city neglect in these areas," Lindsay reports. "Even minimum services are not provided; police foot patrols are provided only when someone makes enough noise about it, and then after a few days the situation reverts to what it was."

On West Sixty-fifth Street, at the time of his own inspections, the city's building department had listed fewer than ten violations, Lindsay said; but he picked out more than a hundred in a single building. "Slums," he repeated, "breed crime, and crime breeds crime. . . ."

So-called "middle-income" housing has caused major and continuing concern for John Lindsay over the years. One of his earliest bills in Congress sought to promote such housing and, simultaneously, to attack the root of scandals. In his first months in Washington he fought successfully for his own plan to clean up the Title I mess; his fight was so effective that one of the nation's principal liberal journals noted that, "while Democratic Congressmen remain silent," Representative Lindsay had "demanded investigation of Title I housing scandals in which Tammany figures were deeply involved."

He had been in Congress only a dozen weeks when he proposed to add his "Public Disclosure" provision to housing legislation. "To correct a serious flaw" in the 1949 housing act, the urban renewal mechanism, and to help restore public confidence in the renewal program, he proposed "full public disclosure of redevelopment proposals submitted by private redevelopers of Title I land before any contract or commitment" between the redeveloper and a local public agency would be permissible.

"We have found in New York that urban renewal is rapidly getting a black eye because it has too often resulted in condemnation of the homes of low-income and middle-income dwellers and the subsequent redevelopment of the resold land into high-rent apartments," he informed Congress. "There is no answer to the question so many have angrily written to me, 'Why are millions of dollars of tax money being spent to turn inexpensive dwellings into expensive ones?' "

He explained that "the redeveloper . . . acquiring the renewal area by markdown sale . . . is being selected by the local public agency without an adequate opportunity being provided to other potential redevelopers, or to the public at large, to study his proposals. Commitments are being made under circumstances operating to conceal from the public just who is redeveloping, what it will cost, what the rents will probably be, and what profit is anticipated."

Citing "one unhappy example," the Washington Square Title I project in New York City, Lindsay said "the names and interests of the investors, made possible by $12-million grants in state and federal funds, were shrouded in secrecy and rumor." The redeveloper, he continued, tore down low-rent apartments and lofts, and uprooted small businesses, only to build huge luxury apartment houses renting for $75 a room, or much more. "Nothing beyond the vaguest information as to the anticipated rents was made available when the commitment . . . was made," said Lindsay. "If this redeveloper had been required . . . to make full and advance public disclosure of its cost, financing, and profit projections, I seriously question whether an enlightened and aroused public opinion would have allowed this to go forward."

The House accepted his plan, though the New York City Committee on Slum Clearance had resisted it on the theory that it would discourage redevelopers.

"In my opinion," Lindsay insisted, "the only redevelopers it will discourage are the ones who have something to hide. When taxpayers' money is involved, taxpayers have a right to know every detail of its use."

The Lindsay plan faltered when it failed to get Senate approval and was deleted in House-Senate conference, but within a few weeks it was an integral part of a new housing bill that won passage. Simultaneously with the final approval Lindsay was warning the Housing and Home Finance Agency that some people, himself included, were determined "to have the operations of the entire program stripped bare for public scrutiny." And in New York City particularly, he charged, in the handling of the Title I program intended to do so much to provide better homes for the millions with "middle-income" prospects, the city administration had merely gone from crisis to crisis. "The time for command decisions from

City Hall in this area of civic need is long overdue," Lindsay said five years before his race for mayor, "and unless prompt action is given to long-range planning, New York City is headed for domestic problems of the gravest sort."

His driving concern for "the single most important group in our population," the middle class, led Lindsay to press, early in his second term, for another new bill which would improve their housing prospects.

He noted that seven out of eight New York City residents have incomes of less than $10,000 and that nearly half fall in the range of $5,000 to $10,000. Such families should be spending $85 to $125 a month for rent, though the number of homes being built in New York at the time was "not even close to being adequate to meet the demands. Increasingly," Lindsay noted, "the city becomes composed of either the privileged or impoverished, leaving the potential leaders, who come largely from the middle group, out in the cold."

His bill proposed a "Federal Limited-Profit Mortgage Corporation" to make direct construction loans (fifty-year, interest up to 4 per cent) to non-profit or limited-profit organizations. Borrowers would be required to put up at least 10 per cent of the development costs and would be limited to 6-per-cent profit. The goal was to build 160,000 moderate-income family units over a four-year period. His bill, similar to the one Senator Javits introduced in the Senate, would have substituted for Title I, which had a forty-year, no-down-payment mortgage provision.

In a letter which he sent to every Congressman he described the high purposes and the specific mechanics of his bill—"a far better, more effective, and far less costly proposal than Title I. The aim of my bill," Lindsay explained, "is to provide federal assistance for housing for families who are not eligible for low-rent public housing but who cannot afford high-cost privately financed housing. Decent and adequate housing for all our citizens at rentals they can afford is the goal I seek."

But his explanations were useless. Though the Senate accepted a similar idea, the House never acted on the limited-profit mortgage corporation. A frustrating parliamentary ruling kept the bill from even being considered. The House instead retained Title I, and because "I do not think that we can have both," Lindsay declined to press his own solution.

Though it was predicated on conditions in New York City, Lindsay's proposal was aimed at the entire country. "Federal legislation should be pinpointed to need," he told the House. "My proposal, which I had planned to offer as a substitute, would have met this specific need, the great need for middle-income housing in the urban and suburban centers of the United States. . . .

"I am one of those who feel that the federal government has a very positive role to play in the field of housing, particularly as the subject affects the exploding metropolis.

"The 70 per cent of our population living in the great urban and suburban centers . . . is a mobile population, which is all the more reason why the federal government has an important role.

"The investment that we make in our cities in terms of their planned growth—the elimination of blight, the building of housing that people can reasonably afford, the promotion of parks and playgrounds—is an investment for the benefit of all Americans, whether or not they live in the cities. . . ."

Congressman Lindsay kept pounding away at the Title I housing abuses, actual and potential, in New York City. But the Democratic leadership in Congress and the Administration were clearly not moved to follow through with meaningful investigations. A month after his bill was rejected, he urged the House subcommittee on housing to call hearings in New York City, at least "to clarify great misunderstandings as to the supervisory responsibility of the federal government where federal funds are involved." He pointed to his vote for the Administration's housing bill, over a Republican substitute, and remarked: "The Title I housing program will continue. It also continues to be abused. In New York City urban renewal continues to erect high-income housing, which middle-income people cannot afford, more often than not at the price of indiscriminate neighborhood destruction. Neighborhoods like Greenwich Village in my own Congressional District, which lend strength to the city because of their neighborhood character, are too often indiscriminately attacked."

Lindsay commented that he had supported the Democrats' housing bill partially because its four-year duration "should at least make possible long-range intelligent planning." He explained he felt he "must support the committee bill over the substitute" also because of the lack of provision for public housing in the latter, and the substitute bill's inability to "fill the gap" in the middle-income housing assistance. He concluded that "the deficiencies of the substitute bill are even greater" than the Democratic committee's bill, "with which I have my disagreements." But he added, "The fact, however, is that in the past we have had no planning whatever in New York City. The program has been short-ranged, hit or miss, veiled in secrecy, and profitable only to the 'insiders.' " He noted "instances of high profits to private sponsors and general corruption of the public purpose behind the housing bill by the erection of high-income, unimaginative housing which the average taxpayer can't afford."

Congress, Lindsay contended, "continues to have a high obligation to determine how taxpayers' money is being spent. The Congress must know, and the public has a right to know, whether there will be further instances of malfeasance and downright corruption, lack of planning, lack of imagination, wholesale destruction of sound neighborhoods, and clubhouse politics. . . ."

And noting suggestions elsewhere in the nation of potential scandals in the urban renewal effort, Lindsay challenged the subcommittee to "seize hold of this problem before it overwhelms your committee and the whole Congress."

Lindsay challenged the Kennedy Administration on numerous aspects of its program, especially its failure to perform on promises in the field of civil rights, and he was bitter against the Democratic leadership in Congress and the White House on the subject of discrimination in housing.

A year after the Democratic Administration entered office, he had taken the President to task in a letter which asked Mr. Kennedy to "live up to your promise and execute . . . an order promptly" which would bar discrimination in all housing programs aided in any way by the federal government. Later the Congressman wrote a letter to a magazine in which he commented stringently on an article that had quoted the President on housing segregation. The author had calmly predicted the Executive Order Lindsay had been demanding. "I wonder," Lindsay wrote, "what kind of an article he would write at the present time in view of President Kennedy's recent refusal to sign such an order when it was placed before him. What kind of leadership would you call this?" (Several months later the President did issue such an Executive Order.)

But John Lindsay's most vigorous declaration on this subject came one June afternoon on the floor of the House of Representatives. In a confrontation with the Democratic majority he bluntly challenged them to perform.

He rose during the debate on the housing bill to propose an amendment to eliminate discriminatory practices, "on account of race, religion, color, ancestry, or national origin," in any public housing where federal funds might be employed. "I am a pro-housing man and have been ever since I have been a member of Congress," he said. "I have also been a pro-public housing man because I know what it means to my district and to the city of New York, and to all the great urban centers of this country."

Speaking directly to housing subcommittee Chairman Albert Rains, who was sponsor of a housing bill Lindsay was committed to support, he remarked, "I will say to the distinguished gentleman from Alabama that I have walked up the aisle with him on housing matters; I have done so in connection with public housing." *

And then, in a candid aside, Lindsay reminded his "friends on the Democratic side" that at times it was not easy to vote with them, "because there is some disagreement on my side of the aisle

* Lindsay's "walk up the aisle" reference was to the practice in the House of having tellers check off members as they file through the well before the Speaker's rostrum, first those in favor of a bill, then those against. Lindsay was underscoring, then, those occasions when he had "walked up the aisle" with the Democrats to vote with them on housing measures. The vote by teller is one of the alternate ways of taking a vote apart from time-consuming roll calls; voice vote and standing count are the others.

[among the Republicans, that is] on the public housing question."

"Having done so," he continued, "now let me say this: that I will vote for programs when I think that they are important to the health and future of this country. But at the same time," he added, "I will expect that you on the majority side will stand up and be counted on a matter of principle regardless of the special provincial pressures you might be under." He was addressing himself primarily to the Southern bloc in the House, including specifically Rains as an Alabaman sponsoring the housing legislation.

His allusion to the "special provincial pressures" was pointed. "Why should we provide federal funds to perpetuate practices of discrimination in one third of this country and, indeed, in many other areas of the country? Do not let anybody suggest for one moment," he warned them, "that this amendment to the public housing section of the bill will kill the whole bill, because it will not. In the first place, it is limited to one section of the bill. In the second place, the distinguished chairman of the committee, the author of the bill, is too much of a statesman and has pride in his bill. In the third place, the leadership would not allow it at this stage of the game, and you know that as well as I.

"So, I can assure you that anybody who suggests to you that you must vote against the amendment, which says that federal funds in public housing shall not be used where there is discrimination, is way off the track—because this housing bill will pass, and you know it as well as I do.

"I will vote for the bill," Lindsay told the Democrats, "and I am willing to take the abuse that I may possibly have to take from my side of the aisle for voting for it. All I ask is that you on the majority side stop this unholy coalition when it comes to matters involving individual rights. . . ."

Here Lindsay revived his charge that three times during the 1960 campaign, Candidate Kennedy had promised "in January, he would have a civil rights bill before the Congress. January came. February, March, April, and May. No civil rights bill. . . ." And when Chairman Celler of Judiciary introduced a bill, Lindsay commented, "the Administration went out of its way to disassociate itself from the bill. So," he added, "when they suggest to you that there is executive power to do what I seek to do by legislation, think twice, because we have had broken promises down the line since January on this question.

"I need not talk further," he ended. "I have walked up the aisle with you. Now let us see you walk up the aisle with me!"

There was no aisle-walking by the majority. But, without question, the taunts from the independent who averred his readiness "to take the abuse" that might be his, stung those whom he urged to "stand up and be counted on a matter of principle."

The "unholy coalition," and the "special provincial pressures" were fully operative that summer afternoon. The Administration's housing bill passed, with John Lindsay's "Yea" among the affirmatives, but without the prohibition he had advocated so stirringly on the use of federal funds to perpetuate practices of discrimination.

❧ ❧ 27 ❧ ❧

Bucking the '64 Tide

Most of the systems flashed anything but green for John Lindsay in the early summer of 1964. His Democratic opponent, who also had the endorsement of the Liberal Party, was a personable woman with reputation, status, and personality of her own who was likely to be more appealing to the voter than the men Lindsay had defeated in 1958, 1960, and 1962. Mrs. Eleanor Clark French, a cousin of the former Mrs. Nelson Rockefeller, was the New York City representative at the UN. Besides, he had not one opponent, but two. The Conservative Party, strong Goldwater partisans, put up Kieran O'Doherty, the young party's former State Chairman, and the virulence of the right-wingers indicated an all-out effort would be made to cut heavily into his vote. Lindsay was the only Republican Congressman who earned their opposition.

Republicans at all levels and all over the country were preparing for the Johnson landslide that was already evident and that was going to swamp many of them. The potential pull of the President's coattails in the 17th District, where the Democrats had an edge anyway, could not be measured. Also, the nature of the Goldwater campaign, and its weaknesses, were beginning to emerge. John Lindsay had announced that he would run "without reference to" the national ticket, but he was obliged nonetheless to appear in the same column on the voting machines. His position cost him the usual financial aid a candidate expects from the national party. And his decision to run on his own record, disassociating himself from the Goldwater campaign, had aroused antagonism and skepticism. Did he mean it? What was the angle? Could he carry it off successfully?

Campaigner Lindsay ended by converting his great liability into a huge and negotiable asset. His independence of the vastly unpopular candidacy of Barry Goldwater was perhaps the wisest political move he ever made, though it was rooted firmly in conviction, or negatively, in distaste. He strummed on his dilemma so effectively that it took a hardhearted voter indeed to resist pulling the lever for Lindsay out of sympathy if not necessarily admiration. Lindsay's campaign literature concentrated on the desirability and technique of ticket-splitting. It showed diagrams of the voting machine and pictures of the Congressman in arm-swinging exhibitions, going from one row to another on the machine, and advising, "Take your time—relax and enjoy it!" Through it, Lindsay even developed a philosophy about the split ticket: "I think the most significant political development in recent years is ticket-splitting," he maintains now. "It is a very healthy thing for the two-party system, because it means that the parties have to offer good candidates regardless of the enrollment statistics. It means they don't dare run a bum."

As the campaign wore on, despite the discouraging omens, Lindsay, though driving tirelessly, was relaxed and loose in contrast to the earnest befuddlement of his two opponents. (Lindsay, to his credit, was never recorded as having said that he was "running scared." He did observe once that he might lose, but this was pretty much on the order of Joe Louis philosophizing that he could lose to Arturo Godoy if Arturo landed one while Joe was yawning.)

It was altogether "a lousy campaign," as he summed it up, finding as its only good by-product the fact that "the public finally is aware of how political machinery runs. It doesn't take great numbers to run the machinery," he pointed out, "but a cadre of organized, disciplined men. If you're not at the job, someone else will be —politics abhors a vacuum. Intra-party fights, of course, have gone on for years, but the public just hasn't been aware of them."

In a series of debates, which he called "churners," because they "get you all worked up," he twitted Mrs. French and O'Doherty. "I'm flattered by the attention I've received from each of these distinguished candidates. Mr. O'Doherty says I engineered most of the Kennedy Administration's program. Mrs. French says I've wrecked it." This particular sally delighted a bewitched group of college girls, but in his street campaigning he seemed to show equal dexterity.

"Why don't you back Goldwater?" a voter would demand. "That's a matter of principle; the Conservative Party has attacked me." "I'm voting for Goldwater, not for you," an elderly woman said; soon after, a man told him, "I voted for you last time. But not this time. Goldwater, I can't stomach him." The Congressman replied, "I'm not supporting him." "I know, but you Republicans let him through the net!"

Mrs. French was billed as "the only candidate who openly opposes Barry Goldwater," and she sought to tie the Goldwater can to Lindsay's coattails. The Lindsay record of siding with the Kennedy-Johnson Administration on two thirds of domestic issues in the two immediately preceding years became his "failure to support the Administration" on one third of the issues.

The Democratic assault was faltering, the Conservative Party's attack was venomous. O'Doherty branded him a renegade, one of a small band who continually crossed party lines to support Administration measures, called him a "crypto-Democrat," and kept up his attack even after the polls were slammed closed and showed the Conservatives with fewer than ten thousand votes. "That was just a preliminary battle," O'Doherty insisted; his own vote became "a stupendous success" in the minds of the Conservatives, among whose other successes at the same time was Barry Goldwater's cause. O'Doherty staked out the future in these words: "The defeat of the Rockefeller-Javits-Lindsay axis—and the prevention of any bid by Lindsay for higher office."

The next year, in keeping with this drive, the Conservatives entered a mayoralty candidate against the Lindsay candidacy. The party's patron saint, William Buckley, was quoted as having told a rally that, as James Baldwin had suggested, dumping garbage out of a window constituted a legitimate ghetto protest, dumping garbage when John Lindsay passed campaigning might constitute a nice protest by the Conservatives. Buckley later denied that he'd said quite this.

The virulence of the Buckley-Conservative drive against Lindsay is, in fact, worth noting. A month before the 1964 campaign came to an end, Buckley's magazine, the *National Review,* published the most detailed of its long series of diatribes against Lindsay, reflecting personal as well as political disdain. Speaking of the Conservative Party, the *National Review* reported that the party had "assigned top priority to Lindsay's defeat for any offices he seeks." As the *National Review* put it, the Conservative opposition threw a shadow . . . across such glittering prizes as it alleged Lindsay had in mind: the Governorship, the Presidency." In the same article the *National Review* promised Lindsay "the implacable hostility of the many friends of Barry Goldwater" and promised this for all time.

Not only was he doing "his savage best" to cut Goldwater's throat during the campaign, but he had broadly hinted that "he will not even vote for the man." The *National Review* sneered that ". . . a day may come when he will look with envy on other ambitious young men, such as Charles Percy of Illinois and Robert Taft, Jr., of Ohio, who voted for Goldwater at San Francisco." Lindsay may one day envy the Percys and Tafts, though presumably not for having voted for Goldwater at the nominating convention. He need not envy their immediate electoral fates; both went down to defeat with their candidate in 1964.

The *National Review* carefully named Lindsay's sins:

—He had assumed leadership of young Northeastern Republican Congressmen "who specialize in providing the Democrats with the margin of victory in close votes." (The allegation was that some of these voted with Lindsay "on the theory that he will reward them with Cabinet appointments. . . .") "It is preëminently Lindsay and his troops who, as a bloc, do the deadly and essential work of the House Democratic leadership."

—"Out of Congress, as in it, Lindsay has kept steadfastly to his ultra-liberal course." ("No civil rights bill, including the one just passed, has ever been enough for John Lindsay. . . .")

—"He is the product of an almost too-perfect set of circumstances: an impeccable background, a glossy foreground. . . ."

—"He has few of the familiar qualities of a leader: wit, daring, imagination, or even oratorical skill. His speaking style verges on a youthful pomposity. . . ."

—"Even his worst enemy would concede he looks the part of a Cecil B. DeMille President . . . almost classically Grecian features . . . mirthless eyes, and the smile (if any) may strike the hyper-sensitive as halfhearted or even synthetic. . . ."

But, added Buckley, "perhaps his humorlessness (for that is what it amounts to) befits one accustomed to brooding over the state of the nation."

—And, finally, the most scarlet sin: Lindsay was found to be, "far more than most of his like-minded colleagues, an odds-on contender for the national leadership of liberal Republicanism in the next decade. . . ."

The personal animosity of the Buckley-O'Doherty drive reached Lindsay through the voters in the 17th District, apparently helping more than hurting for it served to emphasize his independence. "I like your stand on Goldwater" was perhaps the single most frequently heard response from voters.

John Lindsay is, in fact, one of the candidates who go out to meet the people. Even though the dimensions of his victory were becoming apparent, he plunged day and night into the rigors of all-out campaigning. "I'm pouring it on heavier than ever," he said as he "officially" opened his campaign in early summer. Campaign headquarters had been opened by the candidate and Bob Price, his manager, in the late spring, when it was already apparent that

Lindsay would have Goldwater as a running mate. Even so, there is an amusing aspect to the "opening" of a Lindsay campaign, for he is eternally at work at it—in the District offices, in speech-making, in public appearances and personal messages, in the odds-and-ends of work for constituents and other citizens in response to one of the heaviest loads of incoming mail received by any Congressman.

Headquarters was a bulging, unbelievably crowded nest of converted rooms in the Hotel Roosevelt. Volunteers fell over each other to process the hundreds of thousands of mailing pieces and palm cards and other printed materials that were stacked in corridors, on desks and in bathtubs. "We lived like animals in this headquarters," Bob Price said with wry humor when it was all over, "so that we would have money for literature. It was literature that did it."

The "literature"—dozens of brightly styled appeals to "Re-elect the District's Pride—the Nation's Hope"—did its part, but it was far more than "literature," as Bob Price, who is the organizational genius, knew better than anyone else. Only careful planning made it possible for some fifteen hundred people streaming into five crowded hotel rooms to give their efforts meaningfully for something they believed in and for another two thousand to be out on the streets, ringing doorbells. This was the organization that Bob Price had created, nurtured, and tended with a hundred hours a week (or more) of his own sweat. Maps showed every building in the District, and Bob Price could tell you who was responsible for each one and what its current status was. It would be good, or Bob Price would learn why.

Price became an Election District captain for the Republicans in the Bronx when he was seventeen and still in high school, and had launched his fourth Congressional campaign at thirty-one. He has a passion for detail but his vision is broad enough to see the wider horizons. Price is a lawyer when he is not practicing politics and he first met John Lindsay when he was in college. He was head of NYU's Young Republicans when Lindsay was the president of the city-wide group. It was nearly a half dozen years, however, before their interests were combined in the 1958 primary. They have been associated in every campaign since, including, of course, 1965's, though Price took a six-week flyer out to Oregon in the spring of 1964 to run Rockefeller's successful primary campaign.

"Bob's definition of a dilettante," said one harried campaign worker, "is someone who takes a weekend off." In any event, the capacity for long hours of labor only caps the highly unusual, and increasingly respected, political abilities that Bob Price has brought to John Lindsay's career. He comes close to being the indispensable man in the Lindsay camp—for past successes, current operations, and future prospects.

A second key figure in the Lindsay operation is a young woman from Pittsburgh, Elizabeth Patterson, widely known as "Barnie" (for her middle name, Barnett). She joined the Lindsay forces in Washington in 1961, and serves as press secretary on one of those twelve-hour workdays that mark the enthusiastic Lindsay staff. In 1962 and 1964, however, she left the Congressional payroll to become "campaign co-ordinator" in the re-election drives; in 1965 she was campaign director, the number-two spot in the entire mayoralty effort. A former English literature major at Wells College, she is, in Lindsay's words, "an able, efficient executive and administrator, gifted in getting people to work together and in developing harmonious, effective co-ordinated action." As buffer between Bob Price and an immensely complicated campaign organization, she has a knowledge of practical politics which makes her a close rival to him as the indispensable element in the Lindsay organization.

John Lindsay, too active a campaigner to maintain a headquarters desk, maintained his "private office" on a sofa in the hotel's hallway near the elevators. From there he would pop off to long hours of meeting the voters and the opposition. One October day, for example, began with a 9 A.M. radio taping, followed in quick succession by speeches at Hunter College, the New York State Theatre, and the American Academy of Arts. (These were not all political appearances.) At 5:30 he began a series of three "housegatherings," which continued until 8:30, at residences on East Twentieth and East Twenty-third Streets, and Stuyvesant Oval.

The "housegatherings" are the Lindsay version of the *Kaffee klatsch* that has come into so much favor with many candidates in recent years. In the Lindsay version all are evening affairs, and the hosts invite not their tight circle of friends, but voters, usually Democrats. So it is a matter of a great deal of cross-pollination at the "housegatherings." Some, but far from all of these, fit the newspaper description: "soignée soirées in lavish penthouses."

And then after that round of parties where the candidate offered an informal series of remarks ("I ask for an absence of indifference," "This campaign is enormously controversial—you hear the angry voices, and there are bumps and bruises; it's not dull, in any event, but I'm not in it to lead a comfortable life or make easy decisions. . . ."), Lindsay was off to a Republican County Committee card party; a "drop by" for an affair sponsored by friends at the Harvard Club; an "if possible" at the opening of a gallery exhibition at Yeshiva University. The hour for the "if possible" (he made it) was 1 P.M. The next day was to begin with a breakfast meeting.

What the day's timetable did not show at all were the unscheduled appearances—the street campaigning, the buttonholing and handshaking on corners and in subway stations; the "drop bys"; the being on hand, not really by chance, when some block would be bustling with people, or a courtyard lambent with the laughter of toddlers and their mothers. And what deserves special mention, the Lindsay technique of canvassing the high-rise apartment buildings in such an area as Stuyvesant Town with its thousands of families. In a single tower of one of these buildings there might be ninety-six families. With a team of two aides Lindsay takes an elevator to the top floor. From that point on, the aides precede him, racing down the fire stairs to a floor below where the team pushes all the doorbells in sight (simultaneously, if possible, to cut down on the racket). As soon as there is a sign of response, the advance man calls: "It's your Congressman, John Lindsay, here to say hello to you. Just a minute, please." Within an instant, the candidate is on the floor himself, shaking hands and offering brief greetings (the advance team, after tossing campaign folders under unopened doors, is already on the way to the floor below to repeat the same routine). Ninety-six families covered, dozens of them receiving personal greetings at their own doorsill from "your Congressman"—all accomplished in fifteen minutes. It requires imagination, mechanical technique, good legs and lungs and humor, and an unflagging zeal for the old campaign try.

And then, after weeks and weeks of driving effort, it was all over so suddenly that the biggest victory of any Republican Congressman in the nation was evident only forty-five minutes after the polls closed. John Lindsay was saying, "I really didn't expect to win this big, but I was confident. It's the biggest victory of my career, and it was important for the party. Now," he said, "we can start to rebuild a two-party system . . . and I intend to play a part in the rebuilding."

The Democratic opponent, Mrs. French, was disappointed with the returns that showed her nearly 100,000 votes behind in a district that cast fewer than 200,000, but she sent the winner a message offering good wishes "for success in your efforts to eradicate Goldwaterism from your party."

The Conservatives were still vowing to dedicate themselves to "the prevention of any bid by Lindsay for higher office." The columnists were writing, "By 1972, he is certain to be a prime candidate for the Republican Presidential nomination—and is apt to be the man who gets it. . . ."

28

Great Expectations

A WEARY and cynical New York political writer, contemplating the pine-plank rows of the press section at the 1964 San Francisco convention of Goldwater Republicanism, turned to his typewriter in the early-morning light of the Cow Palace. It was almost deadline time for his paper across the continent and virtually no readers of his paper, or any other in the East, could have been strong enough to endure the eight-hour convention session, especially after the purposely dreary two-hour reading of the platform.

The session had also included the bitter and futile struggle on the convention floor to amend the platform. It was too bad, he wrote, that these amending efforts had been deliberately scheduled too late for Eastern TV-viewers, because two New Yorkers had given the most effective speeches of the convention when they argued for the civil rights amendment. They were Joseph Carlino, then Speaker of the State Assembly, who was defeated in the Johnson-Democratic sweep, and John Lindsay.

"One of these years," the political writer forecast, "you may see Lindsay at a convention as the candidate."

His prediction was far from the first or the last association of Lindsay's name with a future national Republican ticket. A gossip columnist has reported that President Johnson and Senator Robert Kennedy exchanged woeful warnings as to which one would next be the likeliest Lindsay foe. A trustee of Vassar College, his wife's alma mater, presented him to a Vassar audience as a man "we fervently hope is a President of our country in the making." Even before his smashing re-election in 1964, columnist Inez Robb called him "a sure Presidential contender in the seventies—if the traditional Republican Party is to be saved. . . ."

If the pre-election projection seemed rosy, it became tinged with inevitability immediately after he won 71.5 per cent of the vote in 1964 over two opponents and in spite of a Johnson landslide. This election made John Lindsay a national figure; he was the biggest winner of any Republican seeking major office. Theodore White said the dimensions of his victory were "almost unbelievable. For him the future opens endlessly bright."

There were other verdicts, hardly less sanguine: "There is general agreement he has a big future in the party. . . ." "One of the most attractive Republicans in the country. . . ." "Lindsay has been catapulted into deserved prominence. With him as standard-bearer, the Republican Party could have great expectations. . . ." "Lindsay's victory establishes him as a man to watch. . . ."

One columnist noted coyly that Republican women seemed intent on helping their party stage a comeback and that they were on the prowl for "a fresh, virile, and viable Lochinvar." Such a hero would need to "stir the emotions as Wendell Willkie did [and be] compounded . . . of Phil Sheridan, Thomas Jefferson, Sir Galahad, Clark Gable, and Cary Grant." And, added the columnist, "they are casting sheep's eyes at the young and dashing John Lindsay. He doesn't meet all the requirements—as who could?—but he is a tide-bucker, young, intelligent, and willing to work hard. . . ."

A national magazine writer echoed that Lindsay is "endowed with the magic to make ladies' heartstrings go *pizzicato*."

In more robust prose Robert Ruark cabled that, "The Republican Party is starving to death for men of Lindsay's calibre—men who call the shots and disregard the flying chips. . . . He is a statesman, young or not, and should be around for a lot of years as Congressman, Governor, who knows? Maybe President."

On the other hand, for every prediction that John Lindsay could, or should, or might have a national future, another barometer reading points to hazards and improbabilities.

These operate in several directions. First, in the House of Representatives, where many dozens of Republicans are senior to him, he is respected but consigned to the "isolation ward" of the irregular. The Lindsays of the GOP draw the lesser committee assignments; for example, no Republican liberals are found in the three most important committees of the House—Appropriations, Rules, and Ways and Means. In the days of Charles Halleck's leadership, a wit said that Halleck's troubles ranged from John Birch at one extreme to John Lindsay at the other.

Lindsay remains, furthermore, and would be for the foreseeable future, a Republican in a Democratic-controlled House, as well as a liberal in a conservative House and a conservatively led party.

As for a Presidential candidate coming out of the House of Representatives, in words paraphrasing one late statesman of the party, that would be one of the most unheard-of things ever heard of. In their day some of the powers of the House, like Champ Clark and Jack Garner, merited attention, but their claim was predicated on seniority, the power of the Speakership and careers of playing the Congressional game. (In more recent times, the Republican Party did turn to a Congressman to fill the second place on the national ticket. Remember William E. Miller of Lockport, New York?) A driver with the magnetic force of Lindsay could conceivably gain the party's backing and project a national image from a rather lowly seat, but the odds are strongly against it.

As for the House seat, Lindsay faced the dilemma of too much success. In his first campaign for office, he won with not much more than 51 per cent of the vote. The second time out he won 60 per cent, boosted it to 67 per cent on the third try, and in 1964 he beat the Democratic candidate by about four-to-one, a margin of better than 70 per cent over two opponents. Lindsay would, as a continued candidate for the House, be in constant danger of failing to better his own successes. Any falling-off would become a minus factor in his credibility as an increasingly popular candidate. Through his first four elections he has built acclaim upon achievement, glory upon invincibility, fame upon a rocket that has never crested. If his margin of victory were reduced, it might suggest that Lochinvar had clay feet.

Within New York State there are tremendous obstacles. He is a New Yorker (which, to upstate "York Staters," means New York City) and the Republican Party's base is already heavily overweighted with men from the city and the adjacent metropolitan area. As of 1965 all the statewide elective officials, including both U.S. Senators, come from just three metropolitan counties. As far as the Senate goes, one seat is held by a close ally, and the other, which is in the opposition's hands, will not be contested until 1970. Junior-grade offices, such as Attorney General and Lieutenant-Governor, have presumably lost whatever appeal they might have had for a man whose name is bandied about as a potential President of the United States.

That leaves the governorship of the Empire State, a vaulting-pit for aspirations and ambitions of dozens of men for a century and a half. The Executive Chamber at Albany represents one of those pleasant political legends which actually are equal parts of mythology and superstition. It is well known that men have made it direct from Albany to the White House but, in fact, only two men managed it: Grover Cleveland, more than eighty years ago, and Franklin D. Roosevelt. Each was a titan in his time, and unquestionably that has lent credence to the superstition that the New York Governor can automatically lay claim to serious consideration for the Presidential nomination. There are, of course, variations which supplement the fable. Martin Van Buren was Secretary of State and Andrew Jackson's Vice-President between his governorship and election as Jackson's successor. Theodore Roosevelt was removed from New York's Executive Chamber to repose, his detractors expected, in the Vice-Presidency before fate opened the White House to him. There were also five defeated candidates—Thomas E. Dewey, Al Smith, Charles Evans Hughes, Samuel Tilden, and Horatio Seymour. Though defeated, each added to the myth that the Governor of New York is entitled to see a President when he looks in the mirror. But if they add to the myth, what of the men who hoped and hoped and never got even a nomination? The names Averell Harriman and Nelson Rockefeller are only the most recent of this long line.

John Lindsay's name began to be mentioned for the Governorship of New York after he had won his first re-election to the House. The Rockefeller divorce announcement in late fall of 1961 touched off the first widespread speculation about a successor. Rowland Evans suggested, shortly after the Rockefeller bombshell, that if Rockefeller were through, the search for candidates from "the left" should begin. The names of Congressman Bradford Morse of Massachusetts and of John Lindsay were cited as "the two young stars of the Republican liberals."

Before Rockefeller's 1962 re-election, one New York writer described Lindsay as "now considered the best Republican gubernatorial material for the future—and even talked about as the party's Presidential hope in years to come." After November, 1962, John Lindsay's name was identified with statewide political plans. He received, and accepted, an increasing number of invitations to Republican and non-political affairs. But Nelson Rockefeller had won, too, in 1962; and now he was pushing for the Presidential nomination, in spite of his remarriage. Even so, some Republicans were trying to persuade Lindsay to look ahead to a governorship race in 1966 and some were wishing he could make the run for President in 1964. "He's young, attractive, vigorous, and progressive," wrote Dorothy Kilgallen, "and that's what they think the GOP needs—someone close to the image of JFK." *

Throughout the hiatus when Nelson Rockefeller made an attempt to get the Presidential nomination in 1964, his office in Albany was eyed by a variety of politicians. It was widely thought

* By 1965 European newspapers were captioning Lindsay photographs as those of "The New Kennedy" ("Bet that burns Bobby up," Lindsay grinned upon seeing one of these). As for the "young" or "youthful" aspect, note that John Kennedy was twenty-nine when he was elected to the House of Representatives; John Lindsay was turning thirty-seven. John Kennedy was halfway between his forty-third and forty-fourth birthdays when elected President and this was John Lindsay's age when he ran for Mayor of New York. The constant references to Lindsay's "youth" probably arise from the economy of line in face and figure, and his "zest."

that Rockefeller might vacate the office for personal or political reasons. Looking at these suppositions, seers saw John Lindsay very much in the Albany picture. One writer forecast a liberal-conservative falling-out within New York Republican circles that would make "ordinary Democratic squabbles look like tea-parties," and with Lindsay the likely liberal contender.

During Rockefeller's ebb tide immediately after his remarriage, when everything seemed even worse than it was, Lindsay came under attack from of all people the right-wingers for having stepped into the void left by the Rockefeller "collapse." William Buckley, the darling of the conservatives, blasted the "Big Ooh and Aah of New York's liberal Republicans, an ambitious and highly skilled void-filler." Buckley conceded Lindsay's credentials as a liberal, but derided him as a questionable Republican.

But the *Herald Tribune,* in the same period (early 1964), noted that Lindsay was "considered by most Republican leaders to be Rockefeller's potential successor."

What were the facts about John Lindsay, Congressman, and Nelson Rockefeller, Governor? Conceivably, if Rockefeller chose to quit the capitol at Albany at a time and under circumstances when it could have any import for John Lindsay, then Lindsay might indeed become the Republican nominee. But no real indication had ever suggested that the Governor had lost his appetite for the powers his office afforded him, much less his appetite for the Presidency. Rockefeller has, in fact, declared his intention of standing for re-election in 1966.

To put the Lindsay-Rockefeller relationship in perspective, some glances at history are required. Each won election for the first time in 1958; each had taken on the entrenched forces of the party's Organization to gain the opportunity for his victory—Lindsay through a primary contest, Rockefeller through steamrollering the leaders. Each was favored by the so-called "Eastern Establishment" of the party; each, though a rebel, was far from a dangerous maverick.

John Lindsay was the first to declare himself a candidate that year and he endorsed Rockefeller the day after the latter announced. It was timely; Manhattan's regular Republicans were by no means certain that they could swallow a Rockefeller. When pizza-chomping, bagel-nibbling Nelson Rockefeller came into the 17th District that fall, they campaigned together, though John Lindsay never has been a public eater, and they have done so ever since, when Rockefeller is on the ticket and when he is not.

In 1959 the Congressman declared himself a Rockefeller man for the 1960 Republican Presidential nomination. This was before Rockefeller's determined drive for delegates, which peaked and fizzled late that year in the face of overpowering Nixon commitments. But Lindsay's commitment to Rockefeller, when both of them had been in office less than six months, specifically excluded Vice-President Nixon.

A year later, just before the convention that nominated Nixon, Lindsay went to some lengths to disassociate himself from a statement supporting Nixon that had been drafted by the twenty-four-member New York Republican Congressional delegation. It occurred at a dinner honoring one of the Congressmen who were about to retire. Without warning, the delegation declared its support for Nixon, at a time when their Governor was strenuously challenging the Vice-President. "I wasn't there and had no forewarning that a social gathering would be turned into a political caucus," Lindsay declared heatedly and publicly. "Had I been there, I would have registered a vigorous dissent." At about the same time, Lindsay had described Rockefeller as possessing "the makings of a great President," at a meeting of the New York County (Manhattan) Republican Committee.

But Lindsay's relations with the Governor, while proper and appropriate, were not those of the all-admiring enthusiast. Shortly after upholding the Governor against more than a score of colleagues who were flocking to Nixon, he told a television interviewer that Rockefeller's quest for the nomination was "unskilled and a little bit clumsy." The Governor, said the Congressman, isn't a professional politician, and he has suffered from a lack of "specialized professional advice" in his rocket-like career. "But I'm for him," Lindsay added loyally.

As Rockefeller pursued Nixon right up to the convention gates, demanding satisfaction on ideological and practical platform commitments, Lindsay let it be known that he and other Republican liberals in Washington thought Nixon had badly needed the pressure of the Rockefeller campaign. This factor, they thought, made it tenable for Nixon to drift leftward in his commitments, and Lindsay later found the platform admirable. The 1960 convention was his first experience as a national convention delegate. Lindsay was not a prominent member of New York's large contingent; but he seized the chance to help lead a movement which hoped to persuade the Governor to nominate Henry Cabot Lodge for Vice-President.

And so, through the early years, Rockefeller was in the debt of the younger man for wide-ranging loyalty, maintained in a variety of changing and difficult situations. Yet Lindsay did not hesitate to speak up when he was in disagreement with the Governor on legislative and other issues. For example, while urging Rockefeller upon the country, he was urging Rockefeller to veto a bill that sought to prevent insurgent political clubs from designating themselves as "Democratic" or "Republican" without their county chairman's permission. Lindsay quarreled with the idea that the legislation would lead to strengthening the party system. It was the kind of regulation that Organization men like, and independent-minded men do not. The Governor, despite his appeal, declined to veto.

In the years between the 1960 and 1964 national elections Lindsay's name was increasingly mentioned for statewide office, at the same time that Nelson Rockefeller was pointing toward national office. Lindsay was in the position of an avowed, if not necessarily ardent, advocate of Governor Rockefeller for the 1964 Presidential nomination. He followed him in his aspiration until the very end of the road in California and even made it possible for his own campaign manager, Bob Price, to manage Rockefeller's primary in Oregon. And when the end of the road was reached, he jumped with Rockefeller and the rest of the Rockefeller delegates to Scranton. But it is important to note that Lindsay had been developing significant bases of his own. As a battler in Congress for a strong civil rights bill he went before the convention in San Francisco with a seconding speech on a platform amendment, just as Nelson Rockefeller did on another amendment.

Lindsay, his own man in Washington, was his own man in New York. He clearly respected the person and privileges and prerogatives of the state's Republican Governor, but he would dissent when the occasion warranted, and in 1963 an occasion made public a difference that almost widened into a permanent breach. At the root of the trouble was a newly created City Council seat, destined to fall to Manhattan Republicans. Richard Lewisohn, leader of the 9th Assembly District, board chairman of the Venus Pen and Pencil Company, and a staunch supporter of John Lindsay, was campaigning for the party's designation and was expected to get it. He had, at Lindsay's urging, already replaced former Congressman Coudert as District Leader. And then came the news that the Governor had sent word to County Chairman Vincent Albano that his cousin, Richard Aldrich, was to receive the nomination. Aldrich had unsuccessfully run, the year before, for Congress in another Manhattan district and the Governor, campaigning for him, had exclaimed, "I love this man. He's a wonderful, wonderful American."

"The word is out," Lindsay said now in mid-1963, that the Governor had told Albano to deliver the county to the wonderful, wonderful American—who was his cousin. Lewisohn threatened a primary fight and John Lindsay said, "As long as you stay, I will stay with you." The squabble became increasingly public and Albano, who was in the middle, said Lindsay must have misunderstood something. But Lindsay retorted, "I most certainly did not misinterpret anything. They wanted to put over Aldrich without any hullaballoo. They wanted me to get Lewisohn out." Rockefeller held a couple of press conferences in which he denied almost everything and commented that "someone is not telling the truth." Lindsay merely repeated that Albano had told him that the Governor "wanted his cousin to have the nomination for City Council and he, the chairman, would have to deliver it."

The Rockefeller-Lindsay struggle was the big political news of the time. Some note was taken that Lindsay was forcing the issue at a time when Rockefeller, just remarried, was trying to re-establish his image, and many people construed the situation as demonstrating that Lindsay was willing to break his political ties with the Governor. The fight could make a shambles of the Manhattan Republican organization and it was viewed as a personal challenge to the Governor.

The county committee endorsed Aldrich, and Lewisohn withdrew a few days later because, he said, "what began as a local party fight, which should be settled in a primary, has become seriously involved with much broader issues and national personalities." A Lewisohn primary victory might have inflicted a mortal wound on Rockefeller because of the timing. The whole thing had reached a point where almost everyone would lose, no matter what happened. In the settlement, a political analyst commented that Lindsay was "a rare political character, whose reputation for sticking by his pledges remains unsullied. . . ."

(Evans and Novak, in the *Herald Tribune,* pointed out that the Governor and Congressman had come close to a break on "a trivial matter"; Rockefeller, they said, was the leader of the Republican moderates, and Lindsay might be the moderate leader of the future. But, they added, to continue his ascent as "one of the brightest Republican stars * in the East, Lindsay needs Rockefeller. . . . Without Rockefeller's support and co-operation, a statewide Lindsay campaign might never get off the ground. But with the help of Rockefeller money and organization, a Lindsay bid for Governor would have to be taken seriously in New York and the nation. It would be a major political event."

Lindsay himself said that the break with Rockefeller was not highly significant and had left no lasting scars. Aldrich finally won the Republican primary over John Lamula by a small margin that was interpreted as a rebuff for the Governor. Lindsay declined to support either Aldrich or Lamula, and after Aldrich's victory limited his aid in the election campaign to lending his name to a published list of supporters. And, as Evans and Novak had hinted, the Governor ultimately made a move that was construed as a slap at Lind-

* On a single day during the controversy, three New York City newspapers said of Lindsay: "The bright light of the city's Republican Party"; "one of the state GOP's brightest stars"; "a rising Republican star."

say. The designation for New York's member on the platform committee in 1964 went to Assembly Speaker Joseph Carlino rather than to Lindsay who was a more logical choice.

(In 1965, when Aldrich declined renomination to the City Council, unsubstantiated reports suggested Lindsay had forced his withdrawal.)

Lindsay continued his strong advocacy of Rockefeller's Presidential cause; they stood shoulder to shoulder at San Francisco, and campaigned together in 1964. With his big win John Lindsay was the lion of the party. The reporters began asking Nelson Rockefeller about Lindsay as a challenger in 1966 to which Rockefeller replied, "I'm not ready to step down." In August, 1965, after State Senator John H. Hughes wrote to Senator Javits urging that Governor Rockefeller be replaced in 1966, Rockefeller announced his intention to run.

The Governor and Lindsay had clashed even when Rockefeller was urging him or Javits to run for Mayor of New York City. Both declined, and Rockefeller peevishly and publicly questioned Lindsay's "conditions" for taking the nomination. There were those who wondered aloud whether Rockefeller really wanted a Republican as mayor. The quality of the Rockefeller-Lindsay relationship, while publicly correct, continues the subject of skeptical speculation among politicians and public alike.

The conclusion has to be that if John Lindsay seeks statewide office in New York, he will do it perhaps with the approval of other Republican leaders but as no man's protégé. His emergence to full status as a politician of top rank in his own right was brought home to scores of the state's political elite one rainy Saturday night in March, 1965, in the crowded ballroom of Albany's Ten Eyck Hotel.

The occasion was the traditional dinner and entertainment of the Legislative Correspondents Association. The Governor and a representative of both major parties always speak. The year before John Lindsay had strolled in, unaware even that it was a black-tie affair; but this night he was one of the three speakers. Going to bat before the most politically sophisticated audience outside the Gridiron dinner, held that same night in Washington, he more than held his own against Senator Robert F. Kennedy and Governor Rockefeller. He teased, twitted, and taunted them with allusions to his own expectations about Albany. One of the usually blasé political writers sent this word back to his paper: "Watch John V. Lindsay. . . . He practically stole the show from the other headliners. His ease of delivery, his charm, his appearance were the envy of every politician. . . . It's hard to believe that the New York Republican Party has such an attractive personality in reserve. . . . He might be needed in the foreseeable future."

Those were in the days when he was "not a candidate" for Mayor of New York or anything else. At the moment in May when he decided that he couldn't resist the temptation to seize the challenge in his own town, he became the central figure in the nation's principal election contest of the year and a national figure in his party. An observer noted that the party's batteries haven't had a charge like this since Eisenhower said he would go to Korea.

The road he had turned down exactly seven years before, when he launched a primary contest as the candidate nobody wanted, had crested an important peak. The political career of John Lindsay stood at mid-course, with a beckoning future that many considered to be of brightest magnitude—a future that would attract many and would be rejected by many others—but one, nonetheless, that would be written on the terms of the man who had defied all the hoary weight of tradition to declare, "as long as I have voice in my body, I will speak for what I believe right."

About the Author

DANIEL E. BUTTON has been a newspaperman since 1939, and has worked on papers in Wilmington, Delaware, and for the Associated Press in New York City. Since 1960 he has been the editor of the *Times Union* in Albany, New York. He has also worked in public relations and was for a time assistant to the president of the State University of New York. He graduated from the University of Delaware and the Columbia University School of Journalism.

Mr. Button has also worked in television, including a tour as co-moderator of a weekly program called "Speak for Yourself," which invited its participants to debate each other informally. John V. Lindsay was twice a guest; on one occasion he appeared with Richard Rovere, and on another with Governor Philip Hoff of Vermont. The *Times Union* sent Mr. Button to the Republican National Convention in 1960 to cover New York State politics—of which Lindsay was very much a part. Later he covered Representative Lindsay's 1964 Congressional campaign.

Daniel Button lives in Albany with his wife, three daughters, and two sons.